EDUCATED IN TYRANNY

EDUCATED IN TYRANNY

Slavery at Thomas Jefferson's University

EDITED BY MAURIE D. McINNIS
AND LOUIS P. NELSON

University of Virginia Press *Charlottesville and London*

University of Virginia Press
© 2019 by the Rector and Visitors of the University of Virginia
All rights reserved
Printed in Canada on acid-free paper

First published 2019

1 3 5 7 9 8 6 4 2

Library of Congress Cataloging-in-Publication Data
Names: McInnis, Maurie Dee, editor, author. | Nelson, Louis P., editor, author.
Title: Educated in tyranny : slavery at Thomas Jefferson's university / edited by
Maurie D. McInnis and Louis P. Nelson.
Description: Charlottesville ; London : University of Virginia Press, [2019] | Includes
bibliographical references and index.
Identifiers: LCCN 2019004596 | ISBN 9780813942865 (cloth : alk. paper) |
ISBN 9780813942872 (ebook)
Subjects: LCSH: University of Virginia—History—19th century. | Jefferson, Thomas,
1743–1826. | Slavery—Virginia—Charlottesville—History—19th century.
Classification: LCC LD5678.3 .E48 2019 | DDC 378.755/481—dc23
LC record available at https://lccn.loc.gov/2019004596

Cover illustrations: Runaway slave ads from 1769 *Virginia Gazette*, with inset detail on right
of *University of Virginia*, 1826 (Benjamin Tanner, engraver), from the Boye map of Virginia
(Albert and Shirley Small Special Collections Library, University of Virginia).

The parent storms, the child looks on, catches the lineaments of wrath, puts on the same airs in the circle of smaller slaves, gives a loose to his worst of passions, and thus nursed, educated, and daily exercised in tyranny, cannot but be stamped by it with odious peculiarities. The man must be a prodigy who can retain his manners and morals undepraved by such circumstances.
—THOMAS JEFFERSON, 1785
FOUNDER OF THE UNIVERSITY OF VIRGINIA

Can we forget the crack of the whip, cowhide, whipping-post, the auction-block, the hand-cuffs, the spaniels, the iron collar, the negro-trader tearing the young child from its mother's breast as a whelp from the lioness? Have we forgotten that by those horrible cruelties, hundreds of our race have been killed? No, we have not, nor ever will.
—ISABELLA GIBBONS, 1867
FORMERLY ENSLAVED AT THE UNIVERSITY OF VIRGINIA

Dedicated to all the people who were enslaved
at the University of Virginia

Aaron, Abraham, Abram, Absalom, Adelaide, Aggy, Agnes, Albert, Alfred, Ambrose, Amy, Anatomical Lewis, Andrew, Ann, Anthony, Araminte, Armistead, Armstrong, Arthur, Aunt Amy, Aunt Mourning, Barbara, Barnet, Barnette, Barrett, Bella, Ben, Bennett, Betsy, Beverly, Bibbianna, Bill, Billy, Binius, Bob, Booker, Brazeel, Bristoe, Britt, Burr, Burwell, Caesar, Caroline, Carter, Cassandra, Cather, Cato, Charles, Charlotte, Claiborne, Clarke, Sally Cottrell Cole, Commodore Lewis, Lucy Cottrell, Cristo, Cross, Daniel, Daphne, Davey, David, Davy, Dick, Dilcy, Dinah, Dorothea, Edmond, Edmund, Edward, Edy, Elijah, Elizabeth, Ellen, Elsy, Elvira, Emily, Eston, Falony, Fielding, Fleming, Mary Fletcher, Flora, Fontaine, Frank, Franky, Frederick, Garland, George, German, Isabella Gibbons, William Gibbons, Gilbert, Giles, Gleaves, Grandma Kidda, William Green, Guy, G. W., Hannah, Harden, Harriett, Harry, Henry, Sally Henry, Thrimston Hern, Hickman, Homer, Horace, Humphrey, Humphry, Isaac, Isacah, Isaiah, Isham, Ishmael, Ishmel, Jack, Jackson, Jacob, James, Jane, Janetta, Jarratt, Jeff, Jefferson, Jenny, Jerry, Jim, Joe, John, John Edward, Johnson, Jones, Joseph, Joshua, Judy, Julia, Julia Ann, Kennedy, Kenny, Kitty, Lancelotte, Lancy, Lavihia, Lawrence, Lewis, Levi, Limos, Linus, Louisa, Lucinda, Lucius, Lucy, Lundy, Madison, Malinda, Susan Maloy, Margaret, Maria, Mariah, Martha, Mary, Mary Jane, Mat, Matilda, May, Micajah, Middlesex, Mike, Millide, Milly, Moses, James Munroe, Nancy, Nathan, Ned, Negro Bob, Nelson, Nicholas, Nimrod, Norman, Old Coly, Old Dick, Old George, Old Man Jack, Old Man Johnson, Old Peter, Old Sam, Pa, Parnil, Patsy, Henry Payne, Jane Payne, Peggy, Peter, Peyton, Phil, Pleasant, Polly, William Preston, Jim Price, Pricilla, Primus, Prince, Prior, Prudence, Queen, Burnly Lee Raphael, Randall, Randle, Reuben, Reubin, Richard, Robert, Roberty, Robin, Roda, Rosalie, Ryland, Sally, Sam, Sandy, Sarah, Sarah Ann, Scott, Sebra, Senior, Sharper, Shelton, Simon, Simpson, James Smith, Sophy, Spencer, Squire, Stephen, Sukey, Susan, Sy, Tad, Tamer, John Taylor, Tepney, Thad, Thomas, Thomas P., Thornton, Thrimson, Thrimston, Trimpson, Tom, Tulip, Uncle Ben, Violete, Walker, Jacob Walker, Warner, Washington, William, Willie, Willis, Wilson, Jack Wilson, Winston, Wyatt, Young Sam, Zach, Zachariah, Zebra, Zebray, Zuba

and the hundreds of others whose names have not survived.

CONTENTS

Foreword by Marcus L. Martin and Meghan S. Faulkner   xi
Acknowledgments   xv

Introduction   1
   Maurie D. McInnis

1. SLAVERY AND CONSTRUCTION   27
   Louis P. Nelson and James Zehmer

2. LANDSCAPE OF SLAVERY   42
   Louis P. Nelson and Maurie D. McInnis

3. EVERYDAY LIFE IN THE YARD   75
   Louis P. Nelson and Benjamin Ford

4. VIOLENCE   97
   Maurie D. McInnis

5. HOTELS   113
   Jessica Ellen Sewell and Andrew Scott Johnston

6. PROSLAVERY THOUGHT   141
   Thomas Howard and Alfred Brophy

7. ANATOMICAL THEATER   171
   Kirt von Daacke

8. FREE PEOPLE OF COLOR   199
   Kirt von Daacke

9. THE AFRICAN AMERICAN BURIAL GROUND   225
   Benjamin Ford

Notes on Contributors   247
Illustration Credits   251
Index   253

FOREWORD

Over the past decade, the focus of the University of Virginia's history has begun to change. The construction of the university and its operation during its first half-century depended upon the labor of enslaved people. But for too long, this fundamental component of history had been ignored. Thanks to the resolute efforts of students, faculty, staff, and local community members, this story is finally coming to light. The past ten years have seen a great increase in scholarship and activities that explore UVA's historical relationship with slavery, including the creation of a presidential commission charged with that task.

In 2007, the University of Virginia's Board of Visitors issued a statement stating its "particular regret" for the university's "employment of enslaved persons" and its "profound respect for the contributions of these women and men." The board also approved the installation of a slate plaque in the passage under the south terrace of the Rotunda honoring the service of both free and enslaved workers during the construction of the University of Virginia's original buildings.[1] It reads: "In honor of the several hundred women and men, both free and enslaved, whose labor between 1817 and 1826 helped to realize Thomas Jefferson's design for the University of Virginia." The installation of the plaque represented a notable milestone for the University of Virginia, but the memorial was soon criticized by many for its inadequacy—its small size, its secondary recognition of the enslaved, and its failure to capture the enormous scope of the roles occupied by enslaved people during the university's formative decades.

Following the resolution and plaque installation, several groups played key roles in highlighting the need to address more adequately the issue of slavery as it relates to the university's history. In 2007 the group University and Community Action for Racial Equity (UCARE) was formed with the goal of helping the university and surrounding communities identify actions that would lead to racial reconciliation. The UVA student group Memorial for Enslaved Laborers (MEL) was established in 2009, centered on advocating for a larger and grander slavery memorial. The UVA IDEA (Inclusion, Diversity, Equity, Access) Fund, an alumni group formed in 2010, also took interest in this work.

The IDEA Fund commissioned a research report titled *Slavery at the University of Virginia: A Catalogue of Current and Past Initiatives* in early 2013. The report documented various projects relevant to the study and recognition of slavery at UVA, and concluded that the development of a larger framework for addressing and investigating the university's history with slavery was crucial in order to ensure that "a more complete and inclusive history of the University of Virginia is presented to students, faculty, staff, visitors, and the community."[2]

In April 2013, Dr. Marcus L. Martin, vice president and chief officer for diversity and equity, presented information on the variety of initiatives related to UVA's historical relationship with slavery, and recommended to the cabinet that an institutional group be formed to explore that relationship further. In summer of 2013, President Teresa Sullivan formally created UVA's President's Commission on Slavery and the University (PCSU) and charged the commission with providing her advice and recommendations on the commemoration of the University of Virginia's historical relationship with slavery and enslaved people. Marcus Martin and Kirt von Daacke were appointed co-chairs of the twenty-six-member commission, which consists of students, staff, faculty, alumni, and members of the local community.

Since that time, much has been accomplished as a result of the PCSU's efforts in collaboration with local community members. The PCSU's Community Relations task force has been an essential part of the commission since its inception. The task force has met regularly for the past several years, with the purpose of collaborating and engaging with local community members on all aspects of the commission's work. The Community Relations task force has helped to plan numerous forums, facilitated discussions, and sponsored events for UVA staff since 2013.

Since the inception of the PCSU, two buildings on the UVA Grounds have been named after enslaved people. The Board of Visitors voted in March 2015 to name a new first-year dorm building Gibbons House after William and Isabella Gibbons, an enslaved couple who worked at the university. The PCSU established an educational exhibit in an alcove on the first floor of and outside the building to teach first-year students about the namesakes of the building and the larger history of slavery at UVA. The building was formally dedicated in summer 2015 and later that same year, descendants of Isabella Gibbons were honored with a reception at Gibbons House. In 2017, Skipwith Hall was dedicated in honor of Peyton Skipwith (1800–1849), an enslaved master mason who quarried stone for use in construction at UVA. Skipwith was owned by John Hartwell Cocke, a member of the Board of Visitors. The site of the building is believed to have been the location of the university quarry where Skipwith was a laborer.

The PCSU has organized or taken part in numerous events promoting education and commemoration. In 2012, archaeologists discovered sixty-seven mostly unmarked grave shafts, which are likely to contain the remains of both enslaved and newly freed African Americans. The graves were left undisturbed. In 2014, the PCSU organized a formal service at the First Baptist Church, followed by an evening vigil led by the Reverend Almeta Ingram-Miller and a choir singing the gospel song "Walk Together Children, Don't You Get Weary." Ingram-Miller led the community in a libation ceremony to celebrate, honor, and remember the men, women, and children buried in the cemetery. Renowned poet Brenda Marie Osbey wrote "Field Work" especially for the cemetery ceremony. The PCSU also conceived of and planned a two-day symposium titled "Universities Confronting the Legacy of Slavery," held October 16 and 17, 2014. The symposium included the African American cemetery commemoration, as well as a full day of panel discussions. The PCSU also collaborated with the Slave Dwelling Project to plan a four-day symposium October 18–21, 2017, called "Universities, Slavery, Public Memory, and the Built Landscape."

In order to engage younger students, the PCSU leadership conceived of a weeklong summer program for high school students called the Cornerstone Summer Institute. The institute ran in 2016 and 2017 with rising sophomores and juniors from all over the country attending the program. Focused on the history of enslaved people at the university and led by faculty and a team of UVA students, the program provided high schoolers with the opportunity to engage in historical investigation, archaeological excavation, and community engagement.

Efforts to memorialize have been at the front and center of the commission's work as well. Over the course of a year, a working group of the PCSU developed a walking tour titled "Enslaved African Americans at the University of Virginia." The full-color brochure and map highlights numerous people, stories, and sites on the Grounds related to early African American life at UVA. Over the course of the 2016–2017 academic year, the PCSU and the Office of the Architect shepherded the process of selecting and working with a design team for the Memorial to Enslaved Laborers. After an extensive community engagement process throughout the year, the firm Howeler + Yoon presented a design concept to UVA's Board of Visitors in June 2017. The Board of Visitors approved the design and instructed the team to proceed with planning and fundraising for the memorial, with construction anticipated to occur in 2019.

We are appreciative of the many students, faculty, staff, and community members who care passionately about this aspect of the University of Virginia's history and who have worked diligently to ensure that the enslaved people who lived and worked here are rightfully recognized and honored. We look forward to continuing to see the changes at the university that result from this work.

Marcus L. Martin and Meghan S. Faulkner
Office of the Vice President and Chief Officer for Diversity and Equity
University of Virginia
July 2017

NOTES

1. Carol Wood, "University of Virginia's Board of Visitors Passes Resolution Expressing Regret for Use of Slaves," *UVA Today,* April 24, 2007, https://news.virginia.edu/content/university-virginias-board-visitors-passes-resolution-expressing-regret-use-slaves.

2. Meghan Saunders Faulkner, *Slavery at the University of Virginia: A Catalogue of Current and Past Initiatives* (Charlottesville: University of Virginia IDEA Fund, 2013), https://vpdiversity.virginia.edu.

ACKNOWLEDGMENTS

This project has been and continues to be the work of a community. In many ways it began with students. Urging a more inclusive and honest history about the University of Virginia, students helped lead the way. They came together and formed the Memorial for Enslaved Laborers (MEL) Committee, sponsored competitions, and encouraged the university to diversify its memorial landscape and thus who is honored on campus. Several students wrote important papers and senior theses (notably Catherine Neale and Caroline Trezza). The University Guide Service created an African American history tour and asked faculty, including myself, to help educate them about African American history at the university.

Inspired by their desire to discover more, in my classes co-taught with Louis Nelson ("Arts and Cultures of the Slave South") and with Kirt von Daacke ("Jefferson, Slavery, and UVA"), we began exploring the university's archives. What we discovered was simultaneously astounding and daunting. Hundreds of linear feet of official records inside of which were threads, hints, and references that collectively helped to tell the history of hundreds of individuals who lived and labored while enslaved at UVA. This grew into a large digital project called "Jefferson's University—Early Life Project, 1819–1870" (http://juel.iath.virginia.edu), which has been supported financially by the Office of the Executive Vice President and Provost and the Jefferson Trust of the University of Virginia Alumni Association. The JUEL project brought together the Albert and Shirley Small Special Collections Library; the Institute for Advanced Technology in the Humanities (IATH); and dozens of students who have worked energetically to uncover this story. Their work has involved first the important task of transcribing the original nineteenth-century texts and tagging those transcriptions for easy searching. But they have also contributed dozens of essays, helped to construct the three-dimensional re-creation of the original buildings at the University of Virginia, and been important partners in shaping the project along the way. The names of all the individuals involved are listed at the end of these acknowledgments, but there are a few who deserve mention here for their special contributions. The first is Worthy Martin (associate professor, Computer Science, and acting director, IATH), who immediately offered to design the database, the website, and guide all technical matters, and who has continued to be at the center of the project. Second is Lauren Massari at IATH who has guided the visual reconstruction of the buildings and helped us see more clearly how the landscape would have appeared in the nineteenth century and understand how we could use those reconstructions to answer important research questions. Third is Julia Munro, who has worked on the project for years, strengthening it in too many ways to list here adequately.

Special thanks also go to President Teresa Sullivan for establishing the President's Commission on the University and Slavery. The research done by JUEL helped to inform the work of the commission, allowing the commission to take that research and amplify the findings through the many important initiatives sponsored by that group. I would also like to thank the University of Virginia Bicentennial Commission for their financial support of the publication.

In the creation of this volume, there are several who deserve special thanks for their assistance with research and preparation: those include Thomas Howard, Stephanie Lawton, Joshua Morrison, Julia Munro, and the staff at the University of Virginia Press. Lastly, I would like to thank my coauthors for their dedication to this work.

Maurie D. McInnis

Names of the individuals who have been part of the JUEL project:

At IATH—Staff: Robbie Bingler, Shayne Brandon, Emily Cone-Miller, Lauren Massari, and Julia F. Munro. Student research assistants: Moses Abraham, Elinor Ackerman, Ellen Adams, Nazar Aljassar, Connor Andrews, Madeline Bartel, Olivia Beatty, Alexandra Bergman, Gwendolyn Bingham, Monica Blair, Patrick Bond, Britt Brown, Samantha Bryant, Alice Burgess, Hahna Cho, Frank Cirillo, Caroline Crossman, Catharine Cain, Catherine Creighton, Kelly Danner, Gwen Dilworth, Meghan Ellwood, Tessa Evans, Joan Fasulo, Rachel Gaffin, Christina Griggs, Noah Harlow, Erin Hernon, Marvin Hicks, Ben Hitchcock, Camille Horton, Thomas Howard, Lauren Johnson, Katherine King, Katherine Landphair-Henneke, Stephanie Lawton, Angela Olive Lee, Sophia McCrimmon, Joshua Morrison, Nathanael

Nelson, Brian Neumann, Rachel Newman, Arden Nguyen, Alison Peltz, Bryan Phan, Dominic Puzio, Emily Richards, Dylan Rogers, Tahiya Salam, Meredith Stanley, Sarah Thomson, Scott Tilton, Victoria Travers, Caroline Trezza, Millicent Usoro, Victoria Valdez, Story Viebranz, Tiffany Vinci-Cannava, Emily Weisenberger, Tom Winters, Tyrabia Womble, and Jasmine Zollar.

EDUCATED IN TYRANNY

INTRODUCTION

Maurie D. McInnis

The University of Virginia occupies a unique place in the history of higher education in America. Frequently described as the most beautiful university campus in America, its history is intimately associated with one of the nation's Founding Fathers. While there are many named after early presidents and revolutionary luminaries, the University of Virginia is the only one that was envisioned, founded, designed, and overseen by one of the nation's first presidents.

Its beginning was inauspicious. In July of 1817, Thomas Jefferson stood in a field about a mile from the Albemarle County courthouse to block out the location of the buildings he planned to erect for "Central College." Having recently purchased land from John Perry, the seventy-four-year-old Jefferson used his theodolite to fix the center of the northern square, "the point destined for some principal building."[1]

Jefferson had been thinking about the importance of education in the new nation for decades; he had even sponsored a bill in Virginia, which did not pass, for expansive primary and secondary education for all white male citizens as early as 1779, a fairly radical concept in its time. He wrote to his friend James Madison, "Above all things, I hope the education of the common people will be attended to, convinced that on their good sense we may rely with the most security for the preservation of a due degree of liberty."[2] Even though not successful in that goal, after retiring from the presidency and returning to Monticello in 1809, Jefferson turned his attention to the designs for an institution of higher learning, Central College (which later became the University of Virginia). Correspondence with colleagues had helped sharpen his plans and he worked tirelessly to build political support for state funding to create a public university. In his mind, this work had a certain urgency. Nearly fifty years after the Declaration of Independence, he worried about the future of American democracy and he thought a broad and liberal education available to all voting citizens was the best way to ensure America's future. As he wrote to a friend, "If a nation expects to be ignorant and free in a state of civilization, it expects what never was and never will be."[3] His decades of work toward establishing a public institution began to take physical shape on that day in 1817, and at the University of Virginia, the moment is often presented as particularly prescient; a sculpture depicts the solitary genius of Jefferson, alone in a field, dreaming the university into existence (fig. I.1).

Importantly, however, Jefferson was not alone on that day, nor was he alone as the work of constructing the university became a reality. From its beginning through the end of Civil War, the University of Virginia was the work of many individuals, including hundreds of enslaved laborers. It began on that July day when Jefferson marked off the "old field"; accompanying Jefferson was his overseer, Edmund Bacon, an Irish builder named James Dinsmore, and "ten hands," a nineteenth-century term used to indicate enslaved laborers. Together the group used twine, shingles, and pegs to mark off the "foundations of the University." After marking it off, Jefferson "set the men at work."[4]

Much of the history of slavery at the University of Virginia is masked by phrases like "hands" and "set at work." From constructing and maintaining the buildings to feeding and caring for the faculty and students, enslaved people brought into existence and then sustained the institution. Additionally, and more abstractly, it was the state's slave-based economy that provided the wealth that made it possible for most of the students of the university to attend (despite Jefferson's interest in educating the "common people" a vast majority of the students came from the state's and the region's slaveholding families). The university's history was thus tied inextricably to the history of the South. Many of its alumni became important southern politicians and intellectual leaders; they were congressmen and governors, leading voices in the proslavery movement, soldiers in the Confederate Army, and political leaders in the Confederate States of America.

Much has been written about the history of the University of Virginia. It holds a special place in the annals of American higher education because of the fame of its founder, the beauty of its architecture, and its unique liberal arts approach to education in a period when most schools were still

Fig. I.1. Robert Fermin, *Thomas Jefferson, 1743–1826*, 2004. Located at the Darden School, this bronze statue of Thomas Jefferson surveying the site for the Academical Village includes a theodolite and tripod but excludes the enslaved "hands."

dominated by the preparation of students for lives as clergymen or lawyers.[5] The prevailing narrative history of the school emphasizes the fact that Jefferson was concerned with the health of American democracy; that he believed that the nation's future depended on a well-educated electorate. As he wrote his friend, "Enlighten the people generally, and tyranny and oppression of body and mind will vanish like evil spirits at the dawn of day. . . . The diffusion of knowledge among the people is to be the instrument by which it is to be effected."[6]

Jefferson's university was unlike any of the others in America at the time, and it set a precedent that has influenced the design of American universities ever since. Part of that legacy is in the organization of knowledge, and part of that legacy is in the architectural setting. Many others have written extensively on these subjects; we know much about the particular genius of Jefferson's plan for public education. What none have addressed in a sustained way, however, is the how Jefferson's designs for the university were intimately linked with his understanding of living in a slave society. The central paradox at the heart of UVA is also the central paradox of the nation, the unresolved paradox of American liberty. How it is that the nation that defined the natural rights of humankind did so within a system that denied those same rights to others based on the color of their skin? And what does it mean to have a public university founded to preserve those democratic rights that is likewise founded and maintained on the stolen liberty of others?

In recounting the university's history, for too long the role of slavery has not been addressed. In 1867, Isabella Gibbons, who was formerly enslaved at the University of Virginia, asked, "Can we forget the crack of the whip, cowhide, whipping-post, the auction-block, the hand-cuffs, the spaniels, the iron collar, the negro-trader tearing the young child from its mother's breast as a whelp from the lioness? Have we forgotten that by those horrible cruelties, hundreds of our race have been killed? No, we have not, nor ever will."[7] Serving then as one of the first teachers in the Charlottesville Freedmen's School, Gibbons believed that those memories would remain fresh. Even though they did remain fresh in the African American community, at the University of Virginia they were quickly and intentionally forgotten. University narratives erased the history of slavery and those who were enslaved. Instead, the focus was placed on Jefferson, the faculty, and the students. In the last decade that has begun to change. This book is an attempt to fulfill Gibbons's admonition that we not forget.

National conversations about the legacy of America's original sin have prompted America's universities to look closely at their own histories. In 2003, Brown University president Ruth Simmons commissioned a report on *Slavery and Justice,* and highlighted the indebtedness of that institution to the revenue from the African slave trade. Craig Wilder's 2013 *Ebony and Ivy: Race, Slavery, and the Troubled History of America's Universities* focused attention on the financial underpinnings that the profits from enslavement provided for America's oldest institutions of higher education, especially those in the Northeast. In the past decade, many other universities have turned their scrutiny on themselves, undertaking projects (often faculty and student led) to understand each institution's indebtedness to slavery: Harvard, Princeton, Yale, William & Mary, Washington & Lee, Emory, the University of South Carolina, the University of Mississippi, to name a few. Most recently, national attention was captured by Georgetown University, where in 1838 Jesuit priests sold 272 people from a Maryland plantation to Louisiana in order to raise money for the college. In a first step toward reparations, Georgetown promised preferential admission status to any descendants of those 272 people.

The majority of America's early universities were intertwined with slavery. Some benefited from gifts given by those who earned money through the slave trade or the business of insuring ships and enslaved persons. Others owned a few people who worked at the institution. Others were supported either directly by slaveowners in the South, or by northern industrialists who profited from the labor of the enslaved. The 272 people sold to raise money for Georgetown is the largest known sale of people to benefit an American university. Many of the descendants of those enslaved people have been identified. The Georgetown history is a pointedly poignant one particularly because of our ability to connect to living descendants today; it allows us to personalize the cost of institutional slavery that might otherwise remain abstract. Additionally, the act of selling people crystallizes the most dehumanizing aspects of slavery and thus focuses a spotlight on American higher education's obligation to acknowledge the broad debt that most of America's early institutions of higher education owe to enslavement.

At the University of Virginia, the role of slavery was much more deeply entangled and even more pervasive, shaping the lives of students, faculty, and the enslaved. In its very inception, even in Jefferson's own imagining of what the University of Virginia could be, he understood it to be an institution with slavery at its core, both in how it operated and in its purpose. He believed that a southern institution was necessary to protect the sons of the South from abolitionist teachings in the North. Jefferson wrote to his friend James Breckinridge and expressed his concern with sending the youth of Virginia to be educated in the North, a place "against us in position and principle." He worried that in northern institutions young Virginians might imbibe "opinions and principles in discord with those of their own country. This canker is eating on the vitals of our existence, and if not arrested at once will be beyond remedy."[8] In other words, Jefferson believed it was important to educate Virginians, and other southerners, in an institution that understood and ultimately supported slavery. As many historians have discussed, Jefferson's own thinking about slavery was enormously complex and contradictory, but it is important to note that at the end of his life, he created an institution that helped to perpetuate the institution by protecting the future leaders of the South from antislavery thought in the North. Ultimately, the southern institution he created also helped shape the articulation and promulgation of an increasingly aggressive proslavery argument.

Revealing the complexity of his relationship with slavery, Jefferson himself had written about the corrupting influence of slavery on the morals of southerners even as he wanted to remove southerners from northern colleges that critiqued the institution. In his *Notes on the State of Virginia*, he had written of the "unremitting despotism," of slavery and noted how "[t]he parent storms, the child looks on, catches the lineaments of wrath, puts on the same airs in the circle of smaller slaves, gives a loose to his worst of passions, and thus nursed, educated, and daily exercised in tyranny, cannot but be stamped by it with odious peculiarities. The man must be a prodigy who can retain his manners and morals undepraved by such circumstances."[9] A painter in the early nineteenth century captured poignantly the violence that enslaved people faced on a daily basis. On the back of a portrait of an unknown individual, the artist created a dual image with the words "Virginian Luxuries," at the bottom (fig. I.2). This chilling image captured the depravity that Jefferson had warned about decades earlier in his *Notes on the State of Virginia*. Most of the students who attended the university had been nursed in the exercise of tyranny at home. When they came to the university, their education in tyranny only deepened.

In fact, Jefferson's own reality was one so intimately connected with slavery that he probably could not imagine a different reality. His earliest memory was being carried on a pillow at the age of two by an enslaved person and when he died in 1826 his last moments were eased by his enslaved butler, Burwell Colbert, who adjusted Jefferson's pillows in his waning hours.[10] He had never known life without slavery and the educational institution he designed in the last decade of his life had slavery at its core. Slavery remained essential to the University of Virginia for the first fifty years of its history until the end of the Civil War brought freedom to the people who lived and labored there. This is the story we will tell in the following chapters.

Jefferson wrote that he imagined his university to be an "academical village," as he called it and as students today still refer to it, a place where faculty and students would live and learn together. Jefferson's design consisted of four

FIG. I.2. *Virginian Luxuries*, unidentified artist, ca. 1825.

parallel rows of buildings, with a massive structure at the north end, called the Rotunda, and open-ended to the south (fig. I.3). Each of the four rows consisted of dormitory rooms for students interspersed with larger structures called pavilions on the inner two rows (the collective space referred to as the Lawn) and larger buildings called hotels on the outer two rows (referred to as the Ranges). The pavilions were designated by Roman numerals, odd on the west side (I, III, V, VII, and IX), and even on the east side (II, IV, VI, VIII, and X). The hotels were designated by letters, A, C, and E on the west side and B, D, and F to the east (fig. I.4). The Rotunda that closed the northern end was intended as a space for meetings and classes and it housed the library. The pavilions served a dual function—classroom space on the ground floor and lodging for the faculty on the upper story. The hotels were intended as dining halls for students and residences for the people hired to serve as hotelkeepers. Jefferson's attention to the university is legendary; he designed each of the buildings, attended to numerous details, visited regularly during construction, specified the curriculum, selected the volumes to be purchased for the library, and guided the selection of the original fac-

Fig. I.3. Aerial view of Academical Village. The view shows the original library, called the Rotunda, dominating the north end of a long lawn flanked on each site by five pavilions. The six hotels stand on the outside ranges, three to the north and three to the south.

ulty. The architecture of each of the principal buildings was distinct: the Rotunda was modeled after the Pantheon in Rome and each of the pavilions and hotels was inspired by a different architectural precedent, most of them derived from published guides to ancient architecture. They were intended to serve as models of good architecture for the benefit of the students. This is the general outline of a history repeated over and over again. It has such broad cultural currency among the University of Virginia community that nearly every faculty member, student, and alumnus could easily repeat it. This is the shared public memory for the University of Virginia community. What is not a part of that commonly shared story, however, is the fact that the university's existence was made possible by a large enslaved population. From the day that Jefferson stood in that field with "ten hands" and "set the men at work," until the day that freedom finally came to Virginia in 1865, enslaved African Americans helped to make the university what it was.

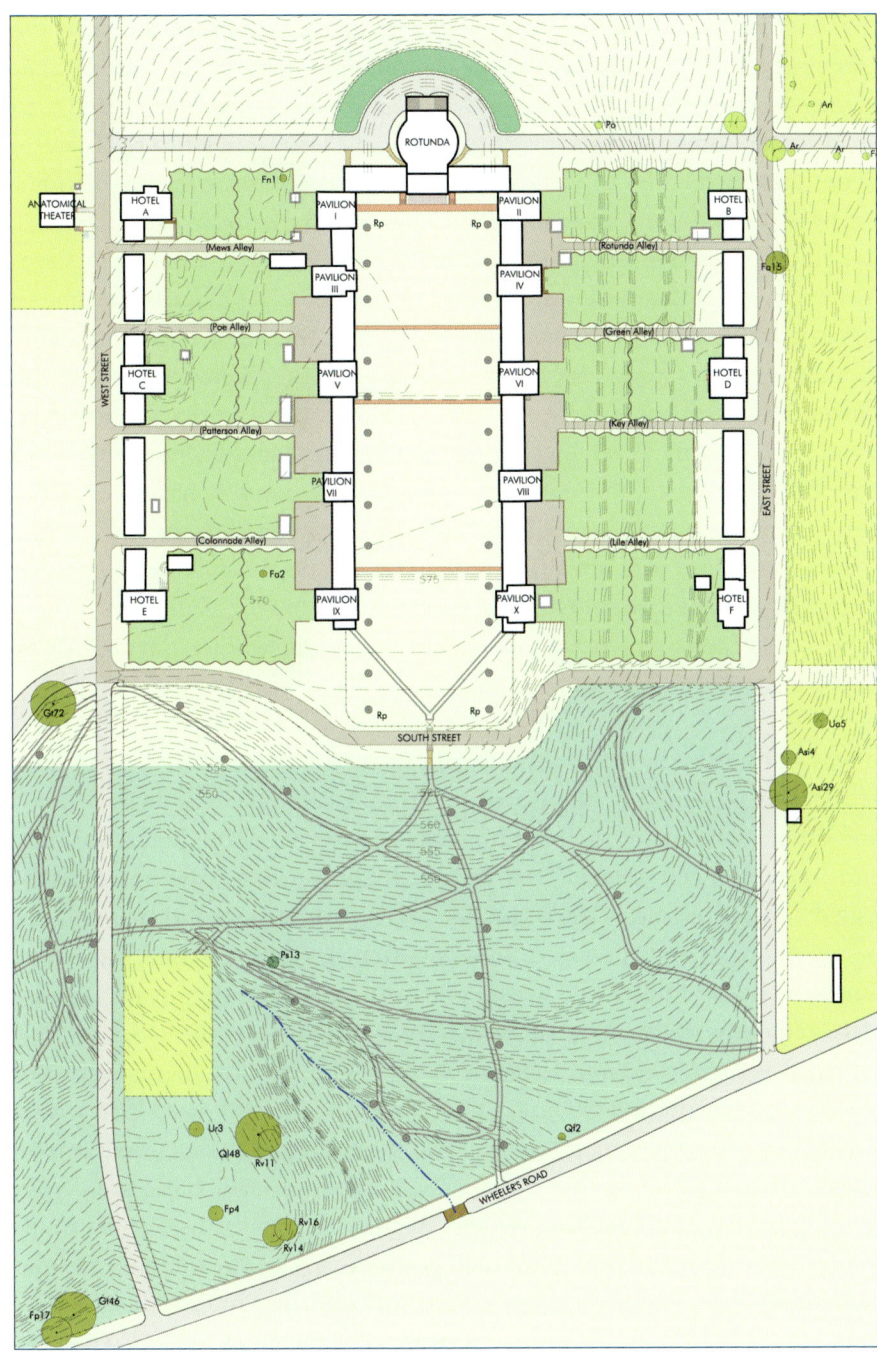

FIG. I.4. Plan of the Academical Village in 1827 from 2013 Cultural Landscape Report of the University of Virginia.

Construction on the university began in 1817 and for nearly ten years the University of Virginia was one of the—if not the—largest construction sites in America. Dozens of artisans—white and black—lived and worked to erect the buildings of the university. Many of these workers were enslaved. Some were owned by the white builders who came to Charlottesville, but the need for both skilled and unskilled labor was immense. In order to secure the labor that was needed, the university hired enslaved labor from slave-owners in Albemarle and the surrounding counties. For many who came to construct UVA, they were dozens of miles from their homes, and probably did not see their families for the months or years they were hired out to the university. Hiring out enslaved labor was a common practice in the American South, bringing in a cash income for the owners. Most of the people who were hired were men; the names of more than one hundred have been rediscovered. Some people were hired for a short term and specific jobs, while others were hired year after year to work at the university. Some provided the grunt work of earth moving, forming terraces and digging cellars; others were skilled artisans working alongside free white workers laying bricks, plastering walls, and shingling roofs.

It was not until 1825 that the university opened its doors to students. The school was governed by the Board of Visitors; Jefferson was its first rector and other members of the board included James Madison, James Monroe, and John Hartwell Cocke. Even before students arrived, the board established a series of rules, called *Enactments,* to govern the institution and the people living there. After a couple of years, the board passed numerous amendments and published a second heavily edited version in 1827. These were regularly updated and provide great insight into the tensions that emerged as the Academical Village grew. The number of students increased steadily over the period from 1825 to the beginning of the Civil War, with a marked increase beginning around 1850, from about 120 in its first year to about 600 just before the Civil War. The number of faculty also grew from the original eight to seventeen in 1860. At first, the faculty lived in the pavilions on the Lawn and they were each given the use of the building and the garden behind to modify as they wished with approval of the board. As the number of faculty soon exceeded the number of pavilions, they also lived in other places nearby.

The first *Enactments* (the rules passed by the Board of Visitors for running the university) specified that the hotels were to be rented to individuals (called hotelkeepers) who were expected to provide for the meals and other domestic needs of the students. The hotelkeepers were allowed the use of the hotel building and the areas just behind each hotel, the workyards, where it was expected that food would be grown, meals would be prepared, and linens would be washed. After the experience of the first few years, a revised version of the *Enactments* added new expectations to the role of the hotelkeepers, now directing them also to closely monitor student behavior. They were told that it was their "duty" to "suppress any disorder or riot." As the years progressed, the board required that the behaviors of both hotelkeepers and students were increasingly monitored and regulated.

The reason for this change is that the early years of the university were marked by significant student unrest and tension between the faculty and the students. The young men who came to the University of Virginia were mostly drawn from the state's planter class.[11] Believing that they were masters themselves, they resented the rules placed on them by the faculty, many of whom they would not have viewed as their social equals. They were certainly not used to discipline, and the *Enactments* spelled out a long list of behaviors they were expected *not* to engage in: drinking, card playing, and gambling at the top of the list. It also spelled out a lot of behaviors they were expected to partake in: wearing a uniform, arising with the ringing of the six a.m. bell, and attending classes. Unaccustomed to such strictures, and feeling as if many faculty rules treated them like a "parcel of children," many of the students expressed their displeasure through riotous means, using the cover of darkness to harass the faculty with noise-making or sometimes with considerably more violent activities. Banging on doors, breaking windows, and burning privies were common activities. The riotous behaviors of the students reached a crescendo when Professor John Davis was shot dead as he tried to unmask a rioting student.[12]

For the first fifty years of the university's history, there were three groups of people living in the Academical Village: faculty and hotelkeepers (and their families), students, and enslaved workers. The enslaved people were owned primarily by the professors and the hotelkeepers. According to census data, the faculty and hotelkeepers collectively owned between 125 to 200 people. In addition, faculty, hotelkeepers, and the institution itself often rented enslaved people from other owners, sometimes for a short-term project and sometimes annually for a period of several years. It is possible that the population of enslaved people living in the Academical Village may have been even larger than reported in the census. As at many other southern universities, from the beginning the students were not allowed to bring personal servants with them. This rule appeared alongside many others in the very first publication of the *Enactments*. The Board of Visitors, with Jefferson as its rector, passed the following regulation months before the university had any faculty or any students: "No Student shall, within the precincts of the University . . . keep a servant."[13] That rule remained in place until the end of the Civil War.

The rule was not, however, one that removed students from the institution of slavery or its "unremitting despotism." It was, instead, part of the system of order that the board and faculty wished to inculcate at the institution. That is, the rule was likely intended to ensure that the faculty would be able to assert control within the Academical Village. If the students had their own personal enslaved attendants, then the faculty would not have any authority over those enslaved workers. In addition, the rule may have been intended to provide a certain degree of social leveling. Jefferson had always imagined that the university would be open and available to students of intellectual merit, not merely those who could afford it. In fact, it was originally intended that many of the early students be supported by scholarships, although scholarships for a small portion of the students were not fully funded until 1845.[14] Through this rule, the students who did not have the financial means to have a personal servant would not be distinct from those who did. The board also passed a uniform rule, which specified that clothing of coarse fabric be worn by every student. This also was intended to have a social leveling effect, or at least to remind students of their place in the hierarchy of the university. Whatever the impetus for the rule that forbade personal servants, it did not work in reality. The students at the University of Virginia acted as if they were masters of any and all enslaved in the Academical Village. Most of the students came from southern slaveholding families where they were accustomed to the relationship of master and servant, and the "unremitting despotism" of slavery remained a defining feature of life in the Academical Village.

In addition, students at the university found themselves at the center of the intellectual debates surrounding the place of slavery in southern society. As the decades progressed, slavery became the nation's most pressing political issue and the university's faculty became some of the nation's leading proslavery voices. In their classrooms, their social clubs, and at public speeches, students at the university were surrounded by conversations that only cemented the notions of mastery they had been taught at home. Former students regularly returned to the university to lecture, and their speeches in support of slavery served as important reinforcement for the messages students heard all around them. In fact, many of the university's graduates became leading politicians throughout the South and thus the university's role in promoting proslavery thought spread far. A UVA alumnus and member of the U.S. House of Representatives, Robert M. T. Hunter, told students on the Fourth of July events in 1839 that slavery was "the only relation in which the two races can coexist in harmony, and operate for the mutual benefit of both."[15] In the inescapable proslavery rhetoric of campus conversations, their education in the tyranny of slavery only deepened.

The pervasiveness of proslavery sentiment is illustrated by student reaction to the visit of Catharine Beecher in 1855. As the sister of Harriet Beecher Stowe, author of the wildly popular and influential antislavery novel *Uncle Tom's Cabin,* Beecher was met with "threatening demonstrations" and "treated to a mock serenade, and Mrs. Stowe was burnt in effigy."[16] The university thus served to do so much more than educate students in the law, languages, and anatomy; the university served to create the South's leading class. Both inside the classroom and out, students received constant reinforcement in the lessons of the proslavery movement that argued for a natural hierarchy based on race. At the University of Virginia, students learned to be southern gentlemen; they learned the skills and attitudes necessary for a position in the South's master class.

The regular daily contact between students and the enslaved was part of the design of the institution from its inception. As the faculty turned their attention to operating the university, they spelled out expectations for the hotelkeepers that governed the expectations of the enslaved. In addition to providing food (and they even specified a minimal menu), since none of the students were allowed to bring their own enslaved servants, each of the hotelkeepers was expected to provide services to the students in their dormitories. These began with lighting a fire by six a.m. and bringing fresh water at the start of the day. It was expected that the rooms be swept, the beds made, firewood or ice delivered as appropriate for the season, in addition to the regular washing of sheets, windows, and so forth. All of these duties were to be performed by enslaved people generally owned or hired by the hotelkeepers. In 1835, the faculty minutes recorded that each hotelkeeper should keep at least one enslaved person to wait on every ten rooms, with up to twenty students.[17]

In general, the hotelkeepers, each of whom generally owned or hired ten to twenty people, assigned different tasks to different individuals. Some were responsible for the duties of food preparation and serving and some were responsible for tending to the students in their dormitory rooms. In general, hotelkeepers had both adults and children who waited at table, in one document described as "three men and several boys,"[18] and in another as "two men, & a servant woman, and a boy & girl about 10 years old."[19]

Only the students dined at the hotels. Faculty members were expected to provide for their own domestic needs and so they also owned people who were expected to take care of daily domestic chores. The workyards behind the hotels and pavilions were the busy worksites of the more than one hundred enslaved individuals who provided for the domestic needs of the faculty and students. Nineteenth-century life was messy. Preparing food for the several hundred people who lived inside the Academical Village (free and enslaved) meant that livestock had to be kept, crops had to be grown, animals had to be butchered, and meat had to be smoked. Cooking involved tending pots over open flames all day long, and laundry involved cauldrons of boiling water, washboards, and clotheslines. As it had at Monticello, this dirty work took place mostly out of sight, primarily in basements of the pavilions and hotels and in the workyards behind these buildings. From the beginning, Jefferson understood these areas to be the necessary work zone for domestic life, expecting the professors to add additional buildings because, as he noted, "a smokehouse is indispensable to a Virginia family."[20] With time, dozens of buildings were added to the gardens: slave quarters, kitchens, washhouses, smokehouses, woodsheds, and privies, among others. As the university became more crowded, there were additional rules passed that were intended to diminish the messiness of life in the gardens. For example, new rules forbade the keeping of animals inside the precincts, and yet complaints continued to be lodged about residents keeping cows and pigs and more broadly about insanitary conditions. The university had been built on a hilltop and the lack of free-flowing water often proved challenging to cleanliness and health. A number of significant epidemics occurred, some resulting in the deaths of both students and enslaved, and when these occurred the enslaved were tasked with additional cleaning measures such as spreading lime or whitewashing buildings. Significantly, having so many people living in such densely packed quarters meant that there were constant points of friction.

For decades a fairly simple narrative, one that focused on the genius and creativity of Jefferson's designs, dominated the early history of Thomas Jefferson's university. Of the popularly available books that told the history of the university, or in the materials the university itself presented in official publications or in the exhibition space of the Rotunda, slavery was never mentioned. The narrative skipped quickly from Jefferson's designs to the Civil War, to the twentieth century. Changing this narrative and uncovering this history has been a multiyear effort of many individuals. Research by local historians, archeological excavations, and papers by students all asked important questions that began to challenge the prevailing narrative. It has required a community coming together to demand change.[21] This volume relies heavily on this broader community effort.

The initial research efforts made it clear that there was evidence to help tell this story, but the challenge is, as it is for so much of the history related to slavery, that the evidence is scarce, incomplete, and scattered. Importantly, we do not have any sources that come directly from people formerly enslaved at UVA. Instead, the information about their lives and experiences has to be pieced together from multiple sources. Local historian Gayle Shulman published one of the earliest papers on the topic. For twenty years, archaeologist and author Benjamin Ford has been excavating this history. His research informs much of the work presented in this volume. Many faculty members, including several of the authors for this volume, had been teaching the broad outlines of this history for many years, but they knew that what was needed was more expansive archival research. That was daunting, however, because of the many thousands of pages of materials in the university archives. No one person could ever read it all or figure out how to make connections between the many fragmentary bits. In 2012, authors Maurie McInnis and Kirt von Daacke began working with Worthy Martin and the Institute of Advanced Technology in the Humanities (IATH) to create the "Jefferson's University—Early Life Project, 1819–1870" (hereafter cited as JUEL, http://juel.iath.virginia.edu). With monetary support from the Office of the Executive Vice President and Provost and the Jefferson Trust of the University of Virginia Alumni Association, they created a searchable digital archive for the university's history. These archives include the university's official records, letters and diaries of students and faculty, and other pertinent materials. Over the years, dozens of students have contributed to this project by transcribing the university's archival materials and creating xml tags that make them easily searchable. The students who have worked on this project have also contributed by writing essays and conducting additional research that allow the threads of evidence to be woven together into a richer and fuller story. This book would not be possible without their efforts and we want to acknowledge their important contributions. The work on the project continues; new materials are added regularly and new discoveries and connections emerge.

Despite the efforts of dozens of people, the story remains fragmentary. It is important to note what the archives tell us and what they do not. The most consistent and prolific sources are the university's official records. These include financial records from the construction period. Here we find notations of the payments made to slaveowners who hired out men they owned to provide construction labor. In these records, we find the names (usually only first names) of more than one hundred enslaved men who helped build the university. Once students arrived, the evidence about slavery is found mostly in the chairman's journals and the faculty minutes. Each of these were kept in large leather-bound volumes and they record two things primarily: first, the academic progress of students, and second, the misbehavior of students. What we miss in these volumes is any sense of regular day-to-day activities, although there are some letters and diaries of faculty and students that provide information about more routine daily matters. In the official documents we get a wealth of information whenever a student broke the rules in the *Enactments*. The faculty acted like a court, gathering evidence and testimony whenever a student was accused of misbehavior. This information is recorded in these volumes and from it we can learn a lot about student interactions with enslaved workers, quite often acts of violence. Sometimes enslaved people are mentioned by name, but often they are referred to only as "Captain Rose's servants," or some other term that describes them merely as property. Even when an enslaved person is mentioned by name, we usually know little else about them. From census records we know how many people were owned and by whom, and in 1850 and 1860, the census recorded the ages and genders of those people. But they are nameless lists. We know little of their lives. We know little of their families, their heartaches, their joys, their struggles, and their hopes. The stories we tell in this volume are built up from these scraps of information. But it is incomplete. The work will continue and we hope in future years we will be able to uncover more stories.

Another important form of evidence comes from the buildings themselves. Jefferson's Academical Village is one of the most intact and unaltered nineteenth-century set of buildings and landscapes in America (except for the Rotunda, which was famously burned in 1895 and later reconstructed). The buildings have been modernized with the addition of plumbing and electricity and technology. Substantial additions, most dating to the nineteenth century, have expanded the pavilions and some of the hotels. Nevertheless, the historic core of each building remains largely intact. The buildings themselves, therefore, are also an important set of documents providing important evidence about the history of their habitation. In 2015, author Louis Nelson and the students in his Historic Preservation course conducted a thorough analysis of the cellars and attics of pavilions, hotels, and student rooms to look for evidence of habitation that might tell us more about the spaces where enslaved people lived and labored. The evidence they uncovered and documented, especially when paired with archival references, has been an important part of understanding the story of slavery at UVA.

Finally, another important aspect of the JUEL project has been to create a three-dimensional digital model of the Academical Village in the period of enslavement (fig. I.5). Because so many of the buildings in the gardens that served the pavilions and the hotels are no longer extant, Lauren Massari at IATH working with JUEL has led the development of a digital model, working to re-create the nineteenth-century Academical Village, and eventually its immediate landscape. This has required the three-dimensional digital reconstruction of portions of the historical landscape; the buildings and structures as well as the major landscape components such as gardens, alleys, walls, and fences that would have been present in the mid-nineteenth-century Academical Village. Creating the digital model has utilized historic images, laser-guided measurements of extant buildings, and drone-guided studies of the topography to aid in reconstructing the proper human perspective. The ongoing digital reconstruction of the nineteenth-century Academical Village allows us to understand better some of the questions that are central to the history we hope to tell.

In 2019, the University of Virginia will begin its official bicentennial celebrations; there was a soft launch in 2017. This is obviously the cause for much

FIG. I.5. Aerial view of the Academical Village generated from the "Jefferson's University—Early Life Project, 1819–1870" (JUEL) digital model of the early university. Those sites in color are fully rendered while those in gray are under development.

celebration. But it should also be a moment for important institutional reflection. The history of the university is bound up and inseparable from the institution of slavery. It is built on the human suffering of those who labored here. For more than one hundred years after freedom came, other African Americans were denied access to the University of Virginia merely because of the color of their skin. It was not until the late 1960s that the university began admitting a significant number of black undergraduate students, later than even most other southern universities. This is a story that has for too long remained untold. Mindful of the upcoming bicentennial, the authors of this volume hope that these chapters will help everyone understand the paradox of freedom and democracy built on the tyranny of slavery that the University of Virginia embodies. One hundred years ago, at the university's centennial celebrations, the pageants, plays, and speeches lauded and mythologized Jefferson (fig. I.6). Only fifty years ago at the university's sesquicentennial celebrations, Jefferson continued to be the focus of the events. The year was 1969, the university had only recently begun to admit African American undergraduate students in sizable numbers, and students were dissatisfied with the official celebrations and organized a counter-event

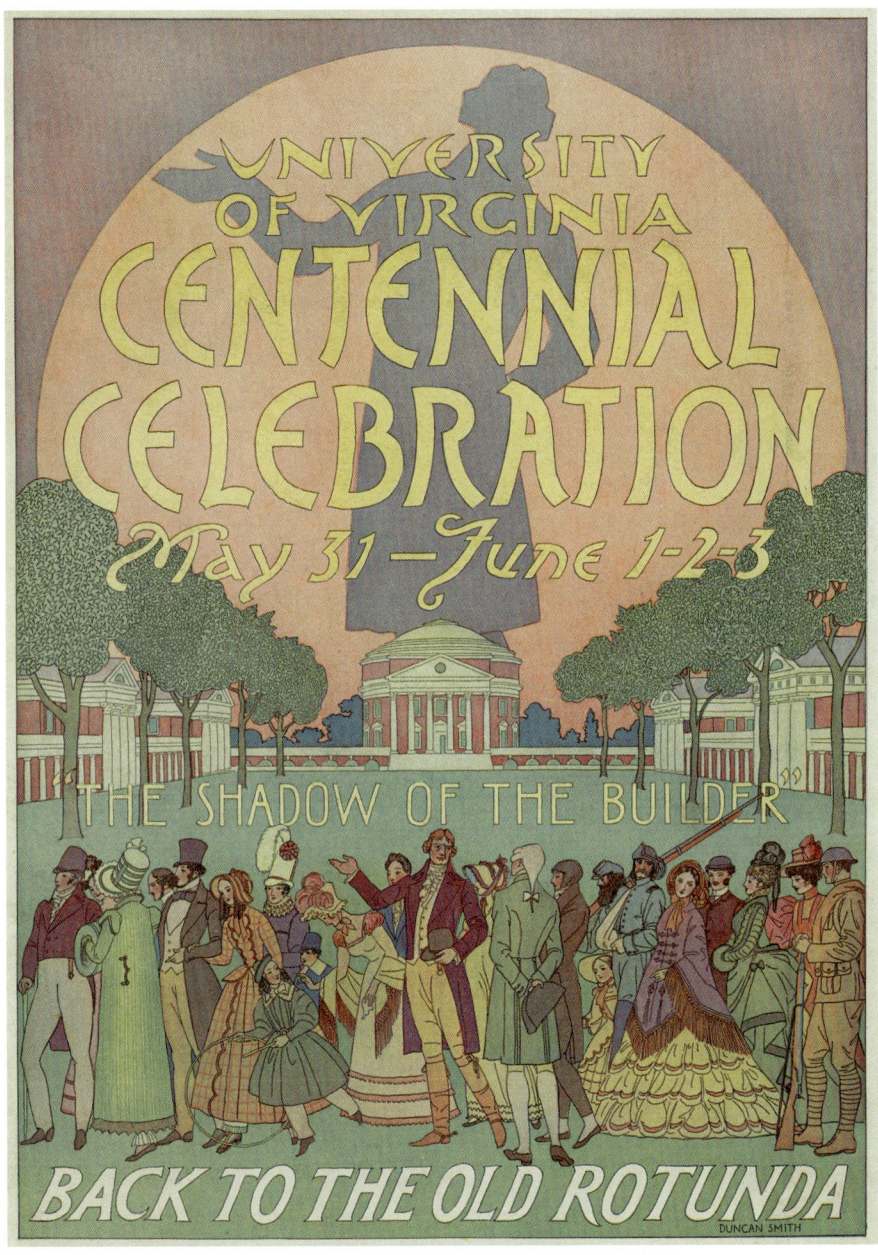

FIG. I.6. "Shadow of the Builder: Back to the Old Rotunda" UVA centennial celebration poster, 1921.

to insist that the university do more to diversify its student body and its curriculum. From the official recognition of the university's history at both of these events acknowledgment of slavery was absent. The current community-wide effort has been an effort to make sure that we no longer forget, as Gibbons called for in 1867. The celebrations of the bicentennial events have been and will be very different. The 2017 opening Bicentennial celebration acknowledged a very different history by including a sequence highlighting the enslaved laborers who built the university, monologues by Jefferson's African American descendants, and a rendition by Andra Day of Billie Holiday's protest song "Strange Fruit" (fig. I.7).

When we began this work, it seemed urgent and too long overdue. As at many universities, African American students at the University of Virginia report encountering an unwelcoming and sometimes even a hostile environment. The institution's long silence about its indebtedness to slavery and another century of segregation undoubtedly contribute to that feeling. The disconnect between the university's story of itself, that it was founded in order to ensure the continuance of democracy, and its history of excluding black students for nearly the first 150 years is palpable.

The continuing legacy of that paradox was brought to the world's attention when on August 11 and 12, 2017, a "Unite the Right" rally including large groups of Neo-Nazi and white nationalist protestors gathered on the campus of the University of Virginia and in downtown Charlottesville (fig. I.8). Their event was intended in part to protest the city's consideration of removing an equestrian monument to Robert E. Lee from a central location in the downtown to a more remote public park. The organizer of the event, Richard Spencer, was likely attracted to the university for several reasons. An obvious connection is that he is a graduate of the University of Virginia. Being a graduate, he was keenly aware of the clash between the city's currently progressive political culture and its history as a bastion of Jim Crow politics and racial oppression. Charlottesville schools participated in the "massive resistance" movement in the 1950s, closing rather than integrating after the *Brown v. Board of Education* decision ordering the integration of public schools. Racial inequality is a legacy still palpable in the city's school system.[22] The University of Virginia remained all male and all white until the late 1960s. It was one of the latest to integrate its undergraduate population, and women were admitted only in 1970.

FIG. I.7. Gale Jessup White and Calvin Jefferson speak at the UVA Bicentennial Celebration, 2017. Behind them stand other descendants of enslaved laborers from UVA and Monticello and James Madison's plantation Montpelier and James Monroe's plantation Highland.

Ever since the August 11 rally at the university that brought white supremacist protestors into conflict with student counter-protestors, the work of this volume has taken on an even greater urgency. While there is much that is still not known about the hundreds of individuals who labored to create and sustain the University of Virginia, we hope that this volume will allow readers to understand how the legacy of slavery is still felt on this and many other college campuses. The scars of that history are written into its landscapes and its buildings. In 2013, President Teresa Sullivan launched the President's Commission on Slavery and the University. That group has played a vital role in reshaping how the institution's history is told and has helped to change the collective memory of the university community. Previously, the university's landscape had largely obliterated any acknowledgment of slavery. The gardens are now beautiful and idyllic retreats. Virtually all of the slave quarter and kitchen and washhouse buildings are gone. The ones that remain have been substantially altered. There are no historic markers that address this history. But that silence has ended. In 2015, the newest residence hall

Fig. I.8. Photograph of white supremacists surrounding students on the UVA Grounds, August 11, 2017.

was named Gibbons House in honor of William and Isabella Gibbons, who were enslaved at UVA. In 2017, a new building for Facilities Management was named for Peyton Skipwith, an enslaved laborer, freed in 1833, who worked as a stonemason at UVA. In 2015, the commission dedicated the newly rediscovered African American Burial Ground. The historical interpretive materials in the Rotunda were substantially redesigned to deal head-on with the history of slavery. In addition, the Board of Visitors approved the design of a Memorial to Enslaved Laborers that will have a prominent location just to the northeast of the Rotunda, near Brooks Hall (fig. I.9). The memorial, currently under construction, will forever serve as a public, physical reminder of the central paradox of the institution and the hundreds of people whose lives and labor enabled the creation of the University of Virginia. These collective efforts will help to change the public memory of the university community.

FIG. I.9. Renderings of UVA's intended Memorial to Enslaved Laborers, 2018.

The work of changing that narrative begins with uncovering, acknowledging, and telling this history. This volume is intended to help everyone understand this story more fully and to serve as a starting point from which additional research can be launched and other stories uncovered as the university and all of America continues to grapple with the legacy of slavery at America's institutions of higher education.

NOTES

1. Thomas Jefferson, "Notes on the Siting of Central College, July 18, 1817," in *The Papers of Thomas Jefferson, Retirement Series* vol. 11, 19 January to 31 August 1817 (Princeton, NJ: Princeton University Press, 2014), 544.

2. Thomas Jefferson to James Madison, 20 December 1787, https://founders.archives.gov/about/Jefferson.

3. Thomas Jefferson to Charles Yancey, 6 January 1816, https://founders.archives.gov/about/Jefferson.

4. Edmund Bacon, "Jefferson at Monticello: The Private Life of Thomas Jefferson," in *Jefferson at Monticello: Recollections of a Monticello Slave and of a Monticello Overseer*, ed. James A. Bear Jr. (Charlottesville: University Press of Virginia, 1967), 32–33.

5. See Garry Wills, *Mr. Jefferson's University* (Washington, DC: National Geographic Society, 2006).

6. Thomas Jefferson to Samuel Du Pont de Nemours, April 24, 1816, https://founders.archives.gov/about/Jefferson.

7. Isabella Gibbons ("Mrs. Isabella Gibbins") letter, March 29, 1867, *The Freedmen's Record* 3, no. 6 (June 1867), quoted in Gerda Lerner, *Black Women in White America: A Documentary History* (New York: Pantheon, 1972), 105. Gibbons was owned by Professor Francis Smith and worked as a cook from 1853 to 1863.

8. Thomas Jefferson to James Breckenridge, 15 February 1821, https://founders.archives.gov/about/Jefferson.

9. Thomas Jefferson, *Notes on the State of Virginia* (London: Printed for John Stockdale, 1787), 270–71. Access to Jefferson's personal copy is available at http://static.lib.virginia.edu/rmds/tj/notes/index.html.

10. Henry S. Randall, *The Life of Thomas Jefferson* (Philadelphia: J. B. Lippincott, 1865), 1: 11; John Meacham, *Thomas Jefferson: The Art of Power* (New York: Random House, 2012), 494.

11. Students at UVA were typically wealthier than their counterparts at other universities, in part because the school was more expensive. See Jennings Wagoner Jr., "Honor and Dishonor at Mr. Jefferson's University: The Antebellum Years," *History of Education Quarterly* (Summer 1986): 167–68.

12. Ronald B. Head, ed., "The Student Diary of Charles Ellis Jr., March 10–June 25, 1835," *Magazine of Albemarle County History* 35–36 (1977–1978): 12. See also Jon L. Wakelyn, "Antebellum College Life and the Relations between Fathers and Sons," in *The Web of Southern Social Relations: Women, Family, and Education*, edited by Walter J. Fraser Jr., R. Frank Saunders Jr., and Jon L. Wakely (Athens: University of Georgia Press, 1985), 107–26. The riots are well covered in Rex Bowman and Carlos Santos, *Rot, Riot, and Rebellion: Mr. Jefferson's Struggle to Save the University That Changed America* (Charlottesville: University of Virginia Press, 2013).

13. Board of Visitors Minutes, 1817–2007, October 4, 1824, http://juel.iath.virginia.edu/resources. For more, see Catherine A. Creighton, "Offences, Punishment, and Early Student Self-Governance at the University (1824)," http://juel.iath.virginia.edu/node/232.

14. A bill passed in 1818 specified an extensive selection process for state scholarship

recipients, but the program was not funded until 1845. See Meghan Ellwood, "A Scholarship for State Students," http://juel.iath.virginia.edu/node/411.

15. Robert M. T. Hunter, "An Address Delivered before the Society of the Alumni of the University of Virginia, at Its Second Annual Meeting, Held in the Rotunda, on the 4th of July, 1839," p. 23, Albert and Shirley Small Special Collections Library, University of Virginia.

16. *Uncle Tom's Cabin; or, Life among the Lowly* (Boston: John P. Jewett, 1852). Quotations from *The Liberator*, June 8, 1855, and June 1, 1855.

17. Minutes of the Faculty of the University of Virginia, 1825–1856, September 12, 1835, http://juel.iath.virginia.edu/resources (hereafter cited as Faculty Minutes).

18. Faculty Minutes, April 28, 1834, http://juel.iath.virginia.edu/resources.

19. Journals of the Chairman of the Faculty, 1827–1864, November 27, 1838, http://juel.iath.virginia.edu/resources.

20. Thomas Jefferson to Arthur Brockenbrough, November 12, 1825, https://founders.archives.gov/about/Jefferson.

21. The efforts of these many people are detailed on the President's Commission website at http://slavery.virginia.edu/a-tip-of-the-hat/.

22. "'You are still black': Charlottesville's Racial Divide Hinders Students," *New York Times,* October 16, 2018.

1

SLAVERY AND CONSTRUCTION

Louis P. Nelson and James Zehmer

Zachariah was exhausted. He was strong, but the task was daunting. His owner, Luther M. George, recently leased him to the university, which had been under construction for two years. Soon after Zachariah arrived on site Mr. Henderson, the overseer for construction, directed him to dig the cellar and foundation for a hotel that stood behind and downhill from the first of the pavilions. Having lived and labored in Albemarle County most of his life, Zachariah had seen the firing of the massive kiln that produced the bricks for the first of the "Academical Pavilions" (now Pavilion VII). As he dug he watched other black men working daily to level the land of the larger worksite. The previous summer they removed huge volumes of earth (records would report nearly 1,000 cubic yards) forming what Mr. Henderson called "terraces." Zachariah watched as these men deployed shovels and barrows to slowly transform the gentle hillocks into the staged building sites for three more pavilions (now Pavilions I, III, and V). Soon thereafter those same men dug foundations and cellars for the next two pavilions (Pavilions II and IV); he learned there were to be ten, five on each side of the terraces. Since only one building now stood completed, Zachariah and his fellow laborers slept on pallets on the floor in the upstairs chambers while the cook struggled to produce meals in the nearly unlit cellar kitchen. Zachariah's daily work excavating the hotel cellar moved quickly until he hit bedrock. For weeks he shoveled the loose earth, all the while knowing that the substantial bedrock also had to be extracted. Once Zachariah began chipping away on the stone, his pace dramatically slowed and Henderson became frustrated. Soon, the earth-moving team from the pavilions was reassigned to work with Zachariah, and with the assistance of these others, the excavation was eventually completed.[1]

FIG. 1.1. Aerial view of Hotel A from the JUEL digital model of the Academical Village. The view shows the deeply excavated cellar.

The deep cellar of Hotel A and its attendant sunken yard (fig. 1.1) are the work of Zachariah's hands. Yet, while he was digging, Jefferson and the Board of Visitors were debating the appropriate sizes for the hotels. The sunken workyard Zachariah toiled so hard to excavate in 1821 was probably the result of the decision to shrink the building plan for the hotel *after* the cellar had already been excavated. And, if that were not frustrating enough, the majority of Zachariah's earned money, more than twenty-five dollars, would go to his owner.

Enslaved laborers—both skilled and unskilled—played a critical role in the construction of the University of Virginia, yet there are few accounts from the period that tell this story. We do not have a surviving journal from James Henderson, who was hired by the university proctor, Arthur Spicer Brockenbrough, to oversee the work of men like Zachariah. Were such a letterbook to survive we might have Henderson describing the daily tasks and habits of Zachariah and other enslaved African Americans. So one of our only options is to read between the lines of account books and to carefully piece together the working lives of enslaved laborers on the construction site through records never intended to be used that way. Zachariah's work, outlined above, comes to us with a bit more detail as a result of the frustrating nature of his task, the shifting of other laborers to the same task, and the resultant payments necessitated by the unforeseen bedrock. This chapter will provide a few glimpses into the lives of a few enslaved laborers and then will make some generalizations about their daily life during the initial construction of the university from 1817 to 1827.

Construction in antebellum America was still dominated by the traditional cultures of craft that had persisted for centuries. In fairly remote contexts, craftsmen undertook a wide range of the tasks necessary to realize a building. But in urban settings, or on major construction sites like the University of Virginia, individuals were either day laborers, often unskilled and taking any work that came their way, or they were skilled artisans, usually having learned that skill through an apprenticeship.[2] Skilled artisans usually fell into categories by building material: sawyers ripped lumber while rough carpenters could frame houses; joiners produced fine, usually interior finished work; brickmakers understood the fine craft of working clay and firing kilns while masons worked bricks up into walls with bonding patterns finished with fine mortar jointing. By the 1820s, smaller building components like glass, some hardware, and paint were commonly manufactured in bulk and transported to the site. But there they would be assembled and installed by specialist artisans: glaziers, painters, and so forth. In the antebellum South, these artisans could be free whites, free blacks, or enslaved, and the majority of construction sites had all three laboring side by side, some earning money for their efforts, others not. Timber-frame construction techniques demonstrate one way that traditional building methodology worked across socioeconomic and cultural differences. In the early nineteenth century, timber framing depended on the fundamental method of securing framing members with a system of mortise-and-tenon joinery. By using roman numerals to identify how various members of a frame were intended to be assembled, any laborer—black or white, enslaved or free—could do this work. The records of the proctor's account books, with their complex array of payments to a wide range of individuals, certainly makes clear that this was the case at the University of Virginia.

The proctor's account books provide important insights into the everyday lives of the numerous enslaved African Americans who labored to build the University of Virginia, but the entries require explication. For example, on December 24, 1821, Proctor Brockenbrough made a draft to pay "Jack for the waggonage of a Hhd [hogshead] of plaster from Milton & Lundy for kiln drying planks." The total was two dollars.[3] This entry is interesting in a number of ways. The first is the reminder that enslaved laborers—skilled and unskilled—were regularly leased to the proctor, as the agent of the university, to undertake work in the construction. For many large construction projects, it was common for enslaved people to be hired from local slaveowners. Sometimes, laborers were hired for an entire year, or they might be hired for a particular project. In these leasing arrangements the earned money was usually paid to the laborer's owner, but occasionally, as in this case, enslaved workers were additionally compensated for accomplishing above-average arduous tasks like digging the Hotel A cellar through bedrock (in this case the compensation was whiskey) or successfully completing unsupervised work like kiln-drying planks. The second is that the entry records that Jack drove the wagon of hogsheads (large wooden barrels roughly four feet long and thirty inches in diameter) to the university construction site from Milton Farm, about eight miles away. Milton Farm was an important port on the Rivanna River and home to a lime kiln. This is a reminder that the construction of the university was a massive undertaking requiring the acquisition of huge volumes of building materials, many of which, contrary to common mythologies, were not produced on site but were produced in workyards all over the region or even across the state. Lastly, the draft was made on Christmas Eve, so perhaps the timing of this payment was related to the upcoming holiday, commonly the only week-long work break during the year, or it could just be simply year-end accounting.

In the following year, the proctor's accounts record a four-dollar payment for "coffin for Rhoda," a poignant reminder of the lives behind the entries in the ledger book.[4] And much like the portage from Milton, this entry reminds us that the university construction site was also a social landscape. One wonders if Rhoda might be among the first African Americans interred in the unmarked graves that comprise the university's African American Burial Ground. As one of the few records to capture the names and work of enslaved African Americans, this chapter depends heavily on Proctor Brockenbrough's construction-era account books. But in using this record, we have struggled to recapture these individuals as people, not numbers.

One of the men who appears most consistently in the construction record is Carpenter Sam, a well-respected artisan on the construction site who was owned by Proctor Brockenbrough. Sam first appears in the records when he is identified as the carpenter charged to begin the tinwork to cover the roof of the newly completed Pavilion VII in 1818, a task he later undertook for the roofs of Pavilion V and Hotels A, D, and F. By 1822, he was very active all around the site contributing to the carpentry work on Hotels A and C and Pavilions V and VII. Either because he was an enormously well qualified artisan or because he was owned by Proctor Brockenbrough, Sam is among the most well paid of the laborers working on site, usually drawing a salary for Brockenbrough of between twelve and nineteen dollars per month. We have no way of knowing, of course, if Sam received any of that money.

By 1824, as work on the pavilions and hotels was coming to a close, Sam built smokehouses around the site to meet the inevitable need for food preservation and storage once the pavilions and hotels were occupied. In this task, Sam supervised three other carpenters, Davey, William, and "young Sam," also owned by Brockenbough, and who may well be the carpenter's son. Later that year, Carpenter Sam was identified as "old" Sam to differentiate him from the younger carpenter of the same name. In 1825, with the smokehouses complete, a team of three carpenters—Old Sam, Young Sam, and Davey—was set to the task of building stables, once again with Old Sam in charge. Sam's services were retained until the opening of the university as the final tasks of construction dwindled to a close in 1827. Through the full decade of construction, Carpenter Sam was a prominent persona on the university's construction site, taking the lead on constructing many of the ancillary buildings necessitated by daily life at the university.[5]

None of those ancillary buildings built by Old Sam and his teams have survived. One artifact that has survived is a saw handle recently found in the attic of Pavilion X (fig. 1.2). The handle bears the stamp "A. S. Brockenbrough." As Proctor Brockenbrough was a white man of significant authority, it seems unlikely that this was his personal saw. Much more likely, this was a saw sold to the university from Brockenbrough's hardware store in Richmond or a saw from that store used by a man owned by Brockenbrough who labored to construct the university. Given the pervasiveness of Brockenbrough's carpenters working across the construction site, this saw might well have been used by Davey, William, or even the father and son team of Old and Young Sam. This saw handle is now on display in the museum on the ground floor of the Rotunda as a reminder of the work they completed.

A majority of the skilled artisans who labored to build the university were owned by builders working in the community but also throughout central Virginia. The 1820 census records that J. M. Perry, who built and lived at Montebello (not far from where Scott Stadium now stands) and also partook in the extensive construction at the university, owned thirty-seven people,

FIG. 1.2. Fragments of early nineteenth-century saw emblazoned with "A. S. Brockenbrough."

thirty of whom were involved in the construction trades.[6] Montebello was close to the university so it seems highly likely that a number of its enslaved laborers and skilled artisans were employed in the construction of the university. The same was true of other builders associated with the university. James Dinsmore and John Neilson each owned six people listed as involved in manufacturing, suggesting that both had skilled work crews of six carpenters they brought with them to their work projects.[7] So when considering the contributions of the enslaved to the construction of the university the question is not "What was built by enslaved labor?" but rather "What was not?" The account books make plainly clear that enslaved labor played a critical role in the process of realizing the Academical Village.

As suggested by the payment to Mr. George for Zachariah's labor and

Fig. 1.3. "Hurrah for Moses" chalked graffiti in the attic of Pavilion I.

to Proctor Brockenbrough for Sam's labor, many of the region's slaveowners tapped into the construction at the university as a means of generating personal income. The daybook records list at least sixteen different enslaved artisans who generated income for the proctor: Jack, Old Sam, Davey, (Young) Sam Jr., Henry, Ned, Dick, John, Aaron, Simon, Lee, Reubin, Burnly, William, Nelson, and Moses. Provocatively, the attic staircase installed in Pavilion I in 1832, when Brockenbrough was still proctor, bears a remarkable inscription scrawled in chalk: "Hurrah for Moses" (fig. 1.3). One wonders if that Moses might be the carpenter of the same name owned by the proctor put to the task of building the staircase.[8] The vagaries of enslavement mean, of course, that we may never know. Again turning to the 1820 census, Luther M. George, Zachariah's owner, owned seven people in that year, a few years before he leased Zachariah to the university.[9] Of those seven, five were men between the ages of fourteen and forty-five. Another man named Raphael was named in conjunction with Zachariah in the Proctor's Daybook associated with the digging out of the Hotel A cellar, so he may also have also been owned by George.¹⁰ George clearly felt that hiring out to the university was a worthwhile investment. A number of the members of the university's Board of Visitors, including former U.S. president James Madison, were also regularly paid for the labor of the people they owned working to build the university.

Leasing people for construction generated and depended on a fairly well established economy.¹¹ One month's work of an enslaved brickmaker, for example, generally earned an owner eight dollars. The greatest labor in brickmaking was molding the bricks, which required throwing the tempered clay into wooden molds and then extracting them to sun-dry in a yard for a few days before being kiln-fired. In the ramp-up to the production of bricks for the Rotunda, Proctor Brockenbrough hired an Irish mason who molded bricks with oil, which created a smoother surface and more uniform color, a fashion employed first on the East Pavilions. The technique produced a more uniform surface but also required greater skill to produce. This unnamed mason, the proctor estimated, was able to mold three thousand bricks per day and could sell those bricks to the construction project at a cost of $4.50 per thousand.¹² As a result, a month's labor of an enslaved man, at eight dollars per month, was a relatively insignificant factor in the economics of brick production, less than 5 percent of gross income. One month of work for an enslaved laborer at a sawmill generated about the same wage: nine dollars. By comparison, hiring an unskilled laborer on a daily rate cost significantly more, between fifty and seventy-five cents per day, or twelve to eighteen dollars a month.¹³ Because renting long-term enslaved labor was much cheaper, the proctor generally hired people for weeks, months, or even a full year at a time. The closing out of accounts in December and the frequency of new hires in January makes clear that much of the economy of construction followed the calendar year.¹⁴

At times the account books list people only as "hand," reducing them just to their capacity as a laborer, but the longer periods of hire, as long as a year or more, meant that those hired at the university became well known. They had the opportunity to build relationships with other enslaved people from around the region. This familiarity meant that many of them, like Zachariah, were listed in the account books by name. In 1824, for example, the proctor hired a team of enslaved masons to begin firing bricks for the Rotunda (fig. 1.4). Their names are recorded: Willis, Sam, John, Ben, Reubin, Nelson, Sharper, Bob, Tom, Lewis, Barrett.¹⁵ The fact of the recording suggests

Fig. 1.4. Rotunda brickwork showing high-quality bricks and precision jointing.

that the individuals' identities and their skills mattered in those accounts. As another example, a man named Burnly was tasked in 1825 with cleaning out all of the construction debris from the pavilions and hotels in preparation for the opening of the university for classes.[16] Many of these named laborers were also clearly recognized for the high quality of their craftsmanship. In 1821, the proctor agreed with a local man, Charles Bankhead, to hire Bankhead's blacksmith, William Green, for ironwork on the construction site.[17] It may well have been Green that fashioned the surviving kitchen crane in the basement of Hotel F.

When Proctor Brockenbrough needed to hire more men to help out with brickmaking, he turned to General John Hartwell Cocke, a planter and friend of Jefferson, veteran of the War of 1812, and member of the Board of Visitors. Brockenbrough knew that Cocke had masons on hand as the planter had just completed his new house at Bremo about forty miles away, under the direction of John Neilson. The proctor was unsatisfied with the small stature of the two men sent from Bremo, as indicated in a letter to Cocke shortly after their arrival: "I wish very much . . . that you will send me two larger boys say Frank and another of the largest size we had of you before," signaling the fact that the proctor knew by name at least some of the enslaved laborers

FIG. 1.5. Detail of Pavilion I from the JUEL digital model of the Academical Village showing the painted heads of Apollo with sunburst as originally painted bright yellow.

who had previously worked on site.[18] And just a few days after Jefferson's death, Cocke wrote to Proctor Brockenbrough and offered Jefferson's "faithful Servant" Burwell, "said to be a good painter—I wish you to offer him any job in his line at the University that he would undertake."[19] Burwell was not only known to Jefferson by name, but in fact was known by Jefferson's peers and might well have been known by name throughout the region.[20] It might well have been Burwell who originally painted bright yellow the masks of the entablature of Pavilion I (intended in the ancient original to be the radiant face of Apollo) (fig. 1.5).

Many of the people, free and enslaved, who built the university were well known within the building trades of central Virginia. In that same letter, Cocke writes also about another of Jefferson's favorite artisans, a white stonemason by the name of John Gorman: "If Gorman does not keep sober & otherwise deport himself well, discharge him promptly—for I am sure, You ... will do better without than with him while drunk or refractory."[21] While Gorman was still employed at Monticello, Jefferson had apprenticed Thrimston Hern, whom he owned, to learn the craft of stonemasonry, after already having mastered carpentry and coopering. Under Gorman's tutelage, Hern became "a tolerable good stone cutter," working with Gorman to finish the paving of the west portico of Monticello and the bases and capitals of the portico's columns. By 1829 Proctor Brockenbrough purchased Thrimston for $600, one of the highest sums paid for those enslaved at Monticello, and rented him to the university to complete the broad flank of steps that led up to the portico of the Rotunda at a much lower price than could be had by white stonemasons.[22] Those stone steps were removed after the 1895 Rotunda fire and some are currently installed as part of the retaining wall for Bayly Drive near the School of Architecture (fig. 1.6).

But reputations cut both ways; notoriety could also work against people if and when they decided to make an escape. Often in an apprenticeship, the enslaved laborers could become skilled artisans with an identity that differentiated them from the majority. Under such conditions, they often gained a degree of recognition to the point that their owner's peers might even know their names and ask to hire their services. As a result, they had the capacity to earn money independent of their owner, and over time, earning the possibility to purchase their own or another's freedom. In 1822, the proctor directed James Harrison to track and find Willis, an enslaved man working at the university who had fled the worksite for Louisa, about thirty miles away. Owned by planter W. Kelley, Willis had worked at the university for at least two years previous, having dug a cistern through rock in 1822 and helped to

FIG. 1.6. Remnants of original Rotunda steps repurposed along Bayly Drive.

fire brick for five months in 1823.²³ He was named because he was well known. Running away was common (fig. 1.7). A few years later when a man named Jones fled the worksite, the proctor simply deducted the lost work from his payment to Jones's owner.²⁴ While there was very certainly a racial hierarchy at play, and also a clear hierarchy between skilled and unskilled laborers, the site was not so large that enslaved workers could not distinguish themselves and be known by name and reputation, which was certainly a liability if one decided to attempt to secure one's freedom.

From 1817 through the early 1830s, the University of Virginia was one of the largest building sites in the new nation and one result of that construction was the necessary production of a prominent male-dominated community of skilled and unskilled laborers—black and white, free and enslaved—who worked side by side, sometimes for years on end. Framed by the seasonal realities of construction and animated by very real frustrations of unanticipated delays and the satisfactions of completion, this site witnessed the labor of hundreds of men through the decade, many laboring to erect buildings they would never be allowed to inhabit once complete. The Academical Village was the product of thousands of tasks and hundreds of projects undertaken by whites and blacks laboring together. Those enslaved who found themselves working here recognized that their situation differed from the more usual circumstances. They enjoyed a great deal more independence and freedom to travel than did their counterparts laboring in the fields of a plantation. And yet many of them were hired from far away, longing to return to their friends and families. Even so, recognition made all the more difficult the possibility of flight as they worked in a world ruled by whites motivated to foreclose any opportunity for real freedom.

The artisans and laborers, white and black, free and enslaved, who participated in the construction of the Academical Village also left a much larger legacy beyond the borders of the University Grounds. Many of these same people migrated to nearly every corner of the Commonwealth of Virginia, taking along with them the architectural lessons and construction techniques they had learned while working at the university. This resulted in a new architectural language, founded in the prescripts of classical architecture, which spread across the state in the form of courthouses, plantation manor homes, churches, and various other significant buildings that would influence the architectural style of Virginia and the United States forever. Such proliferation depended on the social and economic structures of slavery.

FIG. 1.7. Page of 1769 *Virginia Gazette* showing runaway slave ads.

The University of Virginia is part and parcel of an incredibly important and visually stunning world heritage site. The pavilions and the Rotunda are rightly interpreted as exemplars of the birth of an American classical architectural tradition and of the Enlightenment theories—political, scientific, social—that were often corollaries to those designs. But the architecture and landscape of the University of Virginia's Academical Village is also an extraordinary remnant of the life and labor of scores of enslaved laborers who lived, worked, and died to realize the construction of this remarkable complex of buildings. Silently, these buildings bear evidence of some named but many more unnamed lives and in this way these buildings are evidence of the history of enslavement at the University of Virginia.

NOTES

1. The vignette of Zachariah is pieced together from two entries in the proctor's account books: "Day Book, 1821–1828," 10/8/1821, p. 17, and "Day Book, 1821–1828" 11/25/1822, p. 107, RG-5/3/2/102, Albert and Shirley Small Special Collections Library, University of Virginia (hereafter cited as "Day Book"). The only major collected source on the subject of the construction of the university is Frank Grizzard, "Documentary History of the Construction of the Buildings at the University of Virginia, 1817–1826" (PhD diss., University of Virginia, 1996).

2. The best source on this subject is Catherine Bishir, "Black Builders in Antebellum North Carolina," in *Southern Built: American Architecture, Regional Practice* (Charlottesville: University of Virginia Press, 2006), 69–112.

3. "Day Book," 12/24/1821, p. 31.

4. "Day Book," 11/25/1822, p. 111.

5. Citations for Carpenter Sam are as follows: "Day Book," memorandum page; "Day Book," 1/30/1822, p. 36; "Day Book," 9/25/1822, p. 72; "Day Book," 11/25/1822, p. 107; "Day Book," 4/10/1823, p. 153; "Day Book," 9/16/1823, p. 210; "Day Book," 9/30/1823, p. 217; "Day Book," 12/29/1823, p. 239; "Day Book," 6/27/1824, p. 271; "Day Book," 7/2/1824, p. 272; "Day Book," 9/18/1824, p. 298; "Day Book," 11/27/1824, p. 310; "Day Book," 12/31/1824, p. 318.

6. *Population Statistics, Albemarle County, Charlottesville, Virginia, Fourth Census of the United States, 1820*, Microfilm M33, Washington, DC: National Archives and Records Administration.

7. Perry assisted with Pavilions I, III, V, and VII; Hotels D and E; and numerous segments of student rooms. Dinsmore assisted with Pavilion III, V, and VIII and one stretch of student rooms. Neilson assisted with Pavilion IX, X, and the Rotunda.

8. For evidence of a carpenter by the name of Moses, see "Day Book," 5/14/1825, p. 345.

9. *Population Statistics, Albemarle County, Virginia.*

10. "Day Book," 7/15/1822, p. 63.

11. For comparable examples in North Carolina, see Bishir, "Black Builders."

12. Brockenbrough to Cocke, 13 April 1825, Albert and Shirley Small Special Collections Library, University of Virginia. Cited in Grizzard, "Construction at the University of Virginia," chapter 10.

13. Grizzard, "Construction at the University of Virginia," ch. 10.

14. See Bishir, "Black Builders," 81.

15. "Day Book," 4/10/1823, p. 153.

16. "Day Book," 1/19/1825, p. 321.

17. "Day Book," 6/25/1822, p. 61.

18. Brockenbrough to Cocke, 13 April 1825.

19. Cocke to Brockenbrough, 17 July 1826, Albert and Shirley Small Special Collections Library, University of Virginia. Cited in Grizzard, "Construction at the University of Virginia," ch. 10. See also James A. Bear Jr., ed., *Jefferson at Monticello: Recollections of a Monticello Slave and of a Monticello Overseer* (Charlottesville: University Press of Virginia, 1967), 102.

20. A similar familiarity among the skilled enslaved African Americans appears also in North Carolina. See Bishir, "Black Builders," 86.

21. Cocke to Brockenbrough, 17 July 1826, cited in Grizzard, "Construction at the University of Virginia," ch. 11.

22. Lucia Stanton, *"Those Who Labor for My Happiness": Slavery at Thomas Jefferson's Monticello* (Charlottesville, University of Virginia Press, 2012), 140.

23. "Day Book," 1/25/1822, p. 35; "Day Book," 6/25/1822, p. 61.

24. "Day Book," 7/18/1825, p. 358.

2

LANDSCAPE OF SLAVERY

Louis P. Nelson and Maurie D. McInnis

When students arrived in March of 1825, construction in the Academical Village was still under way. It was not until 1826 that the Rotunda would be completed, but the pavilions and Lawn rooms were habitable. In a short period of time, the demographics of the Academical Village shifted. During the construction years, there were several dozen free and enslaved laborers who worked to construct the dozens of buildings and a few domestic servants who provided those workers with food and laundry services. Then a much larger community arrived: students, faculty, and hotelkeepers, and enslaved workers owned by faculty and hotelkeepers. Most had no idea what they might find when they arrived. What they discovered were dozens of brick buildings, many but not all of them finished, making a "village" that rivaled many small towns. For most of them, these buildings were grander than anything they had seen, except maybe their county courthouse. It must have made quite an impression, this grand collection of buildings standing in the midst of the tobacco, wheat, and cornfields of the Piedmont.

Jefferson had decided to locate the university in a rural setting, more than a mile from Charlottesville, a town that was little more than a small county seat when the university was founded. That decision necessitated that the university be able to supply nearly all of its own daily needs, including the growing and preparing of food and the keeping and butchering of animals. Jefferson's choice of the term "village" is telling. His architectural plans for the university drew heavily on what he knew from living on plantations his entire life and his ultimate solution created a community that was simultaneously a plantation but with the density of an urban setting.

The design for the University of Virginia built on Jefferson's many decades of architectural experiments in a slave society. In these, he determined how

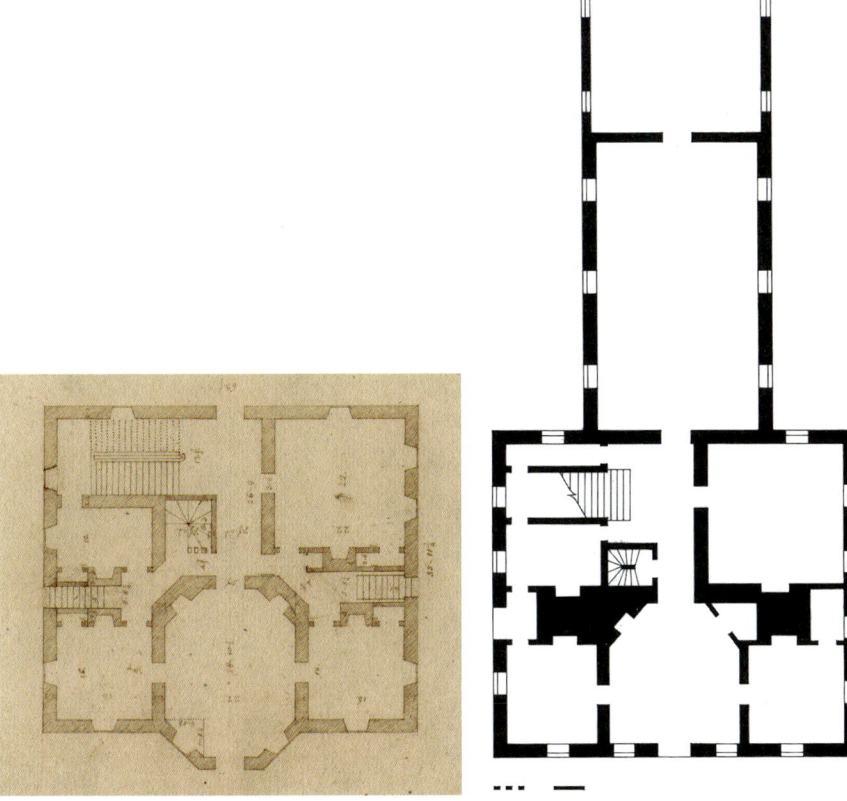

Fig. 2.1. Thomas Jefferson, finished plan for unexecuted remodel at the Governor's Palace, Williamsburg, Virginia, 1779–80 (*left*); Mark Wenger, plan of the first floor, Governor's Palace, Williamsburg, Virginia, after 1750 (*right*).

best to mask slavery by creating separate public, private, and enslaved zones in buildings and landscapes. For example, just as he took office as the governor of Virginia in 1779, Jefferson began a series of sketches for the remodeling of the Governor's Palace (fig. 2.1). Jefferson's unbuilt designs included the insertion of a service passage that would have allowed for the movement of enslaved domestics into and through the governor's residence without having to use the main entrances or passing through the public entertaining rooms.[1] When he redesigned Monticello after his return from France in 1796, he made similar alterations. The design for the house has clearly demarcated zones: public, private, and enslaved (fig. 2.2). The entry hall, parlor, and dining rooms were the public rooms of the house where he received visitors.

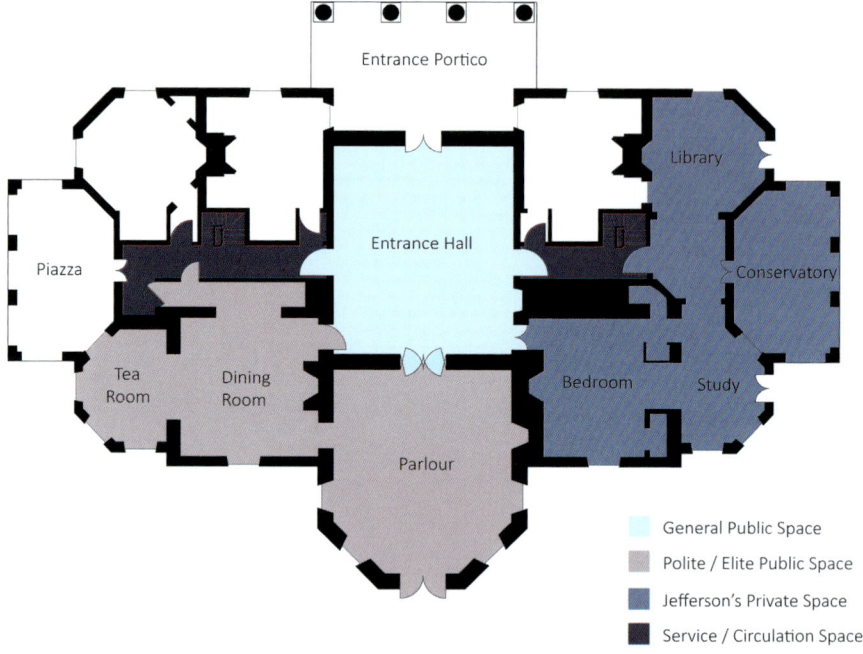

FIG. 2.2. Plan of main floor, Monticello, showing zones of privacy.

These were aligned along one axis of the house; along the other were the private areas, including his suite of rooms, referred to by one of his grandchildren as the "sanctum sanctorum." Traversing these wings were hallways, generally not visible from the public rooms, where the enslaved could accomplish their work unseen. These hallways connected to the stairs that led down to the service level where the kitchens, storerooms, stables, and other service rooms were located.

The changes Jefferson made at Monticello to mask slavery were most obvious in the dining room where he installed a number of devices that allowed him to diminish the number of enslaved attendants necessary to wait on table (fig. 2.3). He installed shelves mounted on a revolving door, so that food could be placed there and then brought into the room either by a trusted enslaved servant or by a family member (fig. 2.4). He also made use of an elevator to transport wine from the cellar and used standing carts, called dumbwaiters, to receive dirty dishes, again diminishing the number of enslaved workers necessary for serving meals (figs. 2.5, 2.6). The intent of

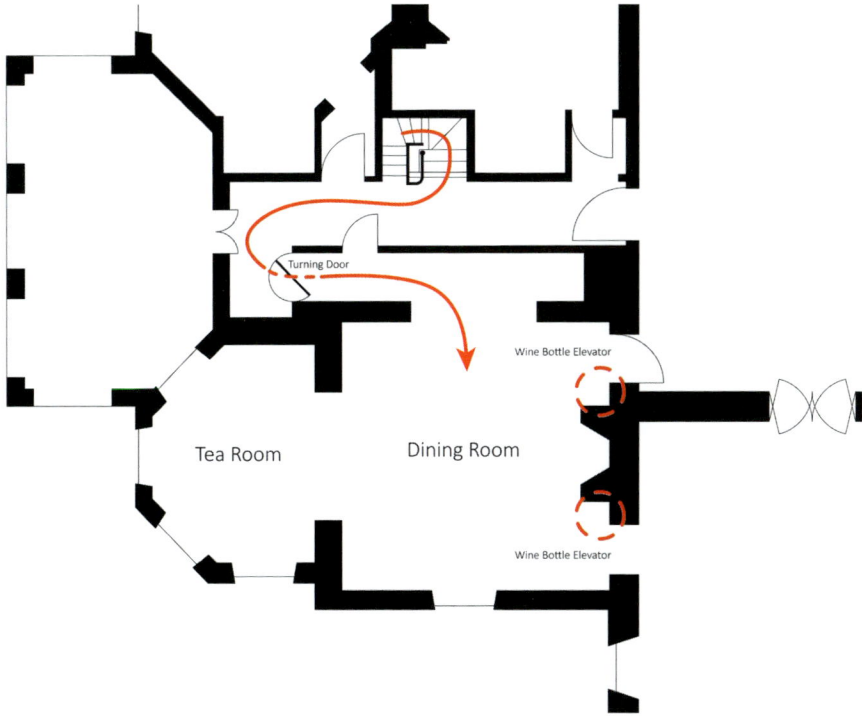

FIG. 2.3. Plan of dining room, Monticello, highlighting fixed service devices.

these modifications was not lost on visitors. Margaret Bayard Smith, who dined at Monticello in 1809, noted that when Jefferson wished to "enjoy a free and unrestricted flow of conversation," he placed a dumbwaiter near every diner, "so as to make the attendance of servants entirely unnecessary, believing as he did, that much of the domestic and even public discord was produced by the mutilated and misconstructed repetition of free conversation at dinner tables, by these mute but not inattentive listeners."[2] She clearly grasped the significance of Jefferson's changes. Conversations at Jefferson's dinner table were often political in nature, and by diminishing the number of enslaved people at the table, it meant that fewer were able to overhear the news of the day. And the news of day, such as the discussions of outlawing slavery that surrounding the Missouri Compromise in 1820, was news that slaveholders often wished to keep from the enslaved.

Importantly for his later work at the university, Jefferson also manipulated Monticello's landscape to mask the visibility of the labor performed by his

FIG. 2.4. Rotating door with service shelves, dining room, Monticello.

FIG. 2.6. Monticello dumbwaiter.

FIG. 2.5. Wine bottle elevator, dining room, Monticello.

Fig. 2.7. Elevated view of Monticello showing partially subterranean service spaces.

enslaved workforce. Famously, his entire row of domestic service spaces, including kitchens, smokehouses, stables, and some quarters, were buried in the embankment, below the level of the main floor of the house (fig. 2.7). As a result, these spaces were entirely invisible from the pleasure gardens above where Jefferson entertained his guests (fig. 2.8). Among those rooms in the basement was the one where Sally Hemings lived, nearby but also hidden away. In this design, the work of the enslaved was largely concealed from the regular daily activities of Jefferson's family and guests.[3]

When Jefferson approached his design for the "Academical Village" he employed a similar strategy, manipulating both the architecture and the topography in order to create separate zones for free and enslaved. Like the lawn at Monticello, the Lawn at the University of Virginia completely masks the labor that took place behind its façade. The front faces of the buildings on the Lawn were primarily intended for faculty and students. The faculty were to live in the upper story of the pavilions and could connect with one another via the upper-story walkway; the students were expected to reside in the dormitory rooms on the Lawn and the Range and take classes either in the Rotunda or the ground floors of pavilions and dine in the hotels; and the

Fig. 2.8. Jane Braddick Peticolas, view of the west lawn of Monticello, 1825.

enslaved domestic workers were expected to inhabit the basements of pavilions and hotels and the enclosed gardens behind, hidden from view. Jefferson's architectural designs separated education and work, free and enslaved. Since the earliest depictions, the university was represented as merely a series of building façades, pavilions marching up the terraces to the Rotunda at the its northern end. These images were generally unpopulated, representing the university as an architectural abstraction (fig. 2.9), an educational ideal with only a scattered few people.

Behind those pavilions were large spaces that are today referred to as gardens. In the earliest plan of the university (often called the Maverick Plan), created before the university was completed, the gardens were bounded by a serpentine wall (fig. 2.10). In the Maverick Plan these spaces are blank. Today they are filled with geometric walkways and ornamental trees and shrubs, pleasure gardens akin to those at European estates (fig. 2.11). These spaces are, however, modern gardens created by the Garden Club of Virginia in 1948, and designed by Alden Hopkins, landscape architect for Colonial Williamsburg. The designs reflected what Hopkins imagined these spaces might

FIG. 2.9. Benjamin Tanner, engraver, *University of Virginia*, 1826, from the Boye map of Virginia.

have been like. But his mid-century vision of pleasure gardens was generally incorrect; these spaces were instead predominantly utilitarian. They were central to life in the Academical Village. What we today call gardens were instead workyards where enslaved laborers were expected to live and labor for the faculty and students at the university. In these spaces enslaved African Americans grew food and prepared it, raised and butchered animals, washed laundry, chopped wood, and struggled to build lives and families.

Census data makes clear the large population of enslaved African Americans who lived in the Academical Village. From the first moment when Thomas Jefferson stood in a field with "ten hands" to mark off the location of the university, enslaved African Americans had been a constant presence. Yet, it is difficult to identify who they were or obtain an exact count because institutional and state records are far from comprehensive. Furthermore, hotelkeepers, faculty, and other staff came and went as did the people they owned and hired. Through the decennial census, the census takers enumerated the people living at the university in 1830, 1840, 1850, and 1860. Prior to 1850, they merely recorded the name of the owner and the numbers of persons owned by gender and broad age categories. Beginning in 1850, the census included the ages and gender of the individuals, but did not record their

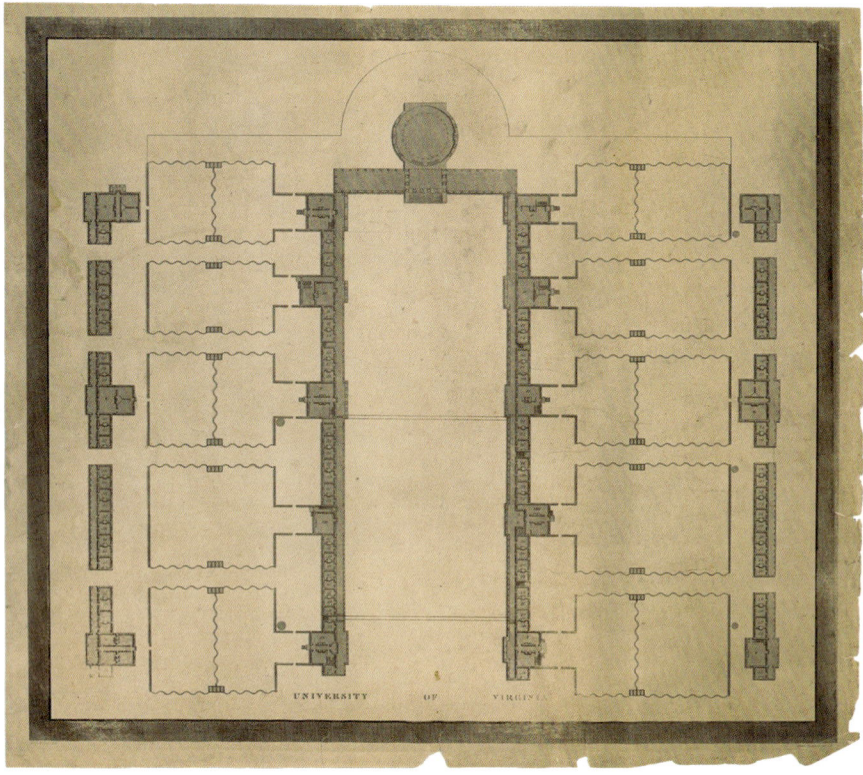

FIG. 2.10. John Neilson, draughtsman, and Peter Maverick, engraver, *University of Virginia* (grand plan), 1822, revised edition, February 1825.

names. The many enslaved people living at the university also included many families; enslaved children were a major presence at the university and were an important part of the labor force. As elsewhere in the South, enslaved children were expected to work in many different capacities in the Academical Village, and they began work at a very young age, usually ten or younger.[4] The written record often commented on the children who waited on students at table in the hotels, but not in surprise, because it was common for young enslaved children to have duties such as service in dining rooms. They probably had many other duties related to food preparation and cleaning. Enslaved children were also expected to run errands. At times, those under eighteen comprised more than one-third of the enslaved population. In 1850, for example, thirty-six of ninety-three enslaved people listed in the census were younger than eighteen. In 1860, the proportion was similar and included three infants under six months of age. The proctor at one point

Fig. 2.11. View of Pavilion II garden in full bloom, 2018.

complained about the number of children who congregated on the Lawn, as they were "in the habit of collecting in groups of a dozen or more, sometimes half naked."[5] We don't know a lot about the interactions between the enslaved children and the white residents, but on more than one occasion various individuals made attempts to provide education for them. At one point, the son of a hotelkeeper was criticized for running "a colored school for Black Children within the University"; it appears that such attempts to educate these children were quickly ended by the faculty.[6]

The census numbers suggest that the population of enslaved people was between 125 and 200 at any one time. The majority was owned by faculty and hotelkeepers and the numbers generally declined over time while the number of students increased. Importantly, these census records should be taken only as a conservative baseline. There were many people who worked at the university but were owned by others and there were many others owned by local businesses whose work regularly brought them to the university. Overlaying the census data onto an 1858 plan of the Academical Village offers a unique perspective on the numeric distribution of African Americans across the university in each of the four decades (figs. 2.12, 2.13, 2.14, 2.15). Comparing the four maps makes clear that the numbers of African Americans in any one pavilion or hotel varied significantly over time. Some of the

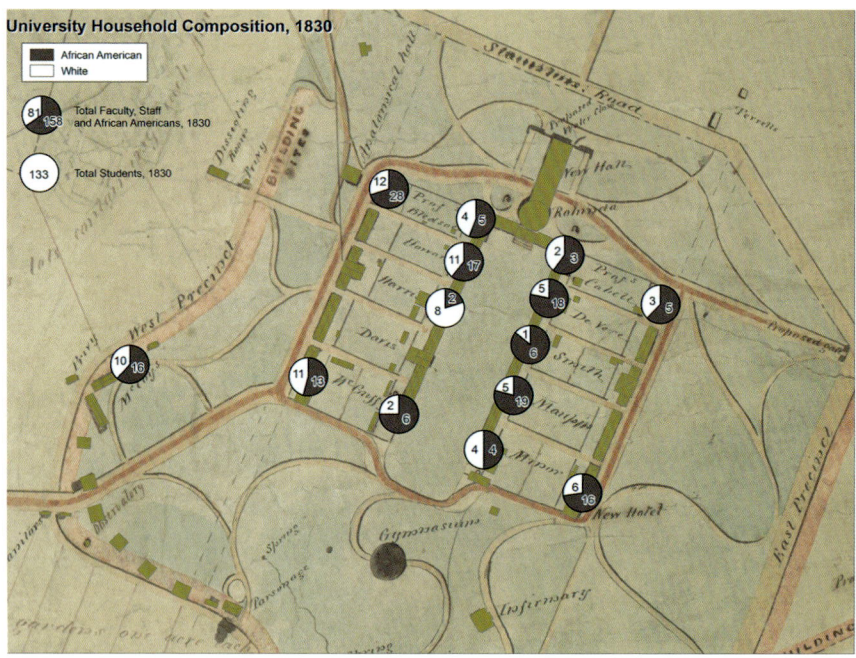

Fig. 2.12. The 1830 census data overlaid on detail of 1858 William A. Pratt Plan of the university.

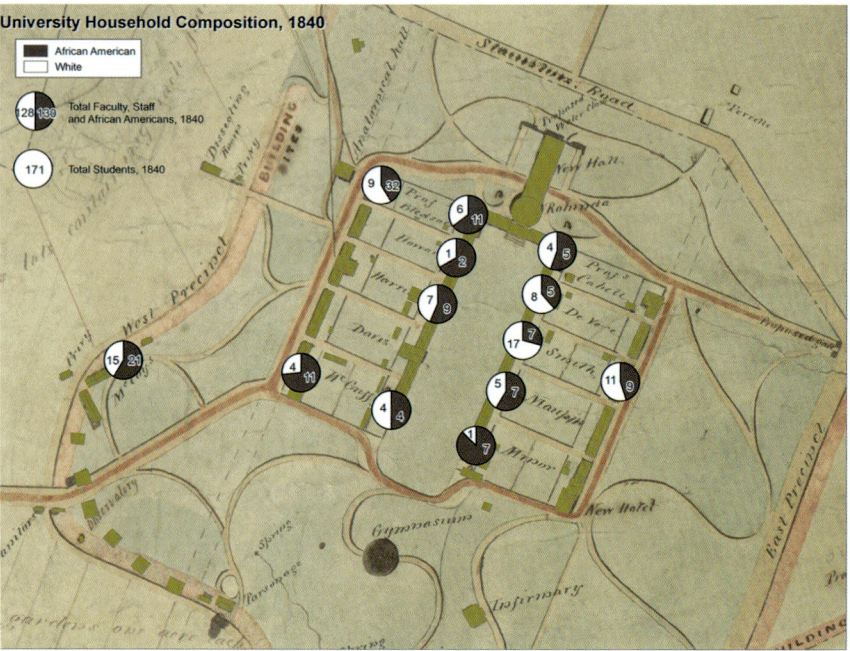

Fig. 2.13. The 1840 census data overlaid on detail of 1858 William A. Pratt Plan of the university.

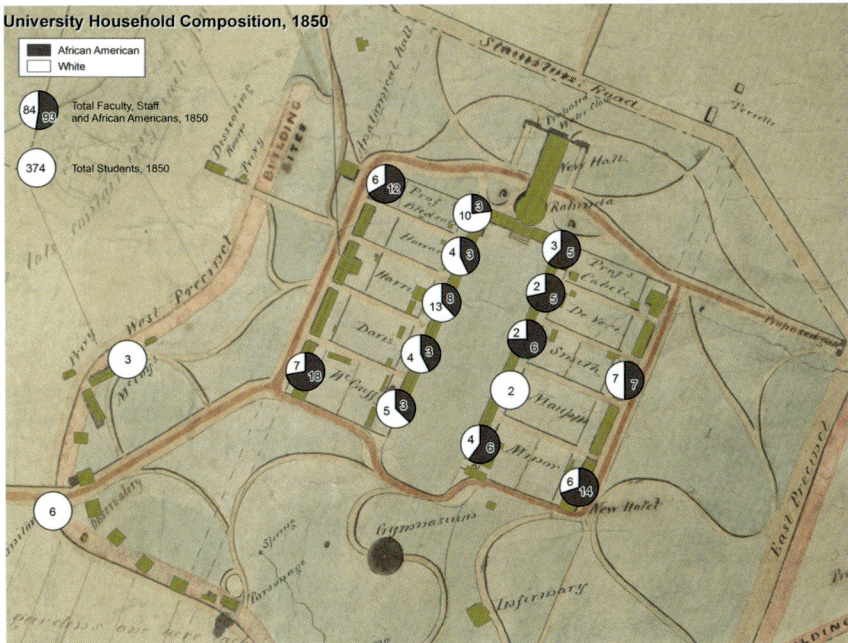

FIG. 2.14. The 1850 census data overlaid on detail of 1858 William A. Pratt Plan of the university.

FIG. 2.15. The 1860 census data overlaid on detail of 1858 William A. Pratt Plan of the university.

faculty owned a sizable number of people while others owned only a few. These maps represent both free and enslaved African Americans, although the number of free blacks is very small. Some of the hotelkeepers hired free blacks to supplement their enslaved workforce. What does not change, however, is that after the students themselves, enslaved African Americans were the second largest population residing within the Academical Village.

The maps provide some sense of the growing population in the Academical Village, but they fail to capture the many other ways that the university changed. Jefferson's plans soon proved inadequate in many respects, and the residents altered and added buildings, moved and erected fences, and expanded and cultivated gardens, in order to meet the needs of an ever-expanding population. As the population grew, both students and the enslaved who served them lived beyond the boundaries of the Academical Village. The many physical changes to the buildings and the landscape provide important information about the lives of the enslaved population, where they lived, and what work they were expected to accomplish.

Having already designed numerous private residences in Virginia, especially his own house on the mountaintop at Monticello, Jefferson knew that each of the pavilions would need a kitchen and some accommodations for the enslaved population. These were essential components of any antebellum Virginia household. Unusually, however, Jefferson placed the kitchen for each of the pavilions and hotels in the cellar. In the American South, kitchens were normally housed in exterior buildings not only to reduce the smell, smoke, and heat inside the residence, but also to reduce the risk of fire. By locating the kitchens in the cellars of the pavilions, Jefferson took advantage of the natural slopes on either side of the Lawn to hide both the people and the work to be done there partially underground, a strategy he had already successfully deployed at Monticello.

Jefferson placed the kitchen in the cellar of Pavilion VII, the first building on the Lawn (figs. 2.16, 2.17). In his design, however, he paid little attention to the requirements of cooking. As a largely subterranean space, the kitchen had little ventilation or light—the only source of natural light was a single door, which gave direct access to the rear workyard. But the limited natural light available for the cook was better than for the other two rooms in the cellar, both of which were fully subterranean. The only natural light for these two rooms would be through the exterior kitchen door, when it stood open.

Presumably Jefferson intended these as quarters where enslaved residents would sleep.

The pavilions he designed soon thereafter, Pavilions I, III, and V, offered greater conveniences for cooking and accommodations than did Pavilion VII (fig. 2.18). With the addition of windows, these kitchens had more natural light. And these cellars included an additional large chamber called a servants' hall; Mary T. Magill described it as "a comfortable room for servants."[7] The servants' hall was probably intended to serve multiple communal purposes such as sleeping, dining, and other necessities of daily life. Despite Magill's describing it as "comfortable," in reality these rooms were dimly lit and frequently damp. Even just a few years after construction, the university's Committee on Inspection resolved that the cellar of Pavilion V was "to be made dry by draining the same."[8] Subterranean, dark, and often wet, these basement spaces were intended by Jefferson as kitchens and other accommodations for slaves, hidden away from the students in the Academical Village.

The pavilions on the east side were built later and in these Jefferson appears to have paid greater attention to accommodating the actual work expected of the pavilion's intended enslaved occupants. The cellar of Pavilion IV included five rooms (see fig. 2.19), with a large kitchen, two fully subterranean rooms that were probably intended for food storage, and two other well-lit chambers. One of these rooms was a private interior chamber with abundant

FIG. 2.16. Section through Pavilion VII from the JUEL digital model of Academical Village.

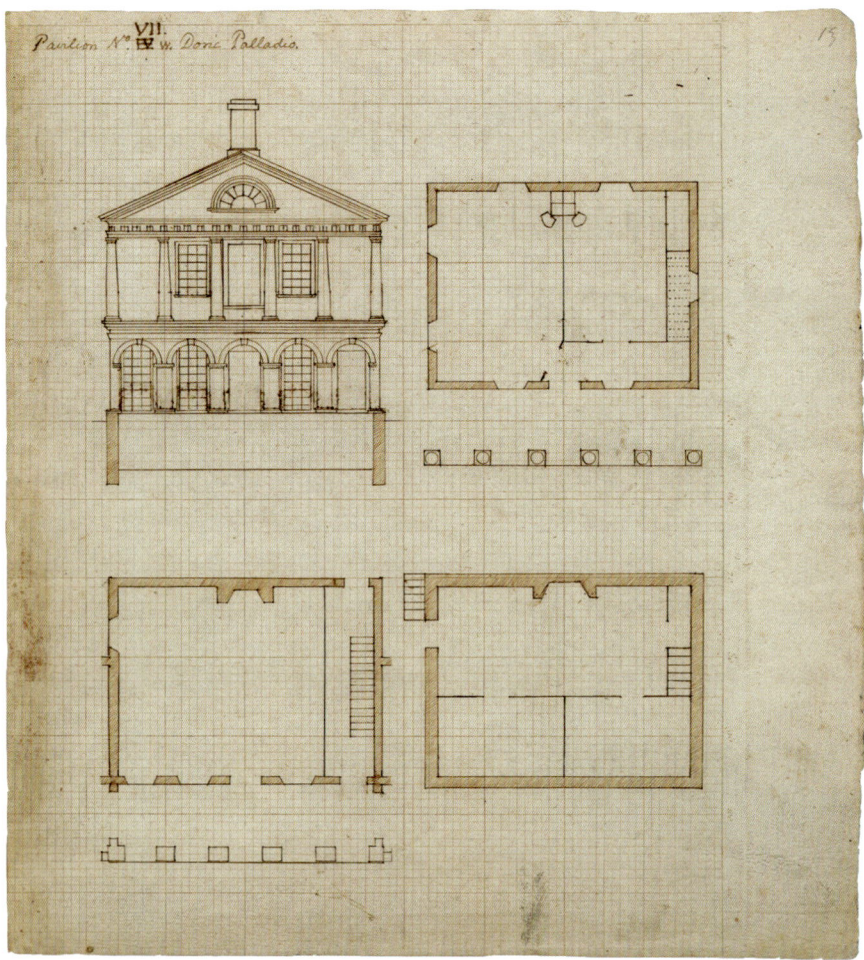

Fig. 2.17. Thomas Jefferson plan for Pavilion VII, 1817. The cellar is the plan in the lower right. In this plan the kitchen (with fireplace) is the largest chamber.

southeastern light and the warmth of a corner fireplace. Lucy Cottrell was likely the first occupant. Professor Blaetterman purchased her along with her mother, Dorothea Cottrell, and their extended family, from Jefferson's estate (fig. 2.20).[9] Lucy probably served as a cook for the professor and his family, and her chamber had direct access to the large kitchen, which was lit by two windows, one each at the north and south end of the room. As cook, Lucy also probably held the keys to the two unlit and unventilated pantries that opened onto the kitchen, which would have been used to store valuable cooking supplies like flour, salt and sugar.[10] Jefferson's designs for the cellars

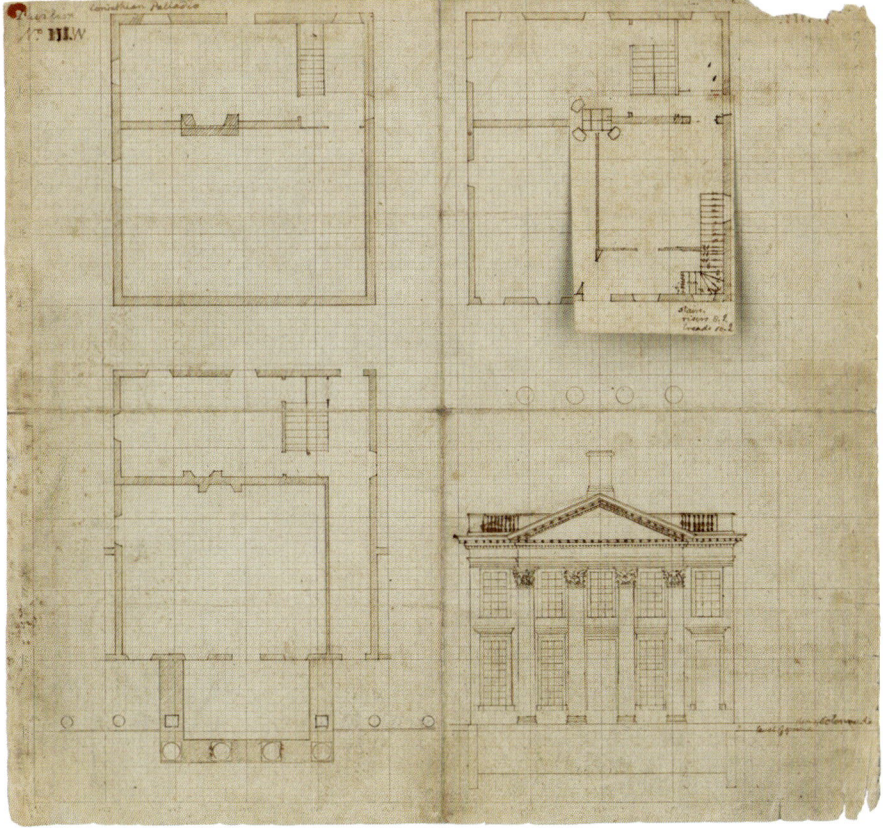

FIG. 2.18. Thomas Jefferson plan for Pavilion III, completed before March 1819. The cellar is in the top left of this drawing. The kitchen is the smaller well-lit chamber while the servants' hall is the larger subterranean and almost entirely unlit chamber.

of the hotels are less well understood, but like the pavilions, each included at least a kitchen and a servant's hall.

The pavilion basements proved inadequate for all of the work necessary to provide for the faculty and their families. Immediately adjacent to the pavilion basements, the spaces behind the Lawn rooms and immediately to the sides of the pavilion cellars became extensions of the working spaces for the enslaved living in pavilions. Over time, many members of the faculty requested to enclose their yard space with a painted wooden fence. The eastern and western ends of the alleys were reduced to narrow public thoroughfares as an early map shows (fig. 2.21).[11] The tall fences would have hidden the work and separated the enslaved from the students who regularly walked

FIG. 2.19. Thomas Jefferson plan for Pavilion IV, completed circa 1821. The cellar in the drawing is at the bottom right. The longitudinal kitchen runs north–south with a window at each end. The two well-lit chambers are to the east while the two unlit subterranean pantries are to the west.

FIG. 2.20. Photograph of Lucy Cottrell holding Charlotte E. Blaetterman, ca. 1850. Purchased from Monticello by Dr. Blaetterman after Jefferson's death, Lucy Cottrell, the cook for Pavilion IV, her mother, Dorothea, and her extended family all lived and worked in the cramped cellar of Pavilion IV.

the alleyways as they moved from dormitory to hotel to classroom (fig. 2.22). Archaeology suggests that these were heavily used work zones. Some were paved with cobble paving, others with bricks. Such paving was useful for the kind of dirty work of food preparation that was likely to have taken place there (fig. 2.23).

Many of these yards included cisterns, a necessary addition given how far the Academical Village was from a reliable source of water. Cylindrical in shape and buried underground, cisterns were repositories for spring-fed and surface water or were filled by downspouts from adjacent buildings. Cistern water was not potable and was used for daily household uses such as laundry and dishwashing, and for fire protection (fig. 2.24).

The garden enclosures behind the pavilions and hotels had always been intended as a primary work zone, and throughout the nineteenth century they served that purpose. From the beginning, Jefferson's garden enclosures were surrounded by brick walls; straight walls on the eastern and western

FIG. 2.21. Untitled map of the Academical Village showing waterlines, pathways, and fences, 1870.

FIG. 2.22. Aerial view of Pavilion IV showing the workyard and the plank fence from the JUEL digital model of the Academical Village.

FIG. 2.23. View of the quartz cobble surface of the workyards and the alley spaces bounded within fences south of Pavilion IV as revealed in an archaeological excavation.

FIG. 2.24. Brick cistern from the east side of the Rotunda under excavation. This was one of several cisterns installed around Grounds to help provide reliable water sources. Filled by downspouts from buildings, the water was nonpotable and used primarily for cleaning, laundry, and fire prevention.

ends of the gardens adjacent to the pavilions and hotels, and ribbonlike serpentine walls on the north and south sides of the garden. Today, the walls have been almost entirely rebuilt. The walls were originally much taller so that the interior spaces of the garden enclosures were nearly invisible from the adjacent alley corridors (fig. 2.25). And they have also been moved to make the alleys more capacious; the original locations were even more restrictive to pedestrian circulation and made the gardens even more secluded, separating the enslaved and the students.

Despite the beautiful geometric paths lined with trees and flowers in the gardens today, the early garden enclosures of the Academical Village were instead utilitarian. Many were used to grow seasonal produce to feed the faculty and students. In 1833 Professor Magill wrote his wife describing the space behind Pavilion III as "sufficiently large to raise most of our vegetables in."[12] By the 1830s, however, it was clear that the original garden spaces behind the pavilions were not adequate to the meet the needs of the residents, and so the Board of Visitors approved the creation of additional "outer garden" space for each pavilion and hotel resident to be located east and west of the Academical Village. These outer gardens were used as kitchen gardens to grow vegetables and to raise hay and grass for livestock. Additionally, it was where livestock were required to be kept, even though many residents continued to keep some animals in the pavilion and hotel garden enclosures.[13] A plan

FIG. 2.25. "In the University Grounds," an 1887 sketch showing a view up one of the alleys.

of the university from 1858 shows both the long thin garden plots and the larger four-and-one-quarter-acre grass lots provided to each of the professors and illustrates how the gardens, pastures, and agricultural tracks that surrounded the Academical Village closely resembled contemporary plantations (fig. 2.26).

Almost immediately after the university opened, the rear garden spaces behind pavilions and hotels were filled with additional buildings. Jefferson expected this. Writing to Proctor Arthur S. Brockenbrough, Jefferson approved the construction of smokehouses and wood yards for each pavilion and suggested that the wood yards be "inclosed in paling" and placed either "in their inclosures [walled gardens], or in a corner on the outside."[14] But these residences would need far more than just smokehouses and wood yards and professors and hotelkeepers almost immediately petitioned for the right to add additional buildings or expand the pavilions and hotels.

The additions and changes to pavilions and hotels happened unevenly and over time, because they were driven by the demands of the individual residents. Rather than decide that each pavilion needed a smokehouse, the Board of Visitors instead thought of these spaces as tenements rented to faculty and hotelkeepers, including not only the building, but also adjacent workyards and the space within the walled garden. The residents of the hotels and the pavilions were thus allowed to use these spaces as they wished, although for major changes they were expected to get board approval.[15] This meant

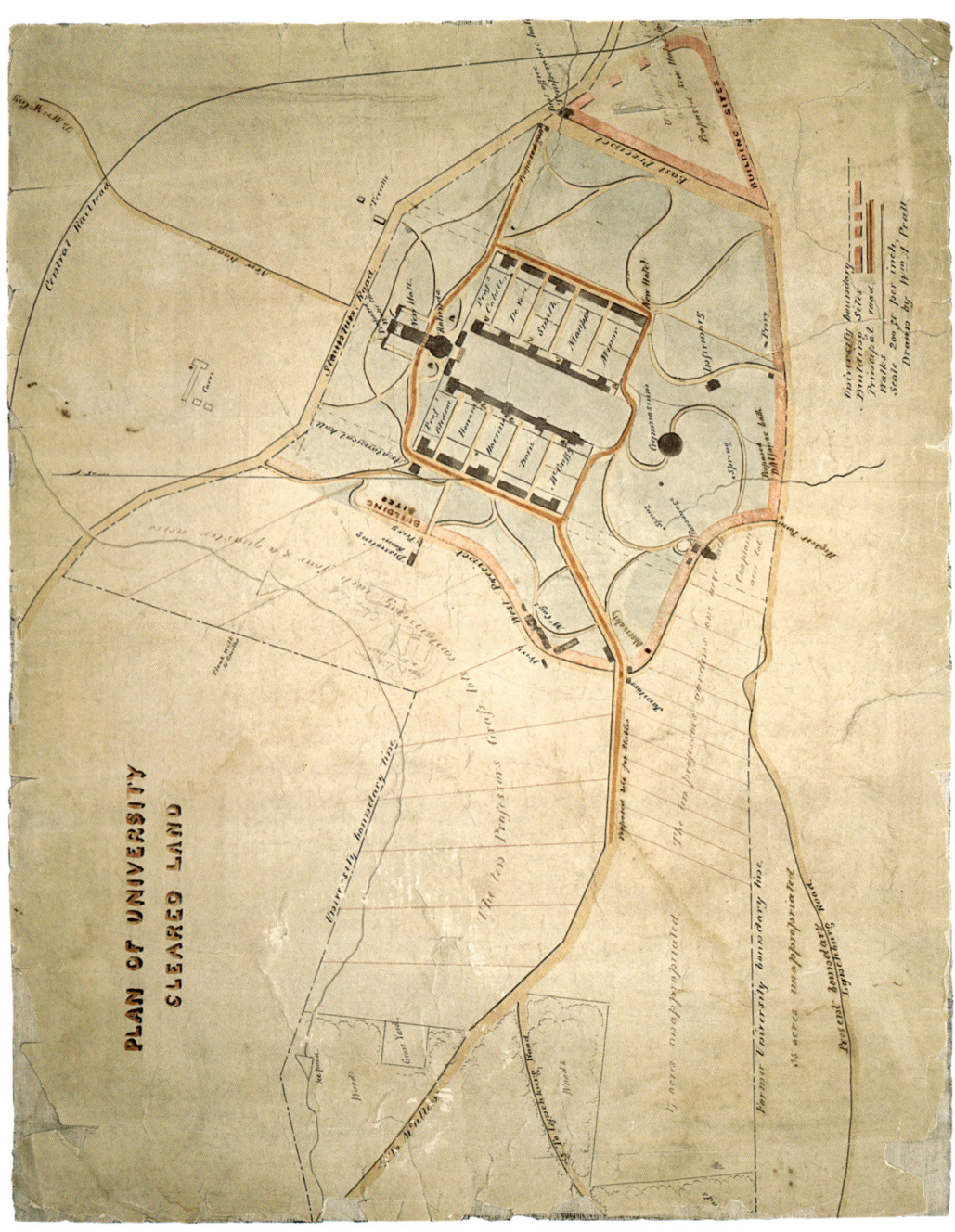

Fig. 2.26. William A. Pratt, "Plan of University Cleared Land," 1858.

that over the decades, faculty and hotelkeepers had considerable freedom to make alterations both by adding additional buildings—generally called offices in the records—to the enclosed gardens or by constructing additions to the pavilions and hotels themselves. Two mid-nineteenth-century views of the University of Virginia illustrate the notable increase of small buildings, some wood and others in brick, in the gardens and yards bounded by Jefferson's famous curvilinear walls (figs. 2.27, 2.28). The view from the west shows that many of the pavilions had additions and most had separate buildings that were erected nearby. In the view from the east, the artist has taken pains to include a number of small structures in the garden enclosures, even though he omits the garden walls from the view. The addition of new buildings began almost immediately after the opening of the university, and over the next quarter century kitchens, washhouses, and quarters were erected to house the large population of enslaved people who kept the university running day in and day out.

In fact, one of the greatest shortfalls in Jefferson's design for the Academical Village was the lack of accommodations for enslaved domestics. Even though Jefferson had provided for numerous servants' halls and sometimes a private chamber reserved for the cook and her family in the cellars, there was precious little space allocated for the other enslaved laborers. Furthermore, faculty and hotelkeepers were not pleased that the space that was provided was located in the cellar. They complained that basements were damp and unhealthy spaces; this environment was thought to promote disease. In a late 1823 letter to James Monroe, keeper of Hotel D George W. Spottswood wrote of his concern for his cellar space, that it "will always be unhealthy. Had I a cabin built for the reception of my servants, after they had done the dutys of the day to retire to, I should be in more comfort and my servants healthy."[16]

These shortcomings were noticed immediately. As early as 1826, only one year after most of the pavilions were occupied, the faculty submitted a series of requests for alterations to their pavilions and gardens. The chairman begged their patience and said that as soon as the funds would allow, the executive committee "will cause the necessary outhouses to be erected, & will consider the propriety of making the proposed alterations in their attics and cellars."[17] In a single passage, the chairman combined the marginal spaces in the pavilions and the gardens as a landscape of slavery and betrayed their known insufficiencies. Without delay, Professors Emmet and Dungli-

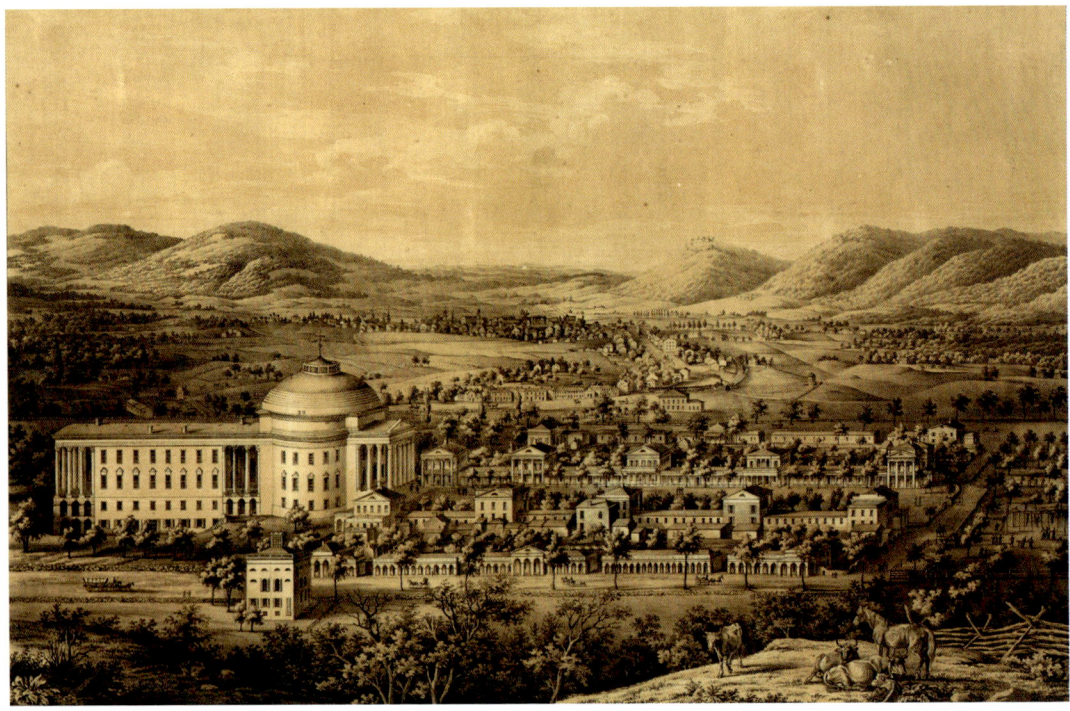

FIG. 2.27. Edward Sachse, draughtsman, *View of the University of Virginia, Charlottesville and Monticello taken from Lewis Mountain*, 1856, published by Casimir Bohn.

son in Pavilions I and X respectively applied for the construction of separate living quarters for their enslaved domestics. By September, both buildings were under construction. The following month, the Board of Visitors issued a policy expanding the offer to all faculty in pavilions and to the keepers of the hotels. The proctor was directed "to cause to be erected additional offices for the accommodation of servants in connection with the Pavilions and Hotels of the University, where they may be desired; not exceeding two apartments [each apartment of only a single chamber] to each hotel or pavilion." Around 1829, Professor John Lomax added a kitchen and quarter building behind Pavilion III (fig. 2.29). It has been considerably expanded since then, but it is one of the few such buildings still standing. For many on the faculty, one such building was not sufficient. In 1830, Professor John A. G. Davis moved into Pavilion III. He owned seventeen people and one building plus the basement proved inadequate to house his family and large group of enslaved workers. Davis later moved to the larger Pavilion X. Numerous

Fig. 2.28. Casimir Bohn, *View of the University of Virginia*, from the east, 1856. This view shows numerous outbuildings but omits the serpentine walls.

other faculty took advantage of the board's offer so that by 1832 two-room quarters stood behind most of the pavilions, namely behind Pavilions I, III, V, VI, VIII, IX, and X.

The pavilions built along the east side of the lawn had fewer offices than those to the west. It seems likely that the steeper slope of the land to the east meant that there was additional cellar space under the Lawn rooms that was used to provide private chambers for enslaved people belonging to the faculty. These rooms were small, had low ceilings, and no windows or light unless the door was left ajar; they would have been miserable accommodations. There was no official record of this, but as with other information about slavery, oblique references in the documents make it clear that these rooms were regularly used as housing. As early as 1828, student Gessner Harrison communicated in a letter that washing and cooking could be done by "a woman who is the wife of a man who occupies my cellar."[18] When there was concern about an epidemic in 1832, the faculty asked the proctor "To have the Dormitories white washed, & the floors well scoured [and] to have such cellars as have been occupied also whitewashed."[19] And in 1840 the university

FIG. 2.29. The Muse, a much altered kitchen and quarter outbuilding behind Pavilion III. The earliest portion of the building was built for Professor John Lomax in 1820.

approved that "the cellar under the dormitory occupied as a study by Professor Bonnycastle to be fitted up for the accommodation of his Domestics."[20]

In addition to the frequent documentary references, the physical evidence also clearly points to habitation. In the cellars under rooms 10, 12, 14, 16, and 18, evidence survives of the early ceilings and whitewashed walls, showing that these spaces had been at some point transformed from marginal leftover spaces into habitable quarters. The cellars below student rooms 10, 12, and 14 were claimed early on by the enslaved domestics owned by Blaetterman, the resident of Pavilion IV just to the north. These cellar spaces opened into Pavilion IV's southern workyard. Most of the cellar rooms used to house enslaved residents were unheated. But in a few rooms (under 2, 4, and 22), it appears that a small chimney and fireplace were installed. There even survives a 1850s plan of the basement that shows the cellar room under student room 36 communicating directly with the cellar under Pavilion VIII, creatively expanding the footprint of the working spaces of the pavilion cellar (fig. 2.30). The fact that faculty were able to transform these marginal cellar spaces into housing for their enslaved domestics probably explains the reason why there were fewer supplementary buildings erected in the eastern gardens. The records do not allow us to know with precision how many people

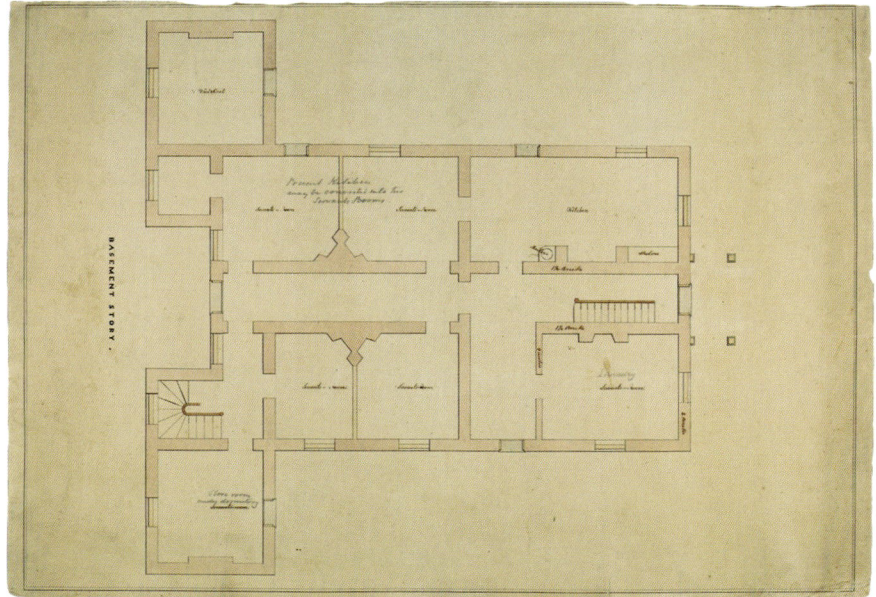

FIG. 2.30. An 1850s plan of the basement story of Pavilion VIII showing the claim of the cellar space under student rooms labeled first "Servant's Room" and then later "store room under dormitory." The plan shows the expanded basement was intended almost entirely for "servants," a period euphemism for the enslaved.

lived in the various spaces. Nevertheless, all of these changes to the Academical Village in its first few decades makes it clear that Jefferson's design for the university provided radically inadequate accommodations for the enslaved domestics who worked in the faculty pavilions.

Hotelkeepers were equally pressed for additional space. Edwin Conway, keeper of Hotel A, owned twenty-eight enslaved individuals in his household in 1830 and thirty-two in 1840.[21] Perhaps because of this, the Board of Visitors approved the construction of a new kitchen and washhouse in the garden behind Conway's hotel in 1829.[22] Even with additional residential space such as adjacent basement and dormitory rooms, a two-room office with garret above would not have provided sufficient living space for Conway's enslaved families. These numbers suggest that eight or more individuals were sleeping in both the cellar kitchen and in the servants' hall, and in each of the two garret rooms of the newly built kitchen-washhouse. If this was the common experience for the majority of the enslaved, the privacy of a single chamber for Lucy Cottrell and her family was unusual. Also in that

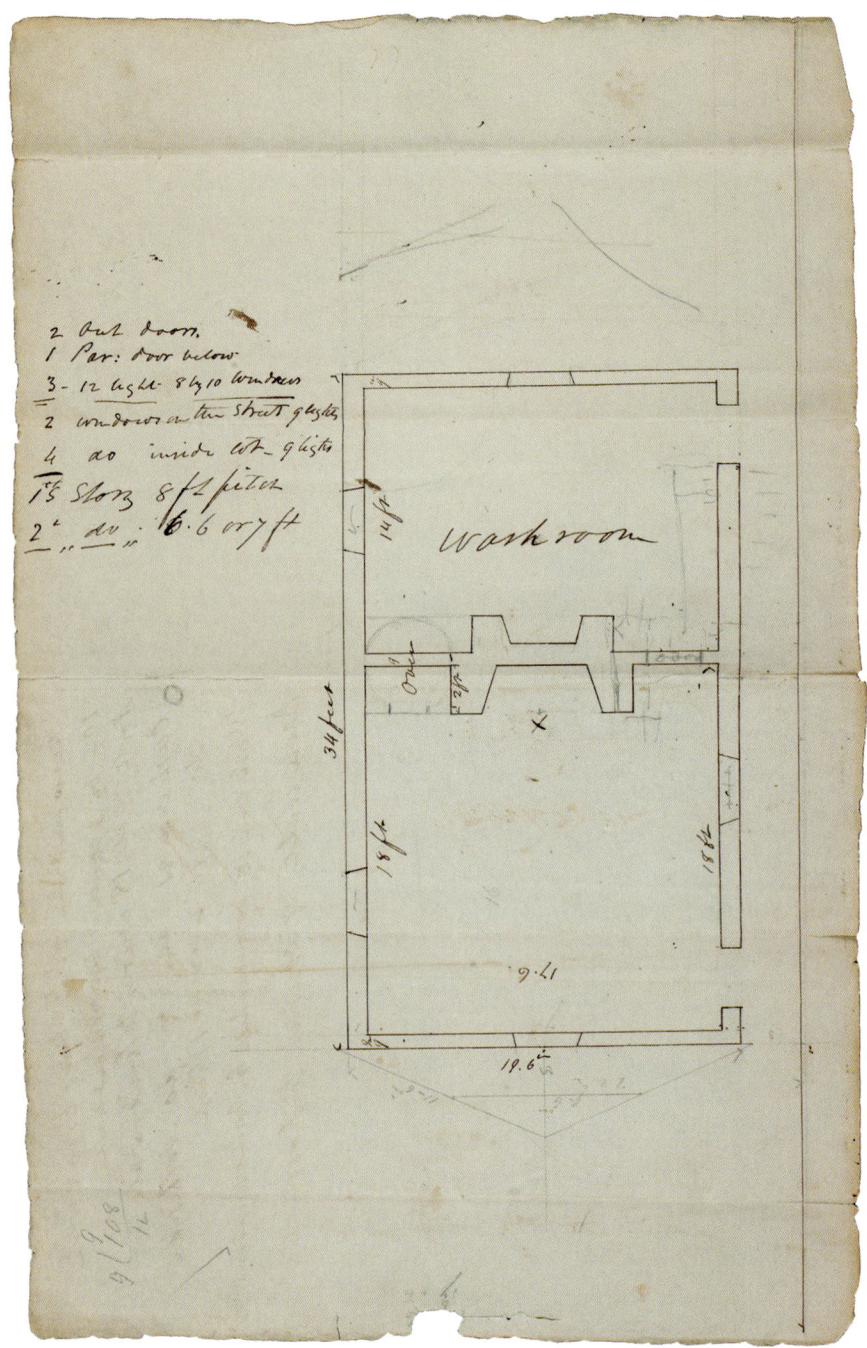

Fig. 2.31. Undated plan for a kitchen building behind Mrs. Gray's Hotel.

same year, Mrs. Gray applied for permission to erect a building, described as "one office with two rooms," behind Hotel E (fig. 2.31). The original sketch provides an idea of the floor plan and indicates that this building was used primarily as a kitchen in the larger room and a laundry in the other. Above it was a loft that would have served as sleeping quarters for the thirteen people Mrs. Gray owned in 1830 and the eleven in 1840.

Between 1828 and 1832 office outbuildings were constructed in the garden enclosures of at least seven of the ten pavilions and five of the six hotels. These additions began to rectify insufficiencies in Jefferson's original designs. This rapid and comprehensive build-out of the space behind each pavilion and hotel implies both that residents desired additional space for washing, cooking, and cleaning, and that they desired to remove enslaved individuals and those chores from inside the white household. As this was common to most nineteenth-century plantations, this desire to move kitchens outdoors is not at all surprising. The noise, smell, and heat of the kitchen were a nuisance to residents and posed a considerable risk of fire.

These newly constructed offices were typically constructed of brick. Small in scale, they were generally square or rectangular, were one to one and a half stories and contained plain, simple interior plans and finishes. The estimate of the carpenter's work and materials required to construct a kitchen and servants' quarter to the rear of Pavilion III is descriptive of most of these structures:

> [T]here will be no plank floor in kitchen it being determined to be paved, the door and window frames to be plain revealed frames, batton doors, partitions of inch plank plained T & groved, stock locks on doores, the upper story to be seven ft high to the collar beems, plain stair base, with a rail around head of staires, doores & windows finished without architraves & no mantles or shelves over fire places, but including 48—lineal of shelving in kitchen.[23]

Like most buildings for enslaved people in the South, the building had little adornment, quite a contrast to the pavilions and the hotels, which had elaborate decorative features in the principal rooms. Most of these buildings ranged in size from 24 × 12 for a double apartment down to 15 × 12 for a single. Like many other such buildings throughout the South, many included a garret accessible by ladder or stair that expanded the livable space. In most cases the two main rooms would have been separated by a wall with a cen-

FIG. 2.32. McGuffey Cottage behind Pavilion IX is the only remaining example of the many two-chamber outbuildings that were built through the early nineteenth century to house enslaved workers.

tral chimney stack with back-to-back fireplaces, one heating each of the two rooms. While many of these apartments were built, there is only one surviving example that retains its early form, McGuffey Cottage behind Pavilion IX, which was built in the 1850s (fig. 2.32). The building included two similarly sized chambers, each an apartment, with a door and window on the elevation facing the rear of the pavilion.

One of the duties of the hotelkeepers was to provide washing for all of the students. Between linens for the dining rooms and beds and clothes for the students, laundry would have been a never-ending task. A washhouse was constructed for hotelkeeper Conway behind Hotel A in 1829–1830, and a combined kitchen and washroom was constructed for Mrs. Gray, keeper of Hotel E, during the same period.[24] Washhouses were typically run and maintained by enslaved women. These independent structures usually contained the features necessary for nineteenth-century laundry: a fireplace or stove for heating water, a large tub with a washboard for scrubbing clothes, and perhaps a flat surface for ironing. Like their kitchen counterparts, washhouses also served residential purposes, housing enslaved families.

As the research into slavery at the university has progressed, it has become increasingly clear the many ways in which the early university was very similar to a plantation landscape. With its newly built kitchens, smokehouses, and washhouses in the garden enclosures; its garden plots and four-acre grassy pastures just beyond; and its large enslaved population, the Academical Village closely resembled other mid-century plantation landscapes. Jefferson's design had attempted to obscure the role of slavery by placing most of the workspace into the cellars of both pavilions and hotels; it was a conscious attempt to visually minimize the physical presence of the laboring black body in his idealized landscape of the university.

But this vision collapsed almost immediately. Slavery spilled out of these cellars to fill the yards and gardens behind and, as later chapters will show, the Lawn and other spaces as well. The density of people and separate households made it simultaneously very much like an urban setting. And since most of these spaces are no longer visible in their original forms, it takes some imagination to repopulate this landscape with large numbers of enslaved African Americans who lived and labored there. Cooks spent long days in their poorly lit and often damp and certainly hot cellar kitchens. Some moved into better lit, newly built kitchens in the gardens. Men and children labored to chop wood and gather water from the cisterns and woodpiles that filled the hard-paved workyards. And at the end of the day, only the very few retired to a private chamber to sleep. The vast majority slept in lots of four to eight in lofts above the washhouse, bunks in the subterranean servants' hall, or on the brick floors of kitchens. These are the spaces that shaped the everyday life for the vast majority of the enslaved African Americans who lived, labored, and died at the University of Virginia.

NOTES

1. Mark Wenger, "Jefferson's Designs for Remodeling the Governor's Palace," *Winterthur Portfolio* 32, no. 4 (Winter 1997): 223–42.

2. Margaret Bayard Smith, *The First Forty Years of Washington Society: Portrayed by the Family Letters of Mrs. Samuel Harrison Smith (Margaret Bayard) from the Collection of Her Grandson, J. Henley Smith,* ed. Gaillard S. Hunt (New York: Scribner, 1906), 387–88.

3. Dell Upton, *Architecture in the United States* (Oxford: Oxford University Press, 1998).

4. Wilma King, *Stolen Childhood: Slave Youth in Nineteenth-Century America* (Bloomington: Indiana University Press), 22–29.

5. Journals of the Chairman of the Faculty, 1827–1864, March 27, 1833, http://juel.iath.virginia.edu/resources (hereafter cited as Chairman's Journals).

6. Chairman's Journals, October 18, 1833, http://juel.iath.virginia.edu/resources.

7. Mary T. Magill, "Dr. Alfred Thurston Magill: A Memorial Sketch by His Daughter," *Alumni Bulletin of the University of Virginia* 4, no. 3 (November 1897): 77–84.

8. Board of Visitors Minutes 1817–2007, July 4, 1845, and August 17, 1837, http://juel.iath.virginia.edu/resources (hereafter cited as Board of Visitors Minutes).

9. Elizabeth C. Blaetterman to Victoria, June 30, 1860, Papers of Francis Lee Thurman, University of Virginia Archives, Alderman Library, Charlottesville, VA.

10. By 1830, Blaetterman owned eighteen enslaved African Americans, ten adults and eight children, who were divided between his pavilion and his small plantation near Keswick called Limestone Farm.

11. Board of Visitors Minutes, July 7, 1840, http://juel.iath.virginia.edu/resources.

12. Magill, "A Memorial Sketch," 77–84.

13. Board of Visitors Minutes, July 21, 1830, http://juel.iath.virginia.edu/resources.

14. Thomas Jefferson to Arthur S. Brockenbrough, November 12, 1825, https://founders.archives.gov/about/Jefferson.

15. Board of Visitors Minutes, December 16, 1826, http://juel.iath.virginia.edu/resources.

16. George W. Spottswood to James Madison, November 29, 1823, James Madison Papers, Library of Congress.

17. Chairman's Journals, October 2, 1826, http://juel.iath.virginia.edu/resources.

18. Gessner Harrison to Dr. Peachey Harrison, September 14, 1828, Papers of the Tucker, Harrison, and Smith Families, Box 2, Albert and Shirley Small Special Collections Library, University of Virginia.

19. Chairman's Journals, August 1, 1832, http://juel.iath.virginia.edu/resources.

20. Board of Visitors Minutes, July 4, 1840.

21. *Slave Census, Population Statistics, Albemarle County, Virginia, 1830 and 1840, Fourth Census of the United States,* https://search.lib.virginia.edu/catalog/u2040113l.

22. Board of Visitors Minutes, July 20, 1829, http://juel.iath.virginia.edu/resources.

23. Estimate of Carpenters Work and Materials, ca. 1831, Papers of the Proctor of the University of Virginia [Proctor's Papers], Box 8, Estimates of Various Expenses, 1831, RG 5-3, Albert and Shirley Small Special Collections Library, University of Virginia.

24. Board of Visitors Minutes, July 20, 1829, http://juel.iath.virginia.edu/resources.

3

EVERYDAY LIFE IN THE YARD

Louis P. Nelson and Benjamin Ford

Even though Jefferson's intention had been to provide separate zones for the faculty, the students, and the enslaved, the reality was that they were tightly packed in together, living in close proximity; that density inevitably led to tensions. In September of 1839, the students residing in Lawn rooms 10, 12, and 14 "complained . . . of very great nuisances created by the use of their cellar by Doct. B's [Blaetterman's] servants & of the yard embracing the cellar in which a cow was frequently penned & fed."[1] Awakened early each morning by the grunting and mooing of the cow being milked and then the stacking of milk pans, these students were annoyed by the work of Marshall and Ben, two enslaved boys who lived and worked in Pavilion IV. What is now a pavilion parking lot was once a workyard occupied by numerous enslaved laborers—and at least one cow—engaged in various activities throughout the course of the day and it sat just below the students' rear windows (fig. 3.1). This kitchen workyard was an extension of the service spaces such as the kitchen and other rooms in Pavilion IV's cellar. As on other pavilions, this space was commonly fenced in and it abutted the taller brick walls that enclosed the rear gardens where additional buildings were added to accommodate the domestic demands of the faculty and hotelkeepers. Nineteenth-century life was labor intensive, noisy, and messy, and much of the work required to provide for a nineteenth-century household was done in these spaces: butchering pigs, plucking fowl, milking cows, grinding grain, and so forth, activities that lead eventually to student complaints. While the Academical Village was a functioning university, it was simultaneously a plantation landscape with a whole world of activity behind the fences and walls that dominated everyday life for the majority of the enslaved who lived and worked at the university.

FIG. 3.1. View of the workyard south of Pavilion IV. It is now a parking lot for pavilion residents.

The labor of providing for the families and students in the Academical Village was never-ending. Nearly all of it was done by enslaved African Americans who prepared food, cared for livestock, washed clothes and sheets, cleaned the yards and gardens, and performed seasonal work such as gardening, chopping wood, and hauling ice. Most of this work took place behind the walls of the enclosed gardens and behind the fences of the workyards. Most of the work and the enslaved working there would have been largely invisible to the students as they traveled around the Academical Village, using the alleyways to move from the Lawn to the Range and spending most of their time in the hotels, pavilions, and dormitory rooms.

As with the original curvilinear garden walls, most of these additional buildings—kitchens and washhouses, slave quarters, privies, and woodsheds—have long since disappeared from the university's landscape but the development of a digital model provides an important opportunity to visualize the many buildings that once filled the gardens of the Academical Village. Using a wide range of evidence, including period images, written accounts, and archeological evidence, our digital team re-created the two most well documented workyards, those behind and between Pavilion VI and Hotel D, in order to visualize how these spaces might have looked. Close behind the

Fig. 3.2. Aerial view of the workyards of Pavilion VI and Hotel D including reconstructions of exterior kitchens in each yard from the JUEL digital model of the Academical Village.

pavilion stood a rectangular—approximately sixteen-by-thirty-two-foot—one-and-a-half-story kitchen overseen by enslaved cook Isabella Gibbons (fig. 3.2). Built around 1831 to accommodate the growing needs of the pavilion household, this structure would have in addition housed many of Professor Harrison's six enslaved workers. With time, other small outbuildings were added. Located in the adjacent workyard was a cistern, a subterranean brick cylinder pargeted on the interior and fed by downspouts from adjacent buildings. A frame covering and manual pump and stock extended above-ground and provided access to the water for use in daily chores and activities. The north yard area was accessed via the rear of the pavilion by a gate in the north brick area wall, and by a door in the kitchen (fig. 3.3).

In the eastern end of the Pavilion VI garden, adjacent to and immediately west of Hotel D, the lower terrace of the garden enclosure contained a small, approximately twenty-by-twenty-foot-square one-and-a-half-story kitchen (fig. 3.4). The kitchen was built to accommodate the needs of the hotelkeeper but also likely housed enslaved families. A smaller eastern washroom addition was added to the kitchen by the mid-1840s. The yard space north and south of Hotel D was enclosed by straight brick garden walls. Brick paths led to and from the kitchen and washroom and the western façade of Hotel D. There was another square brick building of uncertain function opposite

Fig. 3.3. Detail view of Isabella Gibbons's exterior kitchen behind Pavilion VI showing the fences, workyard, and the cistern from the JUEL digital model of the Academical Village.

Fig. 3.4. View of the exterior kitchen with adjacent washroom behind Hotel D from the JUEL digital model of the Academical Village.

the kitchen (fig. 3.5). These two buildings defined and framed the workyard behind the hotel. In both instances, the auxiliary buildings were drawn very close to the rear of the original building leaving fairly large open spaces beyond for smaller gardens and other functions. The final office was the privy, which in the reconstruction appears as the small two-doored building in the very back of the garden, as far removed from the other spaces of the

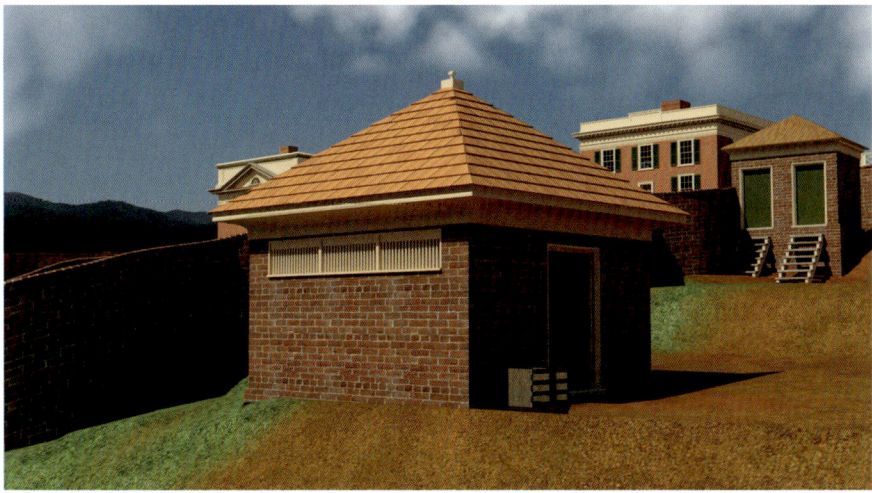

FIG. 3.5. Second outbuilding of uncertain function in the workyard behind Hotel D from the JUEL digital model of the Academical Village.

yard as possible. The perpetual stench of the privies was a consistent concern; those used by the students were so bad, in fact, that the faculty recommended a complete rebuild of all privies with better ventilation in 1849.[2]

The apparent absence of a smokehouse from the gardens of either Pavilion VI or Hotel D might have been mitigated by the very large smokehouse built by Professor Blaetterman behind Pavilion IV. In 1835, Blaetterman had begun the unauthorized construction of a brick smokehouse. For three days in November, the professor's hired bricklayers constructed a smokehouse in the yard directly behind his pavilion. Given a contractual agreement between the professor and Edwin Conway, the hotelkeeper of Hotel A, Blaetterman's motives for the smokehouse may have been both to process and store meat for his family's consumption and to rent the building for use by other professors and hotelkeepers. Although a square smokehouse appears behind Pavilion IV in the 1850s view, few specific physical details of the smokehouse survive. Although not identical to all pavilion workspaces, this reconstruction of the spaces associated with Pavilion VI and Hotel D gives a reasonable likeness for the typical spaces occupied by most enslaved African Americans throughout the course of their day.

Of the daily chores, food preparation was by far the most constant and labor intensive. There were many cooks living in the Academical Village, most of whom were women. Each hotelkeeper had a cook and often several assistants to prepare food for the students and each of the faculty also had a cook for his household. Their work entailed not only the daily cooking and serving of meals, but also the preparation of more long-term foodstuffs such as butter, cured meats, and dried herbs.

In the fall of 1829 Professor Gessner Harrison, resident of Pavilion VI, told his mother how well he was eating as a bachelor as his servant Charles was an excellent cook who prepared toast, cornbread, spare ribs, and coffee on a regular basis. In order to economize, however, Harrison decided to purchase a large amount of meat. "My man Charles said he could cure pork as well as any body, and thinking it might save me something, or at least contribute to my convenience & comfort I concluded to buy my pork & make my own bacon. My family being small (Charles & myself), I bought 361 pounds and it is now put away."[3] Nineteenth-century households in the South relied heavily upon cured pork as a protein source. Typically, hogs were butchered and cured once a year and then stored for use throughout the year. Butchering and curing pigs was a noisy, smelly, and messy activity. Charles and the other enslaved workers at the university who cured pork would have done this work in the gardens next to the smokehouses throughout the Academical Village. At the university, the cellars of pavilions were often fitted out with iron bars and strong lockable doors to protect valuable foodstuffs such as cured and salted meats, sugar, flour, and other dry goods (fig. 3.6). Such fortifications were some insurance against theft from enslaved laborers seeking to supplement their typically inadequate rations.

Whether in the cellar or in the newly constructed buildings in the gardens, kitchens would have been the hub of nearly round-the-clock activity. The external kitchen of Pavilion VI was run by Isabella Gibbons, an enslaved woman owned by Professor Francis H. Smith, and her assistants from 1853 onward.[4] A typical day for cooks like Gibbons started early and lasted late into the evening. She and her helpers would start a fire early each morning and keep it going all day, cook and prepare food, bring food from the kitchen to the dining room, and clear plates, dishes, and cutlery for washing in the vicinity of the kitchen. Such constant activity would have generated considerable noise and smell. The faculty noted this problem during a mid-century inspection of the Grounds:

> . . . in the immediate vicinity of the gates communicating with the back yards of most of the Pavilions & Hotels. . . . In those places the servants

Fig. 3.6. Detail of originally exterior window frame in the cellar of Pavilion X. The mortises or pockets would have accommodated iron security bars.

generally throw out the slops from the kitchens, soap suds and other refuse matter, and although such deposits are frequently carted off by the Proctor's orders yet a considerable portion of the putrescible matters always soaks into the soil and becomes a fruitful source of offensive exhalations.[5]

In an attempt to keep their own working spaces clean, enslaved laborers threw refuse over the garden gates into the narrow public alleys that provided access between the Lawn and the Range. Complaints of offensive odors were a common problem in such a crowded space. In 1835 Mr. Pickett, a student living in a dormitory adjacent to Hotel D, "complained very much of his dormitory that it was rendered very unpleasant by its proximity to Capt. Perrow's kitchen and to the Post Office."[6]

Enslaved individuals living in hotel households performed food preparation on an expanded scale to accomplish the feeding of students three times a day, as well as the household of the keeper, and these activities spread well beyond the kitchen. In 1832, Hotel A keeper Edwin Conway ordered the butchering of animals for consumption in the yard behind the West Range dormitories. The chairman of the faculty, upon hearing of the setup in so public a place, requested that keeper Conway "remove, immediately, the slaughtering apparatus which he had placed near the bottom of Mr. Davis's [Pavilion III] garden."[7]

And food preparation spilled into otherwise unoccupied spaces of the pavilions. Inspection of the attic of Pavilion II revealed rows of early nineteenth-century nails driven into the attic framing near the front and rear windows. These nails are spaced in such a way as to accommodate the hanging of something light, possibly herbs for drying (fig. 3.7). Like cellars, many of the attics and other marginal spaces, unprogrammed by Jefferson, might have easily been overtaken as spaces of slave accommodation and labor.

Many of the physical alterations and additions that occurred in the pavilions appear to have been made in response to the requests of the cooks. It was difficult to get from Lucy Cottrell's kitchen in the basement of Pavilion

Fig. 3.7. Detail of drying nails along a collar beam in the attic of Pavilion II.

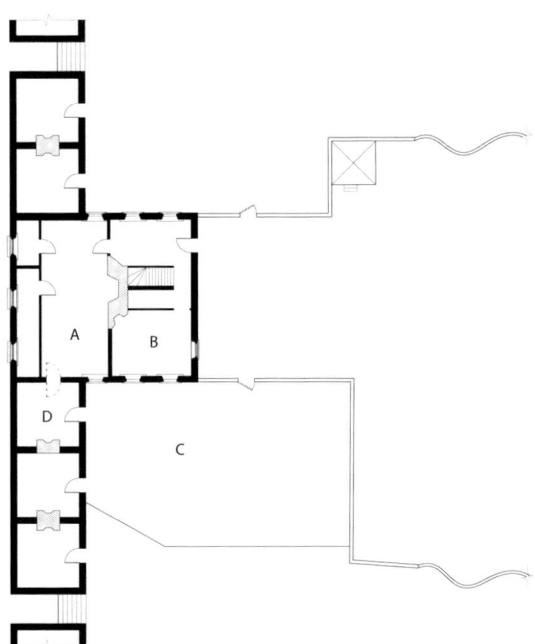

Fig. 3.8. Plan of cellar and southern workyard of Pavilion IV showing: (A) Lucy Cottrell's kitchen, (B) Lucy Cottrell's chamber, (C) the southern workyard, and (D) the cellar of a student room quickly converted into a convenience passage from kitchen to workyard.

IV to the workyards adjacent to and behind the pavilion. In order to get to the pen that housed the cow (the same cow that figures in the chapter's opening vignette), Lucy would have had to go from the kitchen and through another cellar room to get outside, then walk around the corner of the pavilion and through the garden gate to get to the cow pen in the side workyard. Sometime in the 1830s, Blaetterman consented to have a door opened between his kitchen and the cellar under student room number 10. Doing so ingeniously provided a direct route from the kitchen to the southern workyard and connected the cellar of Pavilion IV to the cellar rooms beneath the student dormitories (fig. 3.8; cf. Jefferson's original plan, fig. 2.19 on page 58). Patchwork repairs in the brick reveal a door that was opened up and then later closed. And further inspection of the surviving original brick floor shows newly laid brick, presumably replacing heavily worn original brick leading to this now-blocked door, evidence of heavy traffic from the kitchen to the south yard through this cellar space under student room 10. The cellars under students' rooms 12 and 14 also served as quarters for Blaetterman's growing slave population on one side and as a stable for a cow on the other.

That a cow was stabled in this space should not be a surprise. Livestock were necessary for running a nineteenth-century household and cows, chickens, and hogs were regularly kept close to the pavilions and hotels. Even though the university eventually passed rules against the keeping of livestock inside the precincts of the university, both faculty and hotelkeepers continued to do so. Enslaved African Americans, adults as well as children, took care of the animals: milking cows, tending livestock, and feeding chickens, cows, and pigs. Throughout the first half of the nineteenth century, numerous sources document that livestock, in particular cattle and hogs, kept within the "precincts" often wandered the Academical Village. In 1833 student J. B. Minor complained about "being greatly annoyed by hogs under his window." The chairman of the faculty went on to note that livestock, and hogs in particular, were "so troublesome" within the Academical Village; it was a complaint repeated many times over the decades.[8] Apparently, some enslaved African Americans also brought their own livestock into pavilion and hotel garden and yard spaces. In 1838 the chairman of the faculty received a report that "several of the servants of the University keep hogs within the precincts." As a result, the proctor was instructed "to see that the hogs were removed without delay."[9] Even as late as 1857, the university proctor was requested to prohibit Anselem Brock, keeper of Hotel A, from continuing to keep poultry and livestock so close to the hotel.

In addition to food preparation, women were usually responsible for washing clothes and linens. All white households, regardless of their size, needed laundry services. In 1828 Gessner Harrison, bachelor resident of Pavilion VI, noted, "A woman who is the wife of a man who occupies my cellar, does my washing, and all the cooking necessary for my servant. I shall pay her at the rate of $2 per month. . . . My laundry is most excellently done. Much better than I have ever yet had since I came to the University. My cotton shirts as they are now brought in to me are fully as neat as my linen ones were when my washing was done by other hands."[10]

Laundry was a manual, labor-intensive activity generally requiring a full day of work for an enslaved laundress and her assistants, and it was usually performed mostly outdoors in the university's garden enclosures and yards. Women had to fetch and carry large amounts of water from a nearby cistern or well to a fire for heating. If not purchased, soap was made beforehand from mixing lye and animal fat. Laundresses washed clothes by stirring and beating them in a tub of hot water, and then by repeated scrubbing on a washboard. Clothes were hung to dry outside in all weather conditions. As required, and particularly as cotton replaced other materials, ironing was incorporated into the laundry routine. Laundresses and their assistants heated an iron over a fire or on a stove and pressed the garments, an activity repeated numerous times for each article of clothing. Answering the complaint of a student, Mrs. Gray, the keeper of Hotel E, testified that she kept "one woman always employed" at laundry chores.[11]

In order to supply the needs of a kitchen and washhouse, as well as for heating in cold weather, supplying wood was a constant activity that had no season. Enslaved men procured wood from university-owned lands beyond the Academical Village. As the chairman of the faculty noted in the spring of 1836, this was a time-consuming and laborious process. "The laborers and wagon of the University have been almost constantly engaged in the business of supplying the students with wood. As their assistance seemed to be essential to that end, I have been obliged to acquiesce in this employment of them, though it has necessarily prevented the cleaning up of the grounds as required by law."[12] Enslaved men made the trip to university lands with horse and cart; selected, cut, and split wood; hauled their load back to the Academical Village; and stacked it in each household's wood yard for curing. In the winter of 1831, Gessner Harrison noted the scarcity of this all-important fuel and the time-consuming role that his enslaved servant Charles, who also cooked for him, played in obtaining a consistent supply. "The weather being such as to make it a difficult business to keep oneself warm & especially when wood is so difficult to procure, I find—no easy matter. The only means I have of procuring, for I can get no one to bring me any, is to send Charles to the woods with my horse & cart—he manages to keep us enough to cook with & for the fire—I have none for my study but have been obliged to bring my books into the sitting room." Cold as Harrison might have been, imagine how cold those unheated basement or garret spaces were for the enslaved who lived there. For pavilion and hotel households wood was stored in the adjacent fenced yard space north and south of each residence. The proctor kept a wood yard for the university in the Pavilion VII garden. This wood supplied the needs of the student population and was delivered by enslaved workers. By the mid-nineteenth century, wood as a heating fuel began to be supplemented by coal.

Significant enslaved labor was also required to keep the gardens and yards clean, a requirement established by the Board of Visitors, who called for regular inspections. Despite this regulation, inspections were done sporadically and were most intense during times of widespread illness.[13] In the late

1840s during a period of cholera epidemic, the faculty required: "1) that the yards and grounds be well swept and sprinkled with lime twice a week; 2) that the apartments occupied by servants and the basement rooms of outhouses generally be whitewashed & subsequently be well ventilated; and 3) that the slops, soap suds and other refuse matter from the kitchens, wash houses and dining rooms be kept in water tight barrels on the respective premises."[14]

This messy work of such cleaning was the responsibility of enslaved laborers. Some of the work was done by people owned by the faculty and hotelkeepers, others by laborers hired by the university who collected sweepings and waste from pavilions and hotels; whitewashed buildings and structures; cleaned out public cisterns, privies, and urinals; and generally kept the university infrastructure in working order. Enslaved individuals within pavilion and hotel households regularly swept the kitchens and washhouse offices and hard-surfaced work areas, maintained livestock enclosures, and generally kept the garden enclosures and yards in a reasonable state of cleanliness.

Probably the most vexing problem in keeping the garden enclosures clean was the problem of human waste. Each garden enclosure had multiple privies, some for the use of the faculty and hotelkeepers and their families and others for the use of the students. Additional privies were also located at various locations on the outskirts of the Academical Village. Privies were typically small frame closets built on a masonry foundation. In use by the hundreds of people living in the Academical Village, they were a frequent source of complaint because of their offensive odors. The board asked that they be inspected regularly; too often the reports found the privies "in a very filthy state and a perfect nuisance endangering the health of the students, and even of those who reside within the limits of the University."[15] Because of this, privies were required to be cleaned on a regular basis. At one point the board asked that they be put "under a regular system of police" that included daily inspection and cleaning. They also required that "the deposits" be moved to another location where it would be "mixed with lime or charcoal . . . to neutralize the offensiveness of the mass, and to dispose of the whole from time to time, as it may be applied for by the neighboring Farmers and Gardeners."[16] All of this difficult and nasty work was assigned to enslaved individuals. The fact that there continued to be complaints about the privies for decades, until the introduction of flush toilets, meant that such expectations for daily cleaning regimes were not consistently maintained.

For enslaved African Americans living within the Academical Village, work and living space were never truly separate spheres. While kitchens and washhouses constructed to the rear of pavilions and hotels had a primary function as workspace, they also just as importantly doubled as living space (figs. 3.9, 3.10, 3.11). Rooms where food was prepared or laundry was ironed and folded also served as space where adults and children interacted and socialized throughout the day. Living conditions in kitchen and washhouses were spartan; small uninsulated rooms, possessing poor lighting and ventilation, and with little privacy. Sleeping space was minimal, limited to semi-private garret space and, where necessary, other publicly shared rooms. In 1855 Francis H. Smith, then the resident of Pavilion VI, received a letter from Allen B. Magruder requesting that a more comfortable sleeping space be arranged for Lucy, an enslaved woman his wife had leased to Smith.

> Lucy's mistress is under the impression from what she had heard from other servants that Lucy's rheumatism is perhaps aggravated by her sleeping apartment being paved with brick, the brick flooring being always liable to dampness. If this be so perhaps it would not be amiss to suggest if you retain her in your service, that a *plank* floor might be put down, over the bricks, which would probably render her less subject to attacks of rheumatism—and make her health better as well as enable her to be more useful in your service.[17]

FIG. 3.9. Mrs. Gray's kitchen behind Hotel E from the JUEL digital reconstruction of the Academical Village.

Fig. 3.10. Ground floor interior of Mrs. Gray's kitchen behind Hotel E from the JUEL digital reconstruction of the Academical Village.

Fig. 3.11. Garrett interior of Mrs. Gray's kitchen behind Hotel E from the JUEL digital reconstruction of the Academical Village.

The fact that Lucy slept on a brick floor implies that it was a ground-floor space, most likely a basement-level room of a pavilion or dormitory, or an office outbuilding.

The rear gardens and side yards of the pavilions and hotels were spaces where the enslaved lived, worked, and slept. Enslaved African Americans spent a substantial portion of their time bounded within these fences and walls. As already suggested, these walls and fences were designed to separate the Academical Village into white and black landscapes, but the necessary interactions of daily life meant that this was only marginally successful. But they were also designed to contain and control a potentially violent population. Only five years after the opening of the university, Nat Turner's Rebellion grimly reminded Virginia's white population that any place with a significant presence of enslaved individuals was a potential tinderbox. Virginia's white population used a variety of tools to maintain control over their enslaved populations. The most obvious was the construction of walls and fences to bound and contain. Another was the constant threat of violence. And the third was surveillance, the ability of masters to visually monitor the activities of those they owned.

The newly created digital model of the Academical Village allows for the first time the opportunity to better understand who could see what in the work spaces of a complex landscape of enslavement in early Virginia. This is important because it helps us understand the opportunities for enslaved people to control aspects of their lives away from the watchful eye of their owner and other whites. It helps us understand their ability to move around, to visit with friends and loved ones, and to engage unseen in entrepreneurial activity.

The reconstructed model for the yards and gardens of Pavilions IV and VI and Hotel D is the most accurate because of the significant historical, architectural, and archeological research that has been conducted on these spaces. It provides important information about the location of buildings in the workyard that no longer survive. With the addition of several buildings and fences that no longer survive, the model reveals what the professors or students could and could not see in the alleyways and gardens when they looked out from their rooms. To explicate this question, the model places a light in each of the rooms used by whites, that is, all of the rooms in the pavilions (save the slave-occupied basements), hotels, and dormitories.[18] The model reveals the areas where it was easy for whites to observe activities in the gardens and alleyways (the lighter areas), and those where it was difficult to see people or activities (the darker areas) (fig. 3.12).[19]

What this model demonstrates is that the higher elevation gave whites in pavilions considerable ability to see into the workyards. From there they could monitor that the people they owned were at work making food, doing laundry, chopping wood, or cleaning privies. But it also revealed that this visibility was not total. The many walls, fences, and buildings created zones that could not be observed from any of the rooms above. This created places where the enslaved could hide their activities or their location from their owners. Furthermore, the fewer buildings in the far larger garden of Pavilion IV meant that the enslaved population working in that yard were far more easily surveilled from the pavilion windows than were those laboring in the garden behind Pavilion VI where there were more buildings (fig. 3.13). The model also laid bare the clear differences between the very elevated pavilions and the much lower hotels; the pavilions had far greater capacity to surveille their workspace than did the hotels. Even so, the areas around the hotels had many fewer opportunities for enslaved workers to hide their activities. The hotel yards were relatively flat, open spaces. The activities of hotel-bound slaves were more easily watched by hotelkeepers and students in the dormitory rooms of the Range.

Finally, the model makes clear that there is a discernible difference between the half of the garden near the pavilion and half closest to the hotel. Despite the elevated position of the pavilion it is noticeably easier to go unseen in the half near the pavilion. There are a number of factors that account for this. One is that the mid-garden serpentine wall blocked the view into that half of the garden from the hotel. Also, numerous structures and fences blocked sight lines creating areas not visible to either pavilion or hotel

FIG. 3.12. JUEL reconstruction of workyards of Pavilions IV and VI and Hotel D of the Academical Village using lights to highlight those zones most easily and least easily surveilled.

Fig. 3.13. View from the upper bedchamber of Pavilion VI into the rear workyard to illustrate visibility.

residents. In addition, by the mid-nineteenth century most of the enclosed garden spaces had mature vegetation, such as shade and fruit trees as well as kitchen gardens. The model does not account for historic vegetation, but it is reasonable to assume that opportunities to escape observation would have been even greater with vegetation.

Perhaps surprisingly, the public alleyways, those east/west corridors that were the pathways that students were expected to take from their hotels back to the Lawn, were nearly invisible to professors and hotelkeepers. Thus, in both daytime and nighttime, the alleys would have been spaces where anyone could reliably move without being easily detected. However, because they were also public spaces white staff and students would regularly pass through, there would be inherent risks in conducting activities intended to escape observation there. Those enslaved who wished to use these alleys as a means of unseen circulation would have exploited the predictable rhythms of use by students and others in a typical academic day, week, and year. During periods of the year when students were not present and pedestrian traffic was significantly reduced, the alleys may have been considered ideal spaces in which to escape white surveillance.

The model helps us interpret the experience of the enslaved living and working in these spaces and they help make sense of much of what we read in the documents. Jefferson's original design for the Academical Village allowed the owners to watch the activities of the enslaved largely unobstructed. As the Academical Village evolved, however, it became more and more difficult to watch the activities of the enslaved in the gardens. As additional outbuildings and fences were added, as the vegetation grew larger and denser, it created more places where the enslaved could move about unobserved. We can only assume that the enslaved were fully aware and chose to navigate these landscapes accordingly. This ability gave the enslaved a small measure of control over their time and their movements.

Quite often, the enslaved turned this greater freedom into opportunities to engage in a variety of entrepreneurial activities that allowed them to earn money. Perhaps most commonly, they profited from the students' prohibited behaviors, getting them alcohol and helping them participate in their favorite pastimes, such as gambling over card playing and cockfighting. Faculty members were constantly worried about the underground economy between students and the enslaved and they found it very difficult to monitor, despite an architectural design that was intended to make such monitoring easy.

This was a constantly vexing problem for the faculty, who tried again and again to control the students' access to alcohol and illicit activities. Supplying the students with alcohol was one of the easiest ways for the enslaved to earn money. In one entry, the chairman complained that when he looked inside the basket of one of Mr. Conway's servants, it had a bottle of rum and a bottle of whiskey. Even though the servant said it was for himself, the chairman was certain it was for students. He asked the proctor to begin monitoring what was in the servants' baskets as they returned from town and that same day the proctor reported that two of Mrs. Gray's servants were carrying rum and wine.[20] At one point, the faculty passed a resolution giving them the authority "immediately to dismiss" anyone bringing alcohol to the precincts, unless it was ordered by the owner, and even more broadly, "to dismiss any servant for misconduct."[21] Their inability to control the enslaved was a constant source of frustration for the faculty and allowed the enslaved to pursue a steady source of income.

In addition to alcohol, the faculty were constantly concerned with gambling. Numerous entries mention their suspicions and most frequently, they believed that the students' misbehavior was facilitated by the enslaved. In one instance, Professor Davis, who lived in Pavilion X on the east side, said he had reason to suspect there was frequent gambling in the rooms of the West Range near Mrs. Gray's hotel at the end of the Lawn. He said "there can be no doubt that Mrs. Gray's Servants gambled, and that the fact [was] well known to the students."[22] But all he had was a suspicion. Whether it was based on hearsay or on movements he heard or witnessed is unclear. What is clear is that he could not confirm these activities because at night the students and the enslaved could move about the Academical Village largely without being seen. Even with the illumination provided by candles, oil lamps, and gas lamps, significant portions of gardens and workyards, alleyways and walkways remained invisible to the faculty. The movements and the whereabouts of both students and enslaved were generally unknown and unknowable to the faculty. Such invisibility made surveillance at night nearly impossible.

In addition to enabling the students' forbidden behaviors, the enslaved also capitalized on the students' desire for better food than what was served by the hotelkeepers. Quite a number created a side business of selling food, often bringing complete dinners in baskets. Charles Ellis recorded in his diary, in a nonchalant way as if it were a common occurrence, a "chicken supper," which consisted of a turkey, half a dozen chickens, and some biscuits. In addition, there was also coffee, which was apparently much better than anything offered by the hotelkeepers as it was the "greatest part of the feast in demand."[23] Alfred T. Howell, a student in 1850, described the many ways in which African Americans tried to earn income: "black men, women and boys are constantly surveying us with every sort of question. Do we want to buy this, that and other or will we have a hack to go to town, or have we not something we would like to send after or no message to send? . . . The U is a regular market place for everything."[24] As African Americans exploited their ability to move unseen, they were able to find multiple ways to earn income from the students.

Those living in the Academical Village were not the only ones to profit from the students. In one case the faculty noted that breakfasts were being supplied by a small boy, "belonging to no one in the University, but living with a free woman, the wife of Dr. Magills' servant, in the basement of Mr. Roger's house." In this short phrase, we learn that there was a young black boy, probably not owned by anyone, living with a free African American woman, who was considered married to an enslaved man owned by Dr. Magill. It is not explained why, but Magill resided in Pavilion III on the west side and the boy, wife, and servant all lived in the basement of Professor Roger's pavilion, on the east side. This points to the fluidity of living arrangements and points out some of the difficulties that faculty faced in trying to oversee the movement of the people they owned. It also demonstrates how porous the movements of free and enslaved were in and out of the Academical Village.[25]

Throughout its first fifty years, the University of Virginia's plantation landscape was bustling with activity day and night. Before dawn the cook and her crew would rise to kindle cooking fires. Enslaved individuals owned by hotelkeepers were required to start fires in student rooms as well. Enslaved children might also be set early to gathering firewood and milking the cows. Through the course of the day enslaved men would be sent to fell trees, and chop, haul, and stack wood. Others would be plucking chickens, tending gardens either behind the pavilions and hotels or in the larger gardens just outside the Village. Some would also be tending the horses or livestock penned in the grassy lots on the other side of the Academical Village. Women and girls could be seen cooking and preparing meals and laboring over washboards and tubs; boys and girls might be collecting the day's milk, feeding livestock, and running errands; and men would performing general improvement and repair to the buildings and grounds. Others would be assigned to clean out the privies and haul away waste. In the late fall and early winter, some of the enslaved would be engaged in the slaughtering, draining, butchering, and smoking hogs. And then late in the day they would retire to sleep on the floors of damp cellar chambers or in the lofts over kitchens and washhouses with little privacy.

The labor conducted in yards and garden enclosures was vital to the maintenance of white households, and consequently to the operation of the Academical Village as an institution. And all the while, these were individuals who understood that they were being constantly watched as they moved through their day. For all of them, the threat of violence was an ever-present reality. Yet these same spaces were also places where living was its own act of resisting the institution of slavery. In these places, the enslaved African Americans who labored at UVA created their own sense of place. Despite the pervasiveness of white power and control, the constant demand for their labor, and the crowded living conditions, African Americans built families and sustained a productive life. Families were raised, meals were shared, and cultural traditions were passed from one generation to another. Measures of independence were gained through hard work and negotiation. Above all, enslaved families never lost sight of the struggle for freedom. For most of them, this did not come until the end of slavery.

NOTES

Resources marked with an asterisk (*) are also available online at http://juel.iath.virginia.edu/resources.

1. Willis H. Woodley to John A. G. Davis, Chairman, September 18, 1839, Papers of the Proctor, RG-5/3/1.111, Box 12, Albert and Shirley Small Special Collections Library, University of Virginia. This is one of several student complaints leveled against Blaetterman that would ultimately lead to his dismissal from the university in 1840. As early as 1836, students stoned his pavilion to express their displeasure with him.

2. *Minutes of the Faculty of the University of Virginia, 1825–1970, RG 19/1/1.461, vols. 1–19, vol. 6, part 7, June 16, 1849, Albert and Shirley Small Special Collections Library, University of Virginia (hereafter cited as Faculty Minutes).

3. Gessner Harrison to Mary Stewart Harrison, December 15, 1829, Papers of the Tucker, Harrison, and Smith Families, 1790–1940, Box 3, Accession 2589, 3825, 3847, 3847-A through H, 3847-J through L, Albert and Shirley Small Special Collections Library, University of Virginia.

4. Gayle M. Schulman, "Slaves at the University of Virginia," 2004, MSS 13201, p. 1, Albert and Shirley Small Special Collections Library, University of Virginia.

5. *Faculty Minutes, vol. 7, 1848–1856, June 2, 1849, p. 31.

6. *Faculty Minutes, vol. 4, 1834–1836, May 2, 1835, p. 92. As the duties of postmaster were the responsibility of the proctor, the post office was located near his office in several dormitory rooms on the East Range during the pre-Emancipation period. The noise emanating from the post office was one of the complaints of Mr. Pickett.

7. *Journals of the Chairman of the Faculty, 1827–1864, RG-19/1/2.041, vol. 3, July 1831–July 1832, March 1, 1832, p. 99, Albert and Shirley Small Special Collections Library, University of Virginia (hereafter cited as Chairman's Journals).

8. *Chairman's Journals, vol. 4, July 1832–July 1833, May 11, 1833, p. 69.

9. *Chairman's Journals, vol. 7, 1837–1838, February 28, 1838, n.p.

10. Gessner Harrison to Dr. Peachey Harrison, September 14, 1828, Papers of the Tucker, Harrison, and Smith Families, Box 2, Albert and Shirley Small Special Collections Library, University of Virginia.

11. *Faculty Minutes, vol. 3, 1830–1834, February 2, 1831.

12. *Chairman's Journals, vol. 6, 1825–1837, April 20, 1836, p. 53.

13. *Faculty Minutes, vol. 1, April 1825–July 1827, August 18, 1826, pp. 73–74.

14. *Faculty Minutes, vol. 7, September 25, 1848–September 29, 1856, June 16, 1849, p. 66.

15. *Minutes of the Rector and Board of Visitors of the University of Virginia, 1817–2002, University of Virginia Text Collection, June 26, 1825 (hereafter cited as Board of Visitors Minutes).

16. *Board of Visitors Minutes, July 28, 1845.

17. Allen B. Magruder to Francis H. Smith, November 30, 1855, Papers of the Tucker, Harrison, and Smith Families, 1790–1940, Box 11.

18. The lighting effect was set to show the historic viewshed of a person standing eighteen inches back from the center of a window.

19. The darkened setting and light cones portrayed in the visualization analysis are not intended to characterize night and day (e.g., time of day). Rather they are used to provide a contrast that illustrates the potential viewsheds from a particular location.

20. *Chairman's Journals, vol. 6, July 1835–July 1837, February 17, 1837.

21. *Faculty Minutes, vol. 4, 1834–1836, February 18, 1837, p. 320; Chairman's Journals, vol. 6, July 1835–July 1837, February 15, 1837, p. 29.

22. *Chairman's Journals, February 17, 1831.

23. Charles Ellis Jr., A Student's Diary, November 7, 1835, http://juel.iath.virginia.edu/resources.

24. Alfred T. Howell to Father, October 1, 1850, and Alfred T. Howell to Morton B. Howell, October 15, 1850, correspondence of Morton Boyte Howell, 1851–1860, MSS 8463, Microfilm M-1725, Albert and Shirley Small Special Collections Library, University of Virginia.

25. *Chairman's Journals, March 11, 1836.

4

VIOLENCE

Maurie D. McInnis

On May 1, 1856, student Nathan B. Noland savagely beat a ten-year-old girl. History has not recorded her name, or what happened to her afterward. The girl was owned by a female relative of a woman who operated a boardinghouse only a few hundred yards away from the Academical Village. On the day of the attack, the young girl had heard a knock on the back door and someone calling her name. Awaiting her on the other side of the door was a student who boarded at the house, a student she had encountered earlier that afternoon as she was walking through the university. When she came to the door, the student grabbed her, pulled her out of the house, threw her to the ground, and mercilessly beat and kicked her; she curled into a ball, crying out loudly. The pain was so great, she passed out.[1]

As with so much of the history of slavery at UVA, what we know comes only from the white authorities, in this case what was recorded by the faculty who questioned the student. The complaint against the student was brought by Lucy Terrell, whose boardinghouse (fig. 4.1) was one of several only a few hundred yards north of the university, concentrated along what is now University Avenue and Carr's Hill. There were also several other houses to the west, near the University Cemetery. By the 1850s, over half of UVA's students lived in boardinghouses rather than in lodging provided by the university. The student, Noland, was from a slaveholding family in Fauquier County. Since Noland boarded at Lucy Terrell's, he probably knew the girl. The beating took place just outside of the university precincts but the faculty believed that they had authority to adjudicate the matter because Noland was a student.[2]

Terrell had been associated with the university for more than two decades. She had previously operated Hotel B from 1835 to 1840, but found it more

FIG. 4.1. Detail of William A. Pratt, "Plan of University Cleared Land," 1858, showing Terrell's boardinghouse.

lucrative, and perhaps less restrictive, to run her own establishment. The property was known as Edgeway: it consisted of at least two buildings just to the north of the university, near the current location of St. Paul's Episcopal Church. As at the hotels, most of the labor was done by enslaved people who cooked, cleaned, and ran errands for the students who boarded there. In the 1850 census, Terrell owned eleven slaves, including five children under the age of ten. In the Academical Village and at the boardinghouses, many of those who waited on the students were children, but enslaved children had no childhood. They began working at a very young age, often younger than ten. In 1860, for example, of the 105 enslaved residents in the Academical Village, forty-five were under the age of eighteen.[3] The girl was owned by a relative of Terrell's, Mrs. Woodson, who lived with her at the boardinghouse and perhaps helped her run the establishment.

The day after he had beaten the young girl, Noland was summoned by the faculty to answer their questions. According to the student's testimony, he encountered the young girl wandering through the university. Nothing was said about her purpose in being there, as it would not have seemed unusual to anyone. She might have been running an errand for Terrell, or she might have been going to visit a friend—the enslaved who worked near the university moved freely about the Academical Village. Whatever her reason, she had become intrigued with a pigeon that she was then chasing as it flitted around the precincts. The faculty asked Noland why he had beaten her, leaving her "for a time insensible, and to require the attendance of a Physician afterwards." In Noland's testimony, he claimed that she had spoken to him with insolence.

The beating this young girl received was one of many acts of violence perpetrated by students on the enslaved people who lived and worked in and around the university. Noland's testimony chillingly reveals the ever-present danger that all enslaved people faced, a danger heightened in the university setting. Unlike life on a plantation, where enslaved people most frequently encountered only the white people who owned them, it was quite different at the university. In this way, UVA was more like an urban setting than a plantation. Here the countless daily interactions between enslaved people and whites who were not their owners meant the enslaved were constantly in jeopardy. Despite laws that protected a slaveowner's property, many whites believed that they had a right to act however they wished against enslaved African Americans, even people they did not own.[4] Noland told the faculty "whenever a servant is insolent to him, he will take upon himself the right of punishing without the consent of the master." The result of this attitude was that the enslaved who lived and worked around UVA had not one master but hundreds, all of whom were steeped in the pervasive proslavery thought that was promulgated at the university. It meant that enslaved people were daily subject to the arbitrary actions of faculty, hotelkeepers, and students and the commands of these different groups were frequently contradictory, making navigating daily life fraught with peril for those enslaved at UVA.

On a day-to-day basis, there were numerous acts of harassment; those generally went unmentioned in the official records unless they resulted in physical harm. In addition, there were numerous accounts of more violent offenses including acts of beating, kicking, whipping, and raping. All were vulnerable, women and children especially so. One of the most stunning aspects of Noland's actions is that it was not the result of some burst of momentary anger. Rather, it was a cold and calculated beating. The student had encountered the girl in the Academical Village earlier in the day. Noland tells us that he asked who sent her, and she replied, "I sent myself." He thought her reply was impertinent so he threatened to whip her. To which she responded, "No you won't," further angering Noland. But he did not strike her then. Rather, hours later, he spoke with Terrell and informed her that he would "chastise" the girl for her "impertinent language." The owner promised to "correct" the girl and "earnestly requested" that he not do so. But Noland was not satisfied. After his conversation with Terrell, he left and only later returned, knocked on the back door, and pulled the young girl out and threw her to the ground before beating her.

Official accounts reveal important aspects of the racial attitudes that enabled some students to act with such inhumanity. Of the many cases captured in the faculty minutes, Noland's attitudes are spelled out in great detail and are particularly chilling in their bold assertion of his perceived right to mastery. The faculty committee was quite taken, not by his assertion of the right to violently beat an enslaved person, but by his assertion that he would inflict harm on the human property of another. "Do you mean to assert the right to exercise your own will and the suggestions of your own passions," they asked him, "in the infliction of punishment on a servant of another person?" In the questioning that followed, he said that he could not promise that he would not do so again, only that he would try to restrain himself "not to whip a servant so severely as I did in this case, but no further." The faculty decided to expel Noland "in view of the danger to the peace of Society & the good order of the University." The latter is important to note, because their concern about the "peace of Society" was not a concern that he had severely beaten a young girl, but that by beating this girl he had damaged the property that belonged to another owner. And he said he would do so again. The "good order" they wished to preserve was a complicated series of layers of white authority.

The faculty, through the *Enactments* passed by the Board of Visitors, had authority over the Academical Village, and this included the students, hotelkeepers, and the enslaved no matter by whom they were owned. In addition to the usual authority that faculty had over the people they personally owned, they also exercised authority over the enslaved owned by others, especially those owned by the hotelkeepers, both in specifying their expectations for their labor, but also in meting out punishments. In addition, the faculty also granted the hotelkeepers certain authority over the students, expecting them to act as agents of the faculty. Noland's beating of the young girl threatened to undermine the authority of hotelkeepers to supervise students and manage the enslaved who worked for them. Additionally, Noland's actions threatened more broadly the structure of southern slave society that protected the property rights of slaveowners and that allowed slaveowners to seek compensation from a perpetrator if their "property," that is if the person they owned, was damaged.

The faculty's decision to expel Noland did not stand. The following day they met again. Before them was a letter written by the student. In it, Noland apologized to the owner of the girl, the other residents of the boardinghouse, and the college authorities. He admitted that it was wrong to "inflict punishment upon a servant belonging to another," but said that he believed that "the correction of a servant for impertinence, when done on the spot & under the spur of provocation, is not only tolerated by society, but with the proper qualifications may be defended on the ground of the necessity of maintaining the due subordination in this class of persons." Part of the defense he offered was that he believed that his right to beat an enslaved person could be defended, especially if it should not exceed a "moderate flogging." Any greater punishment, he suggested, should be directed to the magistrate if the owner failed "to take proper measures."[5] Defending his actions by saying it was "tolerated by society" and that it was a "necessity" to maintain the racial order was apparently persuasive to the faculty and "in view of the contrition expressed," they rescinded their decision to expel him.

The faculty's decision to allow Noland to continue at the university is telling. Noland's argument that his actions were justified in order to maintain the racial hierarchy was persuasive. The decision of the faculty speaks to the violence that upheld the system of slavery and that generally went unquestioned. Noland's apology was not to the girl, but to the owner of the girl. His defense was rooted in the conversations that were part of campus life and southern society. In the debating societies and in the school's literary magazines, students argued for the superiority of whites; they argued for a natural hierarchy. Noland presented his defense to a group of faculty, several of whom were leading intellectuals and authors in the proslavery movement, including Albert Taylor Bledsoe and James P. Holcombe.[6] They probably agreed with many of Noland's assertions, especially the assertion of "the necessity of maintaining the due subordination in this class of persons." What Noland maintained followed their own arguments for the rightness of a natural hierarchy based on chattel slavery for those of African descent. To them, if there was a crime in this savage beating, it was a crime against Miss Terrell and Mrs. Woodson for damage to their property.

The faculty's response also points to the larger culture of violence that was part of nineteenth-century life, especially on a college campus. UVA was not unusual in the amount of disharmony that existed between faculty and students. Mostly the children of planters, the students were used to being treated as masters and young patriarchs. At the university, however, they were not at the top of the hierarchical ladder, the faculty were; some students responded by testing that authority. The faculty expected them to wear a "uniform," a suit coat made from cloth not befitting their status as gentlemen. Even more loathsome to most students was that they were expected to answer the call of the bell, rung to wake them at 6 a.m. in the morning and to announce the changing of classes and other important times throughout the day. For many students, the only bells they would have known previously were the bells on their local churches, and the bells on their own plantations that were used to mark the workday for the enslaved. To be a student at UVA was to no longer be the master of your day and your activities. It is clear that many students resented their new status.

It is important to note that violence and unrest on nineteenth-century campuses was common, both in the North and the South. With some regularity, students pushed back on the authority of the faculty by rioting, banging on doors, throwing bricks through windows, and otherwise vandalizing property. They burned barrels of tar and privies. They fought with each other and with townspeople, and duels (though forbidden) still took place. There were even several instances when they beat a faculty member, most famously when two recently expelled students "horse-whipped" Gessner Harrison, who was chairman of the faculty. Apparently the students were angry at their recent dismissal.[7]

In another instance, students Madison McAfee and J. H. Harrison threatened Professor Charles Bonnycastle when he tried to stop them from "murdering his servant Fielding." The students claimed that Fielding was "exceedingly insolent." They had both encountered Fielding outside of the university precincts, on the road into Charlottesville, and for his "insolence" beat him with stick and club and pursued him for additional beatings because Fielding made efforts to defend himself by threatening to throw a stone. When Bonnycastle grabbed McAfee by the collar of his coat, a witness said that

McAfee yelled, "any man who would protect a negro as much in the wrong as Fielding is not better than a negro himself." He also threatened to "whip Mr. Bonnycastle." The students argued that by intervening in the punishment they were inflicting upon Fielding that Bonnycastle had "thrown off the garb of a Professor and assumed that of a man recklessly interposing to screen his servant from merited chastisement."[8]

Once again a student was asserting his right to mastery over an enslaved man owned by another. The faculty found themselves caught between two imperatives. One was the authority of faculty over students. The second was a general acceptance that whites had authority over African Americans, without regard to ownership. In this instance, due to the "peculiar circumstances" of the incident the faculty chose not to do anything about the students' threatened actions against Bonnycastle, and on the charge of beating Fielding merely said that the matter was in the hands of the authorities.[9] There is no evidence that the authorities ever did anything.

Most students spent their years at UVA focused on their education. For the hundreds of students who attended UVA, most are never mentioned as engaging in acts of violence. But some were frustrated, angry, and violent. They wished to reassert their status; the enslaved were easy targets. Numerous attacks by students on enslaved people are noted in the university archives, and it is likely many more occurred than are noted, because such acts were, as Noland pointed out, "tolerated by society." Because of the sources available, we have considerable evidence about student violence against the enslaved, but we know virtually nothing about the actions of faculty or hotelkeepers against the people they owned or the others living in the Academical Village. Complaints were only recorded when the slaveowner complained to the faculty about the actions of students and when the faculty felt there was enough evidence to investigate the matter. Given that the faculty did not consider evidence from an enslaved person admissible, it means the records probably do not capture most of the violent events.

The faculty's responses over the decades were inconsistent. Even in some of the most extreme acts of violence, the faculty often did nothing or turned the matter over to the magistrates. There is little evidence that the local authorities ever did anything. In other cases, the punishments voted on by the faculty were surprisingly slight. Noland's dismissal was reversed when he apologized. He was not punished in any way for the severe beating of a ten-year-old girl. He did not even have to pay a fee to Terrell for the harm done to her property. McAfee and Harrison were not punished for their severe beating of Fielding and their disrespect toward Professor Bonnycastle. Meanwhile, students were regularly dismissed for inattention to their studies, what the faculty often referred to as "academic lassitude," for drinking and playing cards habitually, for not wearing the specified uniform coat, and for other minor but habitual forms of misconduct. In one colorful example, students Johnston and Gray were dismissed from the university for riding their horses under the arcades and up the stairs of the Rotunda while intoxicated.[10] Meanwhile, numerous students received little more than a verbal admonishment for the physical harm they did to enslaved people.

While most of the recorded violence done was at the hand of individual students, the faculty acting as a corporate body also sometimes punished or voted to punish the enslaved. In one of the most pointed examples, the faculty ordered that a man named Thornton, who was either owned or hired by a bookseller whose store was nearby, receive "39 lashes at the public whipping post." Thornton is described as having committed a "fraud" and that some students had had "things stolen from their rooms." The only specific item mentioned was a uniform coat.[11] In later entries, the chairman complained that Thornton, "who is in the habit of gambling, and stealing," has not been punished, even though he has asked the proctor twice to do so. It seems that the whipping post referred to was the county whipping post located in downtown Charlottesville, as no other reference is made to a whipping post in the university archives (fig. 4.2). As whipping was a common punishment inflicted on enslaved people, many counties had a whipping post near the courthouse. The more common form of punishment enacted by the faculty was the banishment of an enslaved person from the Academical Village. The faculty made such decisions wishing to assert their control over the "good order" of the Academical Village by removing an enslaved person whom they believed was assisting the students in their illicit activities. Records reveal, however, that it was very difficult for them to enforce such decisions. In the case of Thornton, who in addition to being whipped they ordered banished, the chairman noted later that Thornton "was found by the Janitor, playing cards with Mrs. Gray's servant Albert, and Mr. Brockenbrough's man Trimpson."[12]

As Noland was telling his story to the faculty, none saw it at all unusual that this young girl who lived in a boardinghouse off-grounds would be wandering around inside the university precincts. Jefferson's design, in theory,

Fig. 4.2. Whipping post in the collections of the Virginia Historical Society, Richmond.

had been intended to make it easy for the professor or the hotelkeeper to watch the enslaved working in the gardens from the back windows of the pavilions or the hotels. But outbuildings and walls blocked sightlines. The alleyways were virtually impossible to monitor. The dark of night provided additional cover (fig. 4.3). Enslaved workers knew that they could use that invisibility to their advantage. Enslaved workers were constantly moving around the Academical Village and back and forth to Charlottesville as well.

This fluidity of movement for the enslaved also meant that the interactions between students and the enslaved who lived and worked in the Academical Village were frequent. Even though students may have felt as if a

FIG. 4.3. View toward the alleys from the ground floor window of a pavilion from the JUEL digital reconstruction of the Academical Village.

certain enslaved servant was "theirs," their interactions with enslaved residents were not limited to the dormitory servant assigned to them or those who waited on table in the hotels. In fact, in the course of any day, students had contact with many, probably dozens of enslaved people. The Academical Village was a small city of only a few hundred residents, and it is clear that everyone knew each other, both free and enslaved. In fact, there was a certain intimacy of familiarity that is hinted at in the documents. One evening after a riot of students, the chairman questioned Lewis (the enslaved bell-ringer owned by the university) about the identities of the students involved. It was dark and the students were wearing masks and yet Lewis was able to name twenty-three students by knowing well their voices and their manners. While the students largely treated the enslaved as if they were invisible, the enslaved watched and listened, and knew the identities and the activities of the students.[13]

We know less about the day-to-day interactions between students and the enslaved. Student Charles Ellis's diary provides some indications. It listed numerous encounters with enslaved people. Albert was assigned to his clean and serve his room, but Ellis's entries also mention numerous other people, usually nameless, such as when "a servant" delivered a letter to him or when "Cook" caught him darning a sock. These numerous references suggest the many daily interactions that took place between students and the enslaved on a regular basis. Given the many duties performed by enslaved people—obtaining and preparing food, chopping and hauling wood, carrying supplies to students' rooms, running errands for students, to name only a few—it meant that the usual forms of surveillance present in a slave society largely broke down. The enslaved were able to use their ability to move about in places where they could not be observed and the fact that their duties meant that they were expected to be in many different places as cover to assert some control in their own lives. But it also meant that they frequently came in contact with students, which put them at greater risk for violence.

Although men were assigned to wait on students in their dormitories, there were many women enslaved who worked at the university as well. In fact, women were usually around one-half of the enslaved living at the university. Their duties often centered on food preparation and laundry or working as domestic servants for the faculty. Even though their duties did not normally have them working directly with students, their presence in the Academical Village made them particularly vulnerable, especially to sexual violence. In fact, some students clearly believed that the enslaved women working at the university were just one of the "Virginian Luxuries" that they had a right to, no matter who the owner was (fig. 4.4).

In one instance, Gessner Harrison, who was chairman of the faculty at the time, complained to the faculty about the loud conduct of several students. According to their own testimony, the students had gone into Charlottesville to Fitch's Tavern where they had become intoxicated. Upon returning to the university after midnight, their "riotous" behavior had awakened the professor when he heard a group of students gathered in a dormitory room and one "knocking at his cellar door [Pavilion VI] & heard indecent propositions made to a female servant." Each of the students was called in to testify before the faculty and most claimed that they had not been noisy and were not intoxicated, or, as one claimed, that he was intoxicated but that it was "accidental." The faculty determined to dismiss one student, because he was frequently drunk at the tavern, and that on that evening he was "excessively drunk." At the same time, they only admonished William G. Carr for his drinking and "indecent conduct in endeavouring to get access to a female servant in a pavilion of one of the professors."[14]

Women were vulnerable throughout the Academical Village, especially so at night when both students and the enslaved knew how to use the cover of darkness to obscure their movements and activities. Standing one night

Fig. 4.4. Detail from *Virginian Luxuries*, unidentified artist, ca. 1825.

around a pump for water, several women who were owned by the assistant proctor were treated with "rudeness and indecency" by a group of students. We have no way of knowing what behaviors are hidden by those words, as the faculty often used euphemistic terminology when discussing matters of a sexual nature. In another instance, G. Tucker broke into Dr. Patterson's pavilion (Pavilion V) in pursuit of an unnamed woman owned by Dr. Patterson. The incident was described only as an "outrage." Clearly it was a significant assault, as the chairman expressed "abhorrence at his conduct."[15]

In another instance, the faculty investigators were more explicit describing the actions of the students, clearly labeling it "a violent outrage [a rape]." According to the notation in the minutes, the victim was described as a "small negro girl, a slave about 12 years old." The minutes do not record by whom she was owned, so it is not clear if she was regularly in the Academical Village or not. The attack took place west of the university, near boardinghouses operated by Colonel Johnson and Mr. Leake, near the University Cemetery. Three university students, George H. Hardy, Armistead C. Eliason, and James E. Montandon, committed the rape. They were discovered by three other students who "interfered to prevent it." In this instance, the students reported the actions of their classmates to the authorities and the faculty voted to expel them from the university.[16]

The vulnerability of women was twofold, not only in the actions themselves, but also in the fact that in these cases the faculty rarely voted on any real punishment for the students. In Harrison's complaint, because "there was no evidence but that of a slave," and because the "offence occurred in the dark" and the students denied involvement, the faculty decided not to do anything.[17] In the second incident, when they broke into Patterson's pavilion, the punishment was light. The student was expected to apologize to Dr. Patterson and his family. The chairman reported that the student "did not seem to be much impressed with the immorality of his conduct." But the chairman's response was merely to "read him a severe moral lecture, & reprimanded him in the strongest terms."[18] Like Noland, who was not punished for his beating of the young girl who belonged to Mrs. Woodson, students knew well that they were rarely held accountable for violent and predatory behavior against the enslaved who lived and worked and around the Academical Village.

But it wasn't only those associated with the university who were at risk. Enslaved residents, including those who did not belong to the university, were vulnerable. Outside of the university precincts, there were numerous places over the decades that served as houses of prostitution, and many of these were staffed by enslaved women. There are several references, often oblique, in the faculty minutes to these places. In one instance, the faculty recorded a very clear recitation of the sort of violence that could occur. According to the faculty minutes, a group of students attacked Mr. Crawford's house and a woman there "was stripped of her clothes." One of the students, George Hoffman, explained that they "insulted and stripped the servant girl of her clothes" because the students were "under the impression that she was one of the women who had infected the students with disease." The faculty decided that Turner Dixon and George Hoffman, "having been implicated in an indecent outrage upon a female," be reprimanded. Their punishment was light, the faculty said, because they "appeared sorry" and promptly apologized to Crawford and paid him $10.[19]

The enslaved who lived and worked at the University of Virginia found themselves in an unusual situation. Their life differed in many important ways from that on a plantation; many of them likely had lived on one prior to coming to the university. Now instead of clear lines of authority, the owner and the enslaved, they encountered a much more complicated social order. The authority of their owner was diluted by their ability to move around and engage in activities with a much larger enslaved community, both those in the Academical Village and those in Charlottesville as well. But they also had hundreds of others—faculty, hotelkeepers, and students—who acted in many instances as if they were the owners. So their situation was that they were owned simultaneously by no one and everyone. They used this ambiguity to carve out more freedoms for themselves, to engage in entrepreneurial activities, and to build families. Nevertheless, the prevailing ideology among the students, faculty, and hotelkeepers was that all of the enslaved were property and that they, therefore, held certain rights of mastery over the enslaved, even if they did not own them. In the violent culture of nineteenth-century student life, students learned that they could act, usually without consequence, in line with the ideological beliefs espoused regularly at the university about the rightness of the South's racial hierarchy. They had been taught that such actions were often defensible in order to maintain "the due subordination in this class of persons." And in case after case of student violence enacted upon the enslaved, the faculty chose to uphold the overarching priority of supporting the racial hierarchy.

Decades after the university's founding, Jefferson's concerns about the impact that slavery could have on the morals of southerners had ample substantiation. Many of the students at the university had clearly been "nursed, educated, and daily exercised in tyranny," just as Jefferson had presaged in his *Notes on the State of Virginia*.[20] As the faculty questioned Noland, they inquired whether he believed he had a right to "exercise his own will and the suggestions of his own passions" in beating the young girl. His answer was yes. The fact that they excused his behavior and that of many other students who hit and kicked men, women, and children and sexually assaulted women means that the "unremitting despotism" of slavery that Jefferson had warned about decades earlier continued to eat away at southern society and deeply infected the University of Virginia.

NOTES

1. The account of the girl's beating is recorded in the Faculty Minutes, May 2 and 3, 1856. Quotations here and in subsequent paragraphs are from this source. See Minutes of the Faculty of the University of Virginia, 1825–1856, May 2 and 3, 1856, http://juel.iath.virginia.edu/resources (hereafter cited as Faculty Minutes).

2. In many ways the faculty served as a judicial authority. The chairman of the faculty often investigated a complaint. That investigation was commonly followed by a meeting of the faculty, who heard testimony from individuals and made disciplinary decisions. Their authority extended over students, hotelkeepers, and the enslaved.

3. See Wilma King, *Stolen Childhood* (Bloomington: Indiana University Press, 1995); *Slave Schedule, Population Statistics, Albemarle County, Charlottesville, Virginia, Eighth Census of the United States, 1860*, Washington, DC: National Archives and Records Administration.

4. There is significant case law that supports this, although there usually had to be permanent damage to the slave, that is, damage to the property of the slaveowner, before there was any finding of guilt.

5. Faculty Minutes, May 2 and 3, 1856, http://juel.iath.virginia.edu/resources.

6. See chapter 6 for a full discussion of proslavery thought at UVA.

7. This incident is more fully described in http://juel.iath.virginia.edu/resources; Journals of the Chairman of the Faculty, 1827–1864, March 20–22, 1839, http://juel.iath.virginia.edu/resources (hereafter cited as Chairman's Journals). For more on student unrest see Rex Bowman and Carlos Santos, *Rot, Riot, and Rebellion: Mr. Jefferson's Struggle to Save the University that Changed America* (Charlottesville: University of Virginia Press, 2013).

8. This incident is discussed more fully at Thomas M. Winters, "Professor Bonnycastle's Slave Is Beaten by Students (1839)," http://juel.iath.virginia.edu/node/320.

9. The extensive testimony about the beating of Fielding is in the Chairman's Journals, February 25, 1839, March 1, 1839, and in the Faculty Minutes, March 2 and 8, 1839, http://juel.iath.virginia.edu/resources.

10. Faculty Minutes, March 30, 1850, http://juel.iath.virginia.edu/resources.

11. Chairman's Journals, September 28, 1829, http://juel.iath.virginia.edu/resources; Chairman's Journals March 23, 1829, http://juel.iath.virginia.edu/resources.

12. Chairman's Journals, March 30, 1831, http://juel.iath.virginia.edu/resources. Thornton appears again in the Chairman's Journals, March 30, 1831, and November 30, 1831, http://juel.iath.virginia.edu/resources. In those instances, he is again linked with Mr. McKennie, who operated a bookstore on the corner.

13. Chairman's Journals, May 19, 1831, http://juel.iath.virginia.edu/resources.

14. Chairman's Journals, June 25, 1829, http://juel.iath.virginia.edu/resources.

15. Chairman's Journals, February 5, 1830, http://juel.iath.virginia.edu/resources.

16. Faculty Minutes, April 24, 1850, http://juel.iath.virginia.edu/resources.

17. Chairman's Journals, November 8, 1830, http://juel.iath.virginia.edu/resources.

18. Chairman's Journals, February 5, 1830, http://juel.iath.virginia.edu/resources.

19. Faculty Minutes, September 20, 1826, http://juel.iath.virginia.edu/resources.

20. Thomas Jefferson, *Notes on the State of Virginia* (London: Printed for John Stockdale, 1787), 270–71. Access to Jefferson's personal copy is available at http://static.lib.virginia.edu/rmds/tj/notes/index.html.

5

HOTELS

Jessica Ellen Sewell and Andrew Scott Johnston

In 1828 an enslaved man working in the dining room of Hotel C was assaulted and beaten by a student. At breakfast the student, Thomas J. Boyd, had asked the man for butter, but found that the butter was not good. When he complained aloud about the butter the man did not answer him, but, Boyd claimed, "spoke to another servant in an insolent tone of voice" after Boyd had left the table, "saying among other things he was surprised that Mr. B having read so many books should not know the difference between water and butter." Boyd apparently fumed about the enslaved man all day, and having had no answer to his letter of complaint to the hotelkeeper Walter Minor, took it upon himself to "chastise" the man after supper. Boyd asked the man to leave the public space of the dining room, which he refused to do, whereupon Boyd beat him with a stick until blood was running freely from his head and the stick broke, meanwhile trying to force him out of the dining room. The beating only ended after Mr. and Mrs. Minor came into the room.[1]

When questioned about his behavior, Boyd, who "expressed his astonishment and Indignation at being called before the faculty for so trifling an affair as that of chastising a servant for his insolence," expanded his complaint well beyond enslaved servants' behavior in the dining room. He "complained of the want of proper attendance by servants in his Dormitory," claiming that one person waited on more than twenty rooms (in defiance of university regulations which dictated a minimum of one servant per twenty students, ordinarily ten rooms).[2] He claimed that water was delivered only twice a day (which met the regulations) and that his room had not been scoured for six weeks (which did not). Because they considered hotelkeeper Minor's service, provided by his enslaved workers, to be negligent, the faculty declined to act against Boyd for his violence, but instead passed a resolution that "Mr. Minor be requested to have his Dormitories attended to."[3]

However, this incident did not end there. In anger at being called in front of the faculty, that evening Boyd verbally attacked Minor, demanding "in a very imperious manner . . . how he dared complain against him to the Faculty," and then "descending to the usual threats and menaces of a bully," in the end going off "uttering threats of taking satisfaction, blood & a good deal of such stuff." He told Minor that "he had not acted the part of a gentleman—that his conduct had been cowardly—that if he ever crossed Boyd's path one or the other shall be whipped." At that, a fellow student, John A. Gretter, called out, "Whip him Boyd—whip him." Gretter explained later that he "was anxious that Minor should be whipped, because he had treated Boyd ungentlemanly in not suffering him to take his slave out to chastise him."

Not only did Boyd and the students who supported him see it as their duty to chastise an enslaved person for what they saw as impertinence, but they also saw it as within their rights to similarly chastise the hotelkeeper for interfering with their rights as gentlemen. In this exchange it was the students, who were served by enslaved servants and hotelkeepers alike, who saw themselves both as those best placed to judge correct behavior and as those whose duty it was to enforce it. The faculty seemed to agree, although they resolved that "a student who insults a Hotel Keeper or other officer for preferring a complaint to the faculty will be visited with the severest punishment permitted by the Enactments," in the case of Boyd they limited themselves to "expressing their high disapprobation of his conduct" and granting Minor's request that Boyd no longer be served by Minor's hotel.[4]

At the University of Virginia, most students were required to lodge in dormitory rooms on campus and were served for all of their daily needs by the enslaved servants of the hotelkeeper to whom they had been assigned, taking all their meals in the hotel dining room. This arrangement meant that the lives of the enslaved, the hotelkeepers, and the students were intertwined. The enslaved, adults and children of both sexes, were either owned or hired by the hotelkeepers to provide the services enumerated by university regulations. Their everyday work revealed the difficulty of negotiating between the demands of the faculty and the *Enactments* that they enforced, the hotelkeepers who owned or hired them, and the students whom they served. The hotelkeepers were usually respectable but poorer gentlemen and women who lived at the university with or without families and had to negotiate between the demands of the university that provided them with their livelihood and the students they served, demands that often were at cross-purposes. The students were largely members of the landed aristocracy, raised to mastery, with a strong sense of self-satisfaction. They defined manhood through autonomy and control of the enslaved, often exercised through violence. They balked at the idea that they should be overseen in any way by hotelkeepers, their social inferiors, who the faculty depended on to control student misbehavior.[5] As a result of the necessary interactions of students, hotelkeepers, and the enslaved, the university's hotels and dormitory rooms were spaces where the sharp edges of slavery were most keenly felt.

THE ARCHITECTURE OF THE HOTELS

Thomas Jefferson's original idea for a university included a separation of functions into individual buildings, rather than having all university functions in one large building, such as at the College of William & Mary, which he had attended. The hotels at the University of Virginia were part of Jefferson's idea of having university functions expressed architecturally through specialized buildings. The hotel buildings served as the dining halls for the students, the residence of the hotelkeepers and their families, the coordination center for the care and tending of the students and their rooms, and the site of labor and accommodation of the enslaved who prepared and served the food, cleaned student rooms, and served the students. In everyday life the hotels and their associated spaces—the workyards, dormitory rooms, and arcades—helped organize the daily activities of the members of all the groups who interacted in the spaces of the hotels: the enslaved, the hotelkeepers, and the students.

The six hotels were built on the eastern and western sides of the university, forming outer perimeter walls with the arcaded rows of student dormitory rooms. Like bastions, the hotels were built at either end and in the middle of the walls, with Hotels A, C, and E on the west side, and Hotels B, D, and F on the east side (see fig. I.4 on page 9). As with the architectural style choices for the pavilions on the Lawn, the architectural style of the hotels was chosen by Jefferson to uplift and educate, yet in a simpler manner. Built of brick with columned entrance portals, the hotels are dignified and serious (figs. 5.1, 5.2). The hotels present a public face to the outside world on at least one side, and for the hotels on the ends of the eastern and western sides, two walls. The other walls of the hotels either help form the entrance

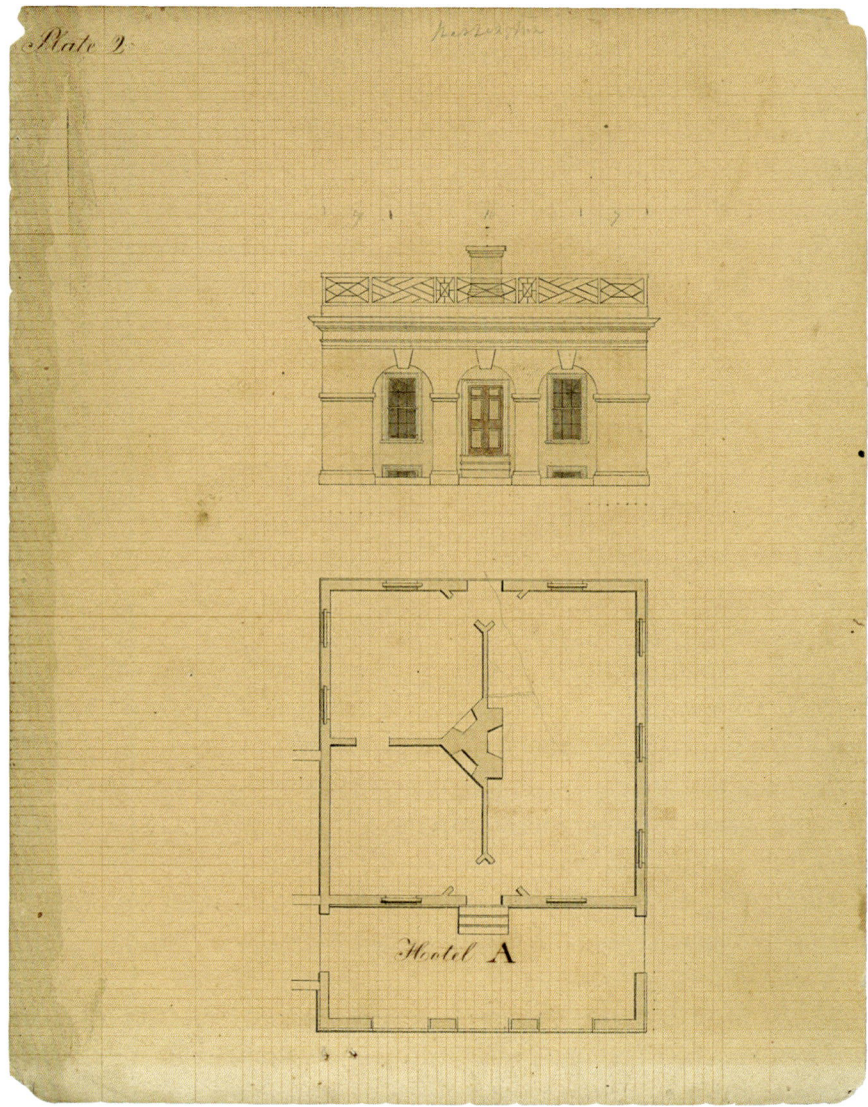

FIG. 5.1. Drawing of Hotel A by John Neilson, undated.

to the alleyway leading to the Lawn, or are walls adjacent to the workyards of the hotels. Associated with the material realities of everyday life, the hotels are sited in the landscape and built with an eye to minimizing their sizable physical presence. The Rotunda and the pavilions, representing the life of the mind, are architecturally dominant, while the hotels, representing the life

FIG. 5.2. Hotel A as built.

of the body, are subservient, well downhill from the Lawn, half buried below grade, and minimally visible above the continuous arcade connecting the Range rooms and the hotels.

Continuing with Jefferson's principle of hiding the enslaved and their work, the design of the hotels places the spaces of work on the lower level, which for many of the hotels was a level set into the ground, with associated workyards also below ground level (see fig. 1.1 on page 28), or hidden behind the wall formed by the hotels and the Range rooms. This same principle continues inside, where most hotels did not have internal stairs connecting the lower level and the main floor. This meant that any work that involved movement of people or things between the floors of the hotel required the use of stairs on the exterior of the building. For the most part this arrangement meant that the service of the dining room required carrying food and serviceware up and then down the exterior stairs. Any request for food that had not already been carried into the dining room would have required a servant to travel a circuitous path out of the hotel and down exterior stairs to the belowground kitchen and then back along the same path to the dining room. Much of the other work performed by the enslaved servicing the student rooms was done using exterior paths, the arcade, and the alleyway.

The plans for the main floors of the hotels vary widely. According to the 1825 Maverick Plan (see fig. 2.10 on page 50), two hotels, A and D, have central passageways, with a large dining room on one side and two chambers (for the residence of the hotelkeeper) on the other. Two hotels, B and C, have the same three rooms (a dining room and two chambers), but the rooms are not separated by a passageway, but instead are divided by a wall and corner fireplaces for both chambers, set together in the center of the hotel. Hotel E has a central passageway like Hotels A and D, with two rooms on either side, two of which were used as dining halls. Hotel F is unique in that the Maverick Plan shows it as having one large main floor room, with attached smaller rooms to the south. Hotel F is also the only hotel with two full floors above ground level, but as with the others it also had a cellar kitchen.

The division of space on the main floor of the hotels (excepting Hotel F) speaks to the complicated interrelationships of the hotelkeepers and their families, the enslaved, and the students. For the hotelkeepers the main floor of the hotel was both residential space and space of work. For students the hotel main floor was their dining and socializing hall. For the enslaved the hotel main floor was a workplace to be carefully negotiated with a variety of white masters barking directions, often at odds with each other. The passageway (for Hotels A, D, and E) is a service space that students could briefly use for accessing the dining room (figs. 5.3, 5.4). Students could also enter the dining hall directly from the exterior. The enslaved and the hotelkeepers and their families could use the hallway for servicing the dining room or the chambers, and for connecting the outside world (to the north and west) to the inside world (the downstairs and the workyards) to the south.

The lower level of the hotels often housed the kitchen, and other chambers (often two) that may have had multiple uses, including storage, workrooms for tasks such as laundry, and places for sleeping, for hotelkeeper families or the enslaved.[6] The lower level in Hotel A is the same plan as the main floor, with a center passage. Beneath the dining hall sat a kitchen with a large hearth centered on the north wall (fig. 5.5), and opposite were two chambers, probably used by the hotelkeeper's family, below the two on the main floor. The presence of a passage between the kitchen and the two chambers allowed for them to be used either as an extension of the private space of the family or as an extension of the service space of the kitchen, much as the passage above served as a filter between the private space of the hotelkeeper and family and the student space of the dining room.

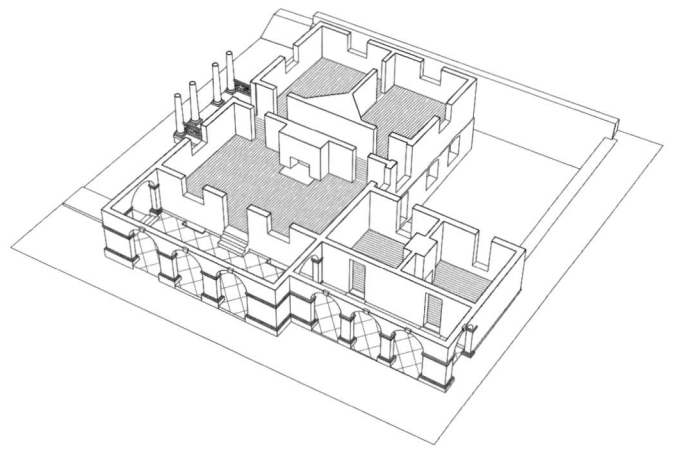

Fig. 5.3. Axonometric of the main floor spaces of Hotel A and adjacent dormitory cellars.

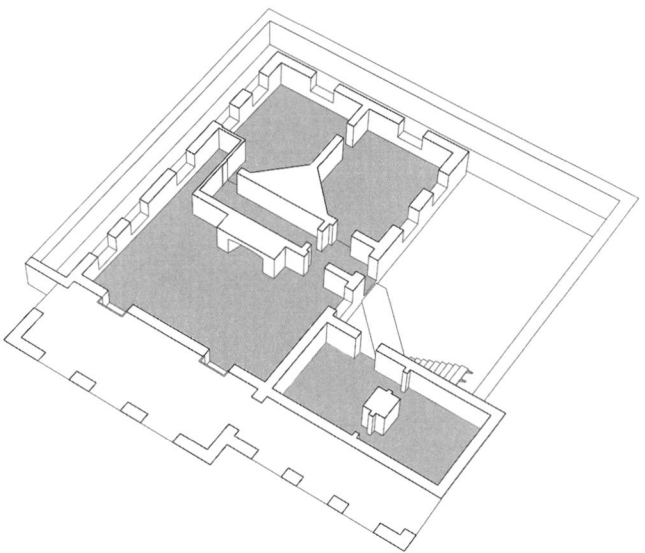

Fig. 5.4. Axonometric of the ground floor spaces of Hotel A and adjacent dormitory cellars.

The hotels were designed by Jefferson and built with the purpose of reproducing the ideal student through providing students meals, clean and furnished living accommodations, and other services for daily life. The design and functioning of the hotels also maintained the institution of slavery, while putting the university itself at a distance from the ownership and control of the enslaved people who maintained its students' bodies and spaces. This ownership and control was delegated to the hotelkeepers. Perhaps due to Jef-

Fig. 5.5. Cellar kitchen in Hotel A before renovation, 2016.

ferson's aversion to the visibility of the work of the enslaved, the workspaces of the hotels, and accommodations for the enslaved, were inadequate in their design and construction. This led the hotelkeepers to struggle with, and frequently complain about, the inadequacy of space for the necessary work.

Hotelkeepers petitioned for more interior and exterior workspace and accommodations for their enslaved workers. For example, in July 1844 Mrs. Gray, the hotelkeeper for Hotel E, sought reimbursement from the university for an apartment for lodging servants that she had built at her own expense at the rear of her hotel. In this case it was resolved that Mrs. Gray would be paid for the building as funds were available.[7] The university also agreed to reimburse Addison Maupin for the brick cottage he planned to build to accommodate enslaved people behind Hotel A in 1853.[8] This building might have been similar to the Crackerbox (figs. 5.6, 5.7), which still stands behind Hotel F and housed a kitchen downstairs and slave quarters above. While the dining room and kitchen of each hotel were the only spaces explicitly designed to house the support work provided by hotelkeepers and their

FIG. 5.6. Kitchen and quarters building adjacent to Hotel F commonly called the Crackerbox.

FIG. 5.7. Kitchen and quarters building adjacent to Hotel F from the JUEL digital reconstruction of the Academical Village.

enslaved workers to students, the spaces this support work needed spilled well beyond their original intended boundaries.

AN ENSLAVED HOTEL SERVANT'S WORK

Service in the hotel dining room comprised only a small portion of an enslaved hotel servant's daily tasks. In addition to aiding the proctor with keeping good order and reporting all offences against the *Enactments,* hotel-keepers were required to supply students with furniture and bedding, prepare three meals a day, with a minimum of two meats and four vegetables at dinner, and care for of all the students' daily needs. This included daily cleaning of all the rooms, with a more thorough scrubbing performed regularly; lighting fires in student rooms; washing and changing students' linens; delivering wood, ice, and water to students; blacking the students' shoes; laundering their clothes; and running any errands the students required.[9] These tasks were all performed by enslaved people, either owned or hired by the hotelkeeper, at a prescribed ratio of no less than one dormitory servant for every twenty students, who ordinarily lived two per room, although in the early years when university enrollment was low many students had a room to themselves.

A hotel worker's day began very early in the morning, at about four a.m.[10] The enslaved people sleeping in a room either in a building behind the hotel or in a basement room of the hotel or an adjacent dormitory room would wake up before dawn and begin their preparations for the day. The cook and her assistant would get up even earlier to stoke the fire and to start making warm rolls or biscuits and cornbread, both of which were required fare at breakfast. She would also put together the rest of the breakfast, separated onto serving dishes for each table: cold loaf bread made the day before, cold meat or fish, butter, milk, molasses, and tea and coffee with loaf sugar, brown sugar, and cream. Soon afterward, the enslaved servants who served the dormitories and waited on table would rise. By five in the morning, they were at their duty, ready to bring water to the dormitories, light fires in each room, and begin their cleaning tasks.[11]

A bell rang at dawn; according to the *Enactments,* students were to "rise at this signal and dress themselves without delay" and hotelkeepers were to ensure that student rooms were "cleaned and set in order . . . at sun-rise," although the *Enactments* allowed that the faculty could "extend the time in the morning for cleaning the dormitories of the students; but not later than the breakfast hour."[12] In practice however, students then, just like students now, often were slow to wake and to rise, and rooms were rarely if ever all cleaned as early as required. Captain Rose, the keeper of Hotel D in 1834, told the faculty that "more than half of the students that board with him sleep until the breakfast-bell rings, and consequently, those rooms cannot be cleaned out before breakfast."[13] In addition, hotelkeepers explained to the proctor in 1831, because of the shortness of the period between the first bell and the beginning of breakfast "to make all the fires and clear up all the rooms, before 7 o'clock would not be possible without either performing the last duty very imperfectly or employing a great number of servants who would be idle for the rest of the day."[14] Hotelkeepers were repeatedly fined for not cleaning rooms early enough and were told by the faculty that "the objection of students to having their rooms cleaned up before breakfast, will not be admitted as an excuse."[15] By 1838, the faculty began to change their attitude, and allowed that as "the failure of the hotel keepers in having the rooms cleaned by the hour prescribed by law, is caused by the delinquency of the students in complying with the law regarding early rising," they would take no action against the hotelkeepers.[16] By 1842, the faculty changed the regulations such that dormitory rooms were to be cleaned no later than nine a.m., thus reflecting what had become standard practice.[17]

Each enslaved servant would have to know the habits of the students he served and arrange his morning tasks to fit them. Some students would be angered by a servant's entering their quarters while they slept and thus waking them. For example, in 1834, when one of Mr. Rose's enslaved servants went into student John Forbes's room to make up the bed in the morning, Forbes "kicked him as hard as he could."[18] A few students also kept animals in their rooms, contrary to the *Enactments,* and an encounter with a fighting cock or a dog might go poorly.[19] Other students such as Thomas Towles, who was admonished by the faculty for repeatedly oversleeping, made use of an enslaved servant as an alarm clock. The person serving Towles's dormitory would enter the room, wake him up, and then make a fire. By that time, Towles had often fallen asleep again; the enslaved attendant would rouse him a second time, although often in vain.[20] In any case, before six a.m., enslaved servants were to bring water and clean towels to the students in the ten dormitory rooms they served, and light fires in those rooms as well, which required cleaning out the ashes from the night before. Lighting the fires, the "most essential duty," could take some time and was difficult, as the proctor provided only "green wood, no kindling stuff," and at times the wood ran low and it was not possible to build a decent fire in each room.[21] Bringing water would have required multiple trips and the fires required wood, which enslaved workers had ideally delivered the day before from the stores provided by the proctor.

After bringing every student water and a towel, lighting all the fires, and cleaning those few rooms that were vacated early enough to permit it, the enslaved servants would hurry back to the hotel to serve breakfast, which commenced at the ringing of the breakfast bell, with the dining room door closing half an hour later and the last warm food served fifteen minutes after that, in the hopes of getting students to class on time.[22] Breakfast was concluded entirely by 7:30, the time of the first morning lecture.[23] All of the dishes and food would need to be carried out of the kitchen, up an exterior staircase, and thence into the dining room by means of the passageway. The enslaved servants would then follow the commands of each student to serve him the food he required.

Students expected fast service and total compliance with their requests, and in the ways of young men in groups, were liable to be rowdy in the dining room, regularly throwing bits of bread at each other and at the people serving them. The students were young men from wealthy slaveholding families, raised to mastery, and quick to take violent offense at even a perceived insult. Some students also cursed at table, particularly at the enslaved servants.[24] However, as many students habitually missed breakfast, the dining room would have been less crowded than the later meals, dinner and supper. After breakfast those students who attended to their studies rushed to their 7:30 lectures, and the enslaved servants were left to clean up the mess they left behind them. They would collect the dishes and bring them downstairs to wash in preparation for their use again at dinner, wash the tables, sweep the floor of thrown bread and other crumbs, and then go back to the dormitories to complete their cleaning tasks.

Some of those serving were adults, but it was also common for children, both boys and girls, to serve in the dining room and sometimes in the dormitories. Generally, enslaved children had virtually no childhood, and were put to work at an early age.[25] These children had relatively low value due to high mortality rates, were underfed and poorly clothed, and had seen much in their short lives.[26] Some of the children may have been at the hotel because their mother or father was also there, but this was not always the case. Enslaved children were at times hired on their own, especially after the age of ten.

Every morning, enslaved men and boys had to clean the dormitory rooms, a task ordinarily completed after breakfast. The faculty enumerated the tasks involved in 1835: "Each room shall be swept clean; the beds made; the ashes removed; the candlesticks cleaned, the washbasin rinsed, and the room put in order; . . . these duties shall be performed daily; and for the better removal of the sweepings etc. each servant shall be provided by the Hotel Keeper with a covered bucket."[27]

At least once every two weeks, enslaved servants needed to put clean sheets on the beds and take the dirty ones to the hotel laundress, who in addition to cleaning the linen for each room was charged with washing clothes for the students, although over time the work of washing students' clothing was increasingly done by free black women working as independent laundresses. The university did not provide the hotels with any specialized space for laundering, making it difficult to do well in wet or cold weather. Bedsheets were sometimes changed less often because of cold weather, which made washing and especially drying sheets difficult, as they would freeze.[28] This could only be remedied by hotelkeepers' making a large investment in extra sets of sheets and also living with the inconvenience of having sheets dried within their own living spaces.[29] Mrs. Gray was able to keep up with the official schedule because she "always has twelve extra sets clean" and when the weather was bad, "she had them dried in her own chamber," but Mr. Rose, who only had seven extra sets, "was not able to obey the law regarding the change of bed linen."[30] Even when washed the sheets were often "in a scandalous condition" because students would get into bed with their shoes on, use their pillows as floor cushions, and make their beds on the floor in front of the fire, staining the sheets with ashes and dirt.[31]

Enslaved workers also had to carry water to the dorms twice a day, deliver the wood supplied by the proctor, and bring up any ice the students had purchased. In addition to these daily tasks, enslaved men and boys serving the dormitories were required to wash the fireplaces and black the andirons in each room weekly, to wash the windows every four weeks, and to scour the rooms at least every two weeks.[32] Many of these tasks were not in fact accomplished on the official timeline, often because students did not want their rooms cleaned. Inclement weather could also be a deterrent, as a great deal of water was used to scour rooms, and at times the water froze to the floor.[33]

At other times the hotelkeepers did not see the point in scouring dormitory rooms because they "would soon become dirty again," because of students' messy habits.[34]

The dormitory rooms were supposed to be inspected weekly both by the hotelkeepers and by the proctor, but rarely were, making it easier for undone cleaning tasks to remain undiscovered. When asked about his duty to inspect the dorm rooms, hotelkeeper Mr. Rose told the faculty that he "avoids going for fear of witnessing something improper on the part of the students."[35] Although the hotelkeepers were tasked with policing the students, they were often fined when students complained about them, and were not treated with respect by the students, who saw them as their social inferiors. As scions of slaveholding families, students' willful behavior had probably rarely been policed, even by their parents, who despised any sort of submission and thus declined to attempt to rein in their sons.[36] In addition, students considered the hotelkeepers as significantly below them in the social hierarchy, and perceived any attempt by a hotelkeeper to police them as an attack upon their honor. This dynamic played out when Major Spottswood, then the keeper of Hotel F, inspected the room of a student named Thomas Hooe at eight a.m. one morning in 1828. Hooe was still in bed, and complained to Spottswood that his fire had not been made. Spottswood told him "you must be more regular in your habits before you complain of want of attention." In addition he complained that Hooe's dog had "dirtied the Room so as to make it highly offensive" and told if Hooe that if he did not get rid of the dog, Spottswood would not send an enslaved servant to clean the room. Hooe threatened to flog the servant if his room was not cleaned and emphatically ordered Spottswood to "begone out of the room." Spottswood replied, "I will go out when you request me as a gentleman," at which Hooe "jumped out of bed put on his Drawers and began to shove Spottswood out," shouting "By G— I will make you." Spottswood was highly offended, replying, "Say what you please but keep your hands off. I will not be ordered as a Servant. Will not go out until you ask me politely." The incident ended with Hooe threatening violence, Spottswood calling him a puppy, and finally with Hooe striking Spottswood with a shovel and his fists.[37] Although Spottswood was asked to leave the university after this incident, what is notable about it is that much of this dispute was about the way that the student addressed the hotelkeeper. He treated him not as a gentleman but as a servant. While the incident between Hooe and Spottswood is an extreme example, students did not take well to being policed by the people who served them, and thus many hotelkeepers decided to take a hands-off attitude toward both student behavior and student rooms, except when their safety or their honor was directly concerned.

In this incident, Hooe threatened to usurp Spottswood's authority over the enslaved servant, much as the student Boyd usurped hotelkeeper Minor's authority in the dispute over butter in the dining room. These incidents show how students thought of the enslaved people who tended their rooms and served them at meals possessively, as if they, not the hotelkeepers, owned them and should thus be able to command them and treat them as they liked. For example, Charles Ellis, who was a student from 1834 to 1836, made casual references to enslaved people in his diary. He wrote of "my servant" waking him in the morning and of "Albert, our servant," arranging their room.[38] Such possessiveness of the enslaved people owned by others only contributed to the feeling held by many students that they had a right to treat the people working in the Academical Village as their own property.

Hotelkeepers, and their enslaved workers, were responsible for not just the hotel, its grounds, and the arcade in front of it, but also the dormitories assigned to them, including the arcades in front of dormitory rooms and the yards behind them.[39] Enslaved workers were required to clean the arcades in front of the rooms served by each hotel as well as the rooms themselves, a job that was made more complex when the dormitory rooms assigned to a given hotel were scattered across the grounds.[40] Cleaning the rooms and the arcades required cleaning the ashes out of the fireplaces in each room, as well as any dirt, leaves, or other detritus, and taking them away from the lawn to "receptacles prepared for that purpose."[41] On one occasion, Lawrence, an enslaved man working for Mr. Conway, was admonished for being "negligent in cleaning the arcades, having swept the offal upon the Lawn, and allowed the ashes &c from the fires used in kindling in the morning to remain on the arcades for days altogether."[42] Unlike the interior of the dormitory rooms, the arcade space was immediately visible, and thus important to keep neat, and cleaning the arcades could also be done with minimal interference from students. Cleaning the arcades too early, for instance when waiting to be allowed into student rooms to clean them, could make for extra work, however, as "sometimes after being swept, wood is thrown upon them," making them messy again.[43] "Throwing" was probably the appropriate term, as wood was reportedly delivered to the students "by throwing it through their dormitory windows."[44] However, arcades could not be cleaned late in the day, as the faculty rules required them to be cleaned by ten a.m., shortly after the rooms were finished.

Students were ordinarily served their midday meal, dinner, from 1:30 to 2:30. This was the major meal of the day, and always included both hot bacon and another hot meat or poultry, soup, four kinds of vegetables, bread, butter, and, three times a week, dessert. In addition to setting up the dinner and serving students at the tables, dinner service often required one or more of the enslaved workers to carve meat at a side table. At home, students would have been attended by a large number of enslaved people, and were thus used to close personal service.[45] In the hotels, they thus complained about an insufficiency of servants to wait on them.[46] Students were frustrated with service in the dining room, where they found the number of people attending them too small, the service often slow and impertinent, and the servants too often dirty.[47] In just one of these complaints, in 1835, the enslaved people serving in the dining room at Captain Perrow's hotel, Hotel D, were described as "mostly children, badly clothed and very filthy in their persons, and therefore not fit to wait on the table."[48] It is likely that enslaved hotel servants were provided minimal clothing and washing facilities by the hotelkeepers, who were operating on a tight budget. In addition, as hotelkeepers often hired rather than owned the enslaved people who worked for them, they may have felt less necessity of providing for their wellbeing.[49] Children were especially likely to be poorly clothed, in part because of their low perceived value, and because slaveowners were uninterested in providing clothing that properly fit their growing bodies.[50]

Students took all of their meals at the hotels, and enslaved servants often found themselves open to abuse while waiting at table. For example, in December 1835 a student named W. W. Harris beat William, a man who worked for Mrs. Gray in Hotel E. The dispute centered on William's service at table and the student's demand for butter. Harris ordered William to give him a plate of butter from another table, and although it was against the house rules, William did so, but afterward took a plate of butter from Harris's table to replace the one he had given Harris, against Harris's orders. Harris then grabbed a stick of wood from the fire and beat William. As a result of this altercation, Harris was suspended for one week, but Mrs. Gray was also ordered to remove William from her employ, although she did not comply for many months.[51] Other incidents also show up in the records. For example, in 1836 students William Grigsby and Richard Carter respectively struck and threw a glass at Colonel Ward's servant in Hotel D for not attending to their orders.[52] Earlier that year, the student T. A. Wilson struck Mr. Conway's servant in the dining room, for supposedly not bringing him water when he requested it, even though other students reported that the servant had complied.[53]

Students' chastisement of enslaved servants in the hotel dining rooms probably extended well beyond those that show up in the faculty records, as the records usually describe either more extreme violence, like that of John Moon, who threw a knife at one of Colonel Ward's servants, or else incidents in which the students talked back to and even cursed the hotelkeepers. Colonel Ward's analysis of Mr. Moon's behavior sheds light on the difficult position enslaved servants were in when serving students at table. Ward argued that the servant was not insolent, but rather "active and attentive," and "it was Mr. Moon's desire to have his exclusive attendance" that made him see the servant as neglectful.[54] In the dining hall of the hotel, twenty to fifty students were served by about four to six enslaved servants.[55] For many of the students, accustomed to a much higher level of service at home, the indifferent care they received in the hotel dining rooms may have felt insulting. The enslaved workers would have been hard-pressed to serve five to ten students each desirous of their exclusive attentions.

The students often expressed dissatisfaction with the enslaved workers bought or hired by the hotelkeepers, but it is likely their complaints stem primarily from the number of workers, not their quality. The hotelkeepers were unable to buy or hire more enslaved workers because their resources were limited to the set fee students were charged by the university for board and related services. The proctor admitted in 1832, when the total numbers of students were still quite low, that money was tight for hotelkeepers because there were too many hotels for the number of students. Were there fewer hotels, he argued, "the business is not only safe but even yields a good profit," but "with four it is scarcely sufficient to support their families."[56] Frequent fines for poor service did not improve matters, but rather made the hotelkeepers' margins even tighter.

In their haste to get their dinner, and uncertain how quickly they might be served, students might snatch potatoes or a plate from a servant, making orderly service more difficult.[57] They were also often dissatisfied with the quality of the food and would voice their displeasure to the servants serving them, as when a student, Littleton Tazewell, insisted on a new plate of food, telling the servant loudly that "nothing but bones had been put on his plate."[58] The one hour of service in the dining room would require multiple trips to serve students meat, vegetables, and drinks, in what was clearly a loud and boisterous atmosphere. The supper service, which began either at six or at seven p.m. depending on the season, was possibly less onerous, as supper was a smaller meal much like breakfast.[59] On those occasions when a hotel-keeper was ill or for another reason was not in the room to supervise, things were particularly chaotic. The chairman of the faculty commented that when Mr. Conway was ill, "there is not only no one, besides servants, to attend to breakfast, but no person to keep order at table at any of the meals. The disorder at table is, I am informed, considerable."[60] The chairman suggested that students might be better behaved if "the wives of the Hotel-keepers should, as well as their husbands, sit at table with the students," but the instances of students verbally abusing Mrs. Gray suggest that the presence of a white woman was not sufficient to quiet students.[61]

After cleaning up from the dinner service, the dormitory/dining room workers had just two official tasks that were specifically to be done in the afternoon—blacking students' shoes and running errands—although their general dormitory tasks such as blacking andirons might well take afternoon time, along with assisting other enslaved workers working in the yards, and service to the hotelkeeper and his or her family. In addition, servants were to bring water to the dormitories twice a day, and the second delivery was probably in the afternoon or evening. While the work that enslaved servants did in the dormitories was nominally under the supervision of the hotelkeepers, who were fined for any dereliction of duty, in practice they went about this work on their own, subject to the orders of students, which they tried to balance with the requirements set out by the university and the hotelkeepers.

The task in which enslaved people were most immediately in the employ of students was running errands, which was officially scheduled for mid-afternoon. The faculty regulations governing the attendance of servants on dormitories proclaimed that "Hotel servants shall not run at all times on students' errands; but one from each Hotel shall call on each Dormitory at a quarter before 3 P.M. to receive students' directions, and at 3 proceed to execute their commissions."[62] It is not clear whether these guidelines were followed, but the wording of the regulations, which specifically refer to servants running errands "at all times," as well as the fact that many students were in lectures at three p.m., suggest that errands might well have been run more often and by more people than the rules suggest. In 1831, Mr. Conway complained to the faculty that "his servants are sent to town at inconvenient times," and that the hotelkeepers had not acted upon the agreement that enslaved servants be forbidden to run errands before three p.m.[63]

Students also asked hotel servants for other services not included in their official duties. When students were ill, they were served meals in their rooms, but many students preferred to eat in their rooms at other times as well. In 1831, for example, the faculty disciplined students for holding "unauthorized festive entertainments" in their dormitory rooms, and asking hotel servants for food to eat in their rooms, mostly roast turkeys or chickens. Both Mr. Conway, hotelkeeper of Hotel A, and Captain John Rose, hotelkeeper of Hotel F, testified that they never prohibited their servants from cooking for students, in spite of this being beyond their ordinary duties.[64] Similarly, in 1836 the chairman of the faculty found that "the servants in the University are in the habit of furnishing expensive suppers to the students" and that a young black boy not employed at the university frequently served breakfast to students, delivering it in a basket that he otherwise used to sell apples.[65] These meals provided extra cash for the people who furnished them, but also created extra work for the servants who cleaned student rooms and the cash-strapped hotelkeepers who controlled them.

Although they commanded the dormitory servants' work freely and with minimal interference from the hotelkeepers, many students, unused to sharing the attention of one servant so broadly, found the service provided insufficient. Even though they were forbidden from bringing personal servants, on more than one occasion students hired servants to supplement the service they received from the hotel servants, particularly in the early years of the university.[66] Records suggest that multiple students hired servants, as when the faculty directed the proctor "to see that all servants hired by the students should be sent away from the Precincts, particularly a boy named German."[67] Although these servants were hired directly by students, on other occasions students made arrangements with hotelkeepers to hire extra servants to serve them. In 1828, five of the students boarding with Major Spottswood in Hotel D paid half the cost of one servant, presumably to give them extra service, while in 1834, twenty-two of the students boarding at Hotel A with Mr. Conway hired a servant, John Taylor, to serve them exclusively. Given the inclusion of Taylor's last name in the records, he may have been a free black man rather than enslaved. They arranged to pay Taylor forty-five dollars "because they had not before sufficient attendance" and Mr. Conway agreed to feed him even though it was "contrary to the Enactments for students to hire servants." The status of John Taylor was somewhat fuzzy, as one of the students who hired him "considers John under Mr. Conway's control" and Mr. Conway stated that he himself had hired Taylor, although the twenty-two students gave him "extra pay" and "John only waits on those students who hire him." The faculty was not convinced that this arrangement followed the *Enactments,* and insisted that Taylor either "leave the university or discontinue his attendance upon the students who have employed him."[68]

In addition to cleaning the dormitory rooms and associated spaces and running errands, enslaved people working for the hotelkeepers were also required to serve the students by blacking their shoes and washing their clothes. While the blacking of shoes was done by the dormitory servants, washing was done by a laundress. Like the cook, the laundress was an enslaved woman who served the students, but for the most part did not interact directly with them. The enslaved people who directly served students appear to have been male, except for at least one little girl who helped serve in the dining room, while enslaved women were engaged largely in labor that was more hidden from the students. There was quite a bit of laundry to be done, as in addition to the students' clothing, the hotel was responsible for cleaning towels and bed linens and the tablecloths and napkins used at meals. There might well have been more than one woman doing laundry for each hotel, as Mrs. Gray's testimony that she "keeps one woman always employed" in washing sheets and pillowcases suggests that another woman might have done the other washing.[69] In spite of the great deal of washing to do, the university did not provide hotels with dedicated space for washing and drying clothes and linens.[70] Students were often unhappy with the laundry service provided by the hotels, and regularly applied to the faculty for permission to have their washing done by an outside laundress. Mr. Conway, the hotelkeeper of Hotel A, argued that students were "not willing to subject their clothes to the inspection of the ladies belonging to the families of the Hotel Keepers," but most evidence suggests that it was not modesty, but rather poorly washed and lost items that made students turn elsewhere.[71] In order to get permission to have their laundry done elsewhere and to thus get a remission of one dollar per month of the fees they paid to the hotelkeeper, students had to show examples of poorly laundered clothing to the chairman of the faculty or the proctor. In the vast majority of cases, the officials agreed about the poor laundry services and allowed the students to have their laundry done elsewhere, thus allowing a de facto amendment to the *Enactments* regarding hotels.[72] The rule was officially changed in 1845, when the Board of Visitors exempted the hotelkeepers from providing for the washing of students' clothes and accordingly decreased the price of board that the students paid them.[73] However, hotelkeepers continued to be responsible for the laundering of bedsheets, towels, and other linens.

STRUCTURES OF POWER BETWEEN STUDENTS, HOTELKEEPERS, AND ENSLAVED SERVANTS

The enslaved people who worked in the dining rooms and dormitories were in a complex position because they in essence had many different masters. They were owned or hired by the hotelkeeper, but the hotelkeeper's authority was only partial. Whether male or female, hotelkeepers were criticized by the faculty and the students for their lack of supervision of the enslaved workers. Female hotelkeepers, like Mrs. Gray, were deemed unable to keep proper control over their servants because of their sex. In her case the faculty requested that she hire a white man to superintend them, which she did not do, pleading the inability to find a "proper person," although the cost would also likely have been a factor.[74] Complaints of indifferent service were sometimes blamed on "there being no white person in the house to superintend."[75] When hotelkeeper Edwin Conway fell ill for a period of time, the chairman was dissatisfied with the quality of the breakfast, "owing to the want of superintendence by the master, mistress, or some one." He also complained that without the presence of Conway order was not maintained at the table.[76] The faculty wanted hotelkeepers to act as a parental influence, hoping that they would dine with students and correct their behavior. At one point the chairman admonished Mrs. Ward for never dining with the students and Colonel Ward for rarely being there, and he urged him to do so, describing it as an "indispensable necessity."[77]

The faculty put the hotelkeepers in a difficult position. Hotelkeepers could only make money by getting the students to select their hotel for services, but the faculty also expected them to act as a correcting parental influence and report on student misbehavior. Not surprisingly, many hotelkeepers saw these as irreconcilable imperatives, especially as students treated them as their social inferiors. As Major Spottswood said when he was called before the faculty, he "does not watch the students," and that if he saw them gambling, he would give information only if called upon, "because he does not think it his duty unless called upon."[78] Another claimed that he has "lost several students for giving them advice against playing."[79] They further argued that as they were "dependent on students" it was not in their interest to try to intervene between students and servants, even when students were breaking rules.[80] The conflict between serving students and enforcing university regulations led a number of people, including some who had previously been hotelkeepers, to open up boardinghouses just next to the university precincts by the late 1830s. Most of these were concentrated just to the north of the university on Carr's Hill and along what is now known as University Avenue. At these "outboarding" houses, as they were called, the proprietors were somewhat free from the scrutiny of the faculty, but they faced many of the same challenges to their authority from the students.

Such conflicting imperatives also meant that the hotelkeepers were less likely to countermand a command given by a student to an enslaved worker. They needed the business.

The faculty sometimes accused the hotelkeepers of facilitating the illicit activities of the students, especially drinking and gambling over card playing, although the hotelkeepers generally denied these charges. Conway admitted to occasionally taking a drink with students in their dormitory rooms. When asked by the faculty how they acquired liquor, Conway said it was supplied by the "servants about the University. All of them there who wait on the Hotels and the other Servants, all servants are admitted into the University." His point was that any enslaved person, even those not owned by faculty or hotelkeepers, had the freedom to enter the university precincts. Thus, it was easy to bring in liquor and sell it to students. He also told the faculty that he did not forbid his slaves from going to town for liquor for the students because "they claimed all the services of his servants who were waiters on their own Dormitories."[81] In other words, Conway admitted that he may have owned the people, but the students controlled them. Hotelkeepers stated that they had "no control over dormitory servants except in [the] dining room," and that "students control them in the dormitories."[82] For the faculty, part of the challenge of regulating the behavior of the enslaved who worked at the university was that it was not clear who was really the master.

This provided both a difficulty and an opportunity to enslaved hotel workers. On the one hand, having in essence up to twenty masters in addition to the hotelkeeper and his or her family members was difficult. A servant who was ordered by students to break the *Enactments* by, for example, running an errand to procure liquor was not in an easy position to refuse. However, not refusing could theoretically result in his being sent away from the university, quite possibly to a position with less autonomy and fewer opportunities for extra pay. A servant also had minimal recourse against the violence that students were quite willing to use. Although students were informed that it was against the law to punish a servant belonging to someone else, they argued that it was within their rights to do so.[83] They saw any enslaved person who served them as theirs to chastise, using as much violence as they deemed necessary.

On the other hand, working in several spaces within and without grounds with varying levels of supervision provided an opportunity for significant freedom to enslaved hotel workers. They had quite a bit of mobility, and moved freely not just around grounds, but also into Charlottesville on errands. In working for the students, servants also found an opportunity to make extra money, whether by running prohibited errands or providing students extra food in their rooms. This money then gave them freedom to buy alcohol, gamble, or otherwise enjoy what personal free time they had.[84] Enslaved workers could have significant autonomy. For example, James Munroe, an enslaved man whose labor was contracted from his owners by a hotelkeeper, personally received a portion of his wages when the rest were sent to his owners and was free to work in taverns in his free time to make more money. In 1847, he used the money he earned to purchase his own freedom.[85]

Enslaved hotel workers in essence had different masters in different spaces. Within the space of the hotel itself, they answered to the hotelkeeper, although the students often also demanded fealty. On the university grounds, they were also under the surveillance of the overseer and janitor. In and around the dormitory rooms, the hotel servants answered to the students and served in essence as personal house servants, albeit to as many as twenty different masters. Between these spaces, and on errands into Charlottesville, enslaved people had considerably more freedom. When they ran the errands that gave them an excuse to travel freely, they traveled without direct oversight, and were free to make purchases and conduct other business for themselves as well as for students. This is made clear by the responses of servants who were caught carrying liquor and explained to the chairman of the faculty that the liquor they were found carrying was for their personal use.[86]

The design of the hotels seems simple on their face—they are tucked down the hill from the Lawn, marking the subservience of the body to the mind, and serve the material needs of the students while spatially compartmentalizing the different players: the students in the dining room, the hotelkeeper in first-floor rooms, and the enslaved people below and behind. However, in practice none of the players followed this idealized model. Jefferson's and the faculty's ideal of monklike students, who rose early, dressed modestly, and never drank or gambled, was a poor fit with the willful dandyish southern scions the university served. Rather than merely accepting the service they were provided with and concentrating on the life of the mind, students challenged hotelkeepers and the enslaved alike to provide them with comfort and obedience. The hotelkeepers were charged by the faculty with the contradictory task of both serving these students and controlling them, and found that their authority outside the physical boundaries of the hotel was minimal. The enslaved were everywhere and nowhere within the hotel, the university, and Charlottesville. There was little concern in the design or operation of the hotels to make the labor of the enslaved rational or efficient. They lived and worked in unrealistic spaces with unrealistic expectations, which rather than housing them, denied their very existence. They moved between spaces and between masters, negotiating between the demands of the hotelkeepers and those of the students, finding both violence and opportunity.

NOTES

1. Faculty Minutes, of the University of Virginia, 1825–1856, June 26, 1828, http://juel.iath.virginia.edu/resources (hereafter cited as Faculty Minutes).

2. Faculty Minutes, September 12, 1835, lays out a requirement of one servant attending no more than ten rooms, a requirement that is repeated in the Faculty Minutes, October 3, 1835, and April 12, 1837. The dormitory rooms could each accommodate two students. See *Enactments* 1827, ch. 2, http://juel.iath.virginia.edu/resources#_ftn3.

3. Faculty Minutes, June 26, 1828, http://juel.iath.virginia.edu/resources.

4. Faculty Minutes, June 28, 1828, http://juel.iath.virginia.edu/resources.

5. On the culture of southern boyhood and manhood, see Lorri Glover, *Southern Sons: Becoming Men in the New Nation* (Baltimore: Johns Hopkins University Press, 2007).

6. Faculty Minutes, November 6, 1835, http://juel.iath.virginia.edu/resources, mention that the cellar room of Hotel F was used "for the accommodation of the servants attached to the hotel."

7. Board of Visitors Minutes, 1817–2007, July 4, 1844, http://juel.iath.virginia.edu/resources (hereafter cited as Board of Visitors Minutes).

8. Board of Visitors Minutes, June 29, 1852, http://juel.iath.virginia.edu/resources; Faculty Minutes, October 27, 1853, http://juel.iath.virginia.edu/resources.

9. Faculty Minutes, October 1, 1842, http://juel.iath.virginia.edu/resources.

10. Mr. Conway testified to the faculty that he sometimes was up at four a.m. to superintend his servants. Faculty Minutes, October 26, 1829, http://juel.iath.virginia.edu/resources.

11. Faculty Minutes, March 5, 1838, http://juel.iath.virginia.edu/resources. Mrs. Gray testified that "she is certain that her servants are at their duty at five o'clock of the morning, and in time to clean the rooms."

12. *Enactments* 1831, p. 42, http://juel.iath.virginia.edu/resources.

13. Faculty Minutes, May 8, 1834, http://juel.iath.virginia.edu/resources.

14. Journals of the Chairman, 1827–1864, November 27, 1838, and January 31, 1831, http://juel.iath.virginia.edu/resources (hereafter cited as Chairman's Journals).

15. Faculty Minutes, May 8, 1834, http://juel.iath.virginia.edu/resources.

16. Faculty Minutes, March 5, 1838, http://juel.iath.virginia.edu/resources.

17. Faculty Minutes, October 1, 1842, http://juel.iath.virginia.edu/resources.

18. Faculty Minutes, January 27, 1834, http://juel.iath.virginia.edu/resources.

19. Chairman's Journals, April 29, 1831, tell of a student, Mr. Winfree, keeping a fighting cock. Chairman's Journals, April 29, 1831, http://juel.iath.virginia.edu/resources.

20. Faculty Minutes, November 5, 1838. Other students also mention asking slaves to wake them, and used their dereliction of this duty as an excuse for not following the *Enactments* as to early waking. See Faculty Minutes, March 31, 1838, and October 27, 1838, http://juel.iath.virginia.edu/resources.

21. Chairman's Journals, January 31, 1831, http://juel.iath.virginia.edu/resources. There was a lengthy wood shortage in the winter of 1835–1836 due to the proctor not having ordered enough.

22. Faculty Minutes, October 31 1836, http://juel.iath.virginia.edu/resources.

23. Faculty Minutes, September 12, 1835, http://juel.iath.virginia.edu/resources.

24. Faculty Minutes, June 8, 1835, and February 17, 1845, http://juel.iath.virginia.edu/resources.

25. See the introduction in King, *Stolen Childhood*.

26. Daina Ramey Berry, *The Price for a Pound of Flesh: The Value of the Enslaved, from Womb to Grave, in the Building of a Nation* (Boston: Beacon Press, 2017), 46. Enslaved children in the hotels were often poorly clothed. See Faculty Minutes, May 14, 1835, http://juel.iath.virginia.edu/resources.

27. Faculty Minutes, September 12, 1835, http://juel.iath.virginia.edu/resources.

28. In the Faculty Minutes for March 5, 1838, Mr. Conway testified that "the cold weather was the cause of the sheets remaining so long unchanged, those in wash were frozen, and having no wash house he had no means of drying them—when the weather would not admit of their being dried out of doors there was no possibility of doing it within doors." Faculty Minutes, March 5, 1838, http://juel.iath.virginia.edu/resources.

29. Faculty Minutes, February 2, 1837, http://juel.iath.virginia.edu/resources.

30. Ibid.; Chairman's Journals, February 18, 1831, http://juel.iath.virginia.edu/resources.

31. Faculty Minutes, February 2, 1837, http://juel.iath.virginia.edu/resources.

32. Faculty Minutes, January 24, 1831, and October 1, 1842, http://juel.iath.virginia.edu/resources. In the early years, the fireplaces were to be washed with potter's clay twice a week, but by 1842, this was changed to once a week. See Faculty Minutes, September 12, 1835, and October 1, 1842, http://juel.iath.virginia.edu/resources.

33. Chairman's Journals, January 26, 1831, http://juel.iath.virginia.edu/resources.

34. Faculty Minutes, January 24, 1831, http://juel.iath.virginia.edu/resources; see also Faculty Minutes, February 2, 1831, and April 28, 1834, and February 2, 1831, http://juel.iath.virginia.edu/resources.

35. Faculty Minutes, January 24, 1831, http://juel.iath.virginia.edu/resources.

36. Glover, *Southern Sons,* 21–34, 45–50.

37. Chairman's Journals, December 19, 1828, http://juel.iath.virginia.edu/resources. See also Faculty Minutes, December 19 and 20, 1828, http://juel.iath.virginia.edu/resources.

38. Charles Ellis Jr., A Student's Diary, January 27, 1836, and February 5, 1836, http://juel.iath.virginia.edu/resources.

39. *Enactments* 1827, chapter IV, http://juel.iath.virginia.edu/resources.

40. Faculty Minutes, October 26, 1829, http://juel.iath.virginia.edu/resources.

41. *Enactments* 1827, chapter IV, http://juel.iath.virginia.edu/resources.

42. Faculty Minutes, January 8, 1838, http://juel.iath.virginia.edu/resources.

43. Faculty Minutes, February 2, 1837, http://juel.iath.virginia.edu/resources.

44. Faculty Minutes, January 24, 1831, http://juel.iath.virginia.edu/resources; see also Chairman's Journals, February 18, 1831, http://juel.iath.virginia.edu/resources.

45. Glover, *Southern Sons,* 174.

46. Faculty Minutes, February 1, 1836, http://juel.iath.virginia.edu/resources.

47. Faculty Minutes, May 14, 1835; June 21, 1836; October 1, 1836; September 30, 1839; and May 4, 1841, http://juel.iath.virginia.edu/resources.

48. Faculty Minutes, May 14, 1835, http://juel.iath.virginia.edu/resources.

49. Jennifer Oast has found that this was often the case for what she calls "institutional slaves," owned by institutions and often rented out yearly. Jennifer Oast, *Institutional Slavery: Slaveholding Churches, Schools, Colleges, and Businesses in Virginia, 1680–1860* (Cambridge: Cambridge University Press, 2016), 1–8.

50. King, *Stolen Childhood,* 15–16; Berry, *The Price for a Pound of Flesh,* 46.

51. Faculty Minutes, December 10, 1835, http://juel.iath.virginia.edu/resources. In the Faculty Minutes for February 3, 1836, http://juel.iath.virginia.edu/resources, Mrs. Gray is admonished for continuing to have William wait on table.

52. Faculty Minutes, October 1, 1836, http://juel.iath.virginia.edu/resources; Chairman's Journal, September 28, 1836, http://juel.iath.virginia.edu/resources.

53. Faculty Minutes, June 21, 1836, http://juel.iath.virginia.edu/resources.

54. Faculty Minutes, September 30, 1839, http://juel.iath.virginia.edu/resources.

55. According to Faculty Minutes, October 26, 1829, Edwin Conway had two servants; Faculty Minutes, February 5, 1834, Mrs. Gray had two servants to attend the dormitories; Faculty Minutes, November 28, 1834, Captain Rose had five servants; Faculty Minutes, February 1, 1836, Mrs. Gray had six servants at meals, including two children; Faculty Minutes, April 12, 1837, Mrs. Gray decreased from three servants to two attending dormitories; Faculty Minutes, September 30, 1839, Colonel Ward had four male servants plus a boy and a girl, http://juel.iath.virginia.edu/resources.

56. Chairman's Journals, September 25, 1832, http://juel.iath.virginia.edu/resources. The authors of the Historic Structure Report on Hotel A agreed, finding that even with increasing numbers of students to serve hotelkeepers made very little profit, at most a few hundred dollars. *Hotel A: University of Virginia Historic Structure Report* (Williamsburg, VA: Meslick, Cohen, Wilson, and Baker Architects, 2012), 28.

57. Faculty Minutes, November 28, 1834, http://juel.iath.virginia.edu/resources; Chairman's Journals, February 18, 1831, http://juel.iath.virginia.edu/resources.

58. Chairman's Journals, March 10, 1836, http://juel.iath.virginia.edu/resources.

59. On the supper hour, see Chairman's Journals, April 30, 1829. For the fare at supper, see Faculty Minutes September 12, 1835, October 1, 1842, and September 27, 1851, http://juel.iath.virginia.edu/resources.

60. Chairman's Journals, March 7, 1836, http://juel.iath.virginia.edu/resources.

61. Chairman's Journals, March 7 and 11, 1836, http://juel.iath.virginia.edu/resources.

62. Faculty Minutes, October 1, 1842, and September 27, 1851, http://juel.iath.virginia.edu/resources.

63. Chairman's Journals, January 28, 1831, http://juel.iath.virginia.edu/resources.

64. Faculty Minutes, February 21, 1831, http://juel.iath.virginia.edu/resources.

65. Chairman's Journals, March 11, 1836, http://juel.iath.virginia.edu/resources.

66. Oast, *Institutional Slavery*, 174.

67. Chairman's Journals, April 16, 1828, http://juel.iath.virginia.edu/resources.

68. Faculty Minutes, February 3 and 5, 1834, http://juel.iath.virginia.edu/resources; Chairman's Journals, February 4, 1834, http://juel.iath.virginia.edu/resources.

69. Faculty Minutes, February 2, 1831, http://juel.iath.virginia.edu/resources.

70. Faculty Minutes, March 5, 1838, http://juel.iath.virginia.edu/resources.

71. Faculty Minutes, February 21, 1831, http://juel.iath.virginia.edu/resources.

72. The only rejection of a request for outside laundry services in the records in the Faculty Minutes for January 30, 1841, http://juel.iath.virginia.edu/resources. Granted requests are mentioned in the Faculty Minutes on October 3, 1835, http://juel.iath.virginia.edu/resources; Faculty Minutes, October 29 and 31, 1836, December 20, 1836, and October 31, 1837, http://juel.iath.virginia.edu/resources. In addition, hotelkeepers were sometimes required to pay restitution for lost or badly done laundry. See Faculty Minutes, February 5, 1834, and March 5, 1838, http://juel.iath.virginia.edu/resources.

73. Board of Visitors Minutes, 1817–2007, July 4, 1845, http://juel.iath.virginia.edu/resources.

74. Faculty Minutes, February 2, 1831, http://juel.iath.virginia.edu/resources.

75. Chairman's Journals, February 22 and 25, 1836, http://juel.iath.virginia.edu/resources.

76. Chairman's Journals, March 7, 1836, http://juel.iath.virginia.edu/resources.

77. Chairman's Journals, November 9, 1837, http://juel.iath.virginia.edu/resources.

78. Faculty Minutes, February 14, 1828, http://juel.iath.virginia.edu/resources.

79. Faculty Minutes, December 22, 1826, http://juel.iath.virginia.edu/resources.

80. Faculty Minutes, February 14, 1828, http://juel.iath.virginia.edu/resources.

81. Faculty Minutes, December 22, 1826, http://juel.iath.virginia.edu/resources.

82. Faculty Minutes, June 26, 1828, http://juel.iath.virginia.edu/resources.

83. Faculty Minutes, May 2, 1856. See also Faculty Minutes, June 27 and 28, 1828; December 10, 1835; June 21, 1836; September 30, 1839, http://juel.iath.virginia.edu/resources.

84. Albert, one of Mrs. Gray's slaves, is accused more than once in the Chairman's Journals of gambling (February 11, 17, 1831, and March 30, 1831, http://juel.iath.virginia.edu/resources).

85. Kirt van Daake, *Freedom Has a Face: Race, Identity, and Community in Jefferson's Virginia* (Charlottesville: University of Virginia Press, 2012), 85–86.

86. Chairman's Journals, February 17, 1837, http://juel.iath.virginia.edu/resources.

6

PROSLAVERY THOUGHT

Thomas Howard and Alfred Brophy

In June 1850, alumni, students, and faculty gathered in the Dome Room of the Rotunda to celebrate Final Exercises. Muscoe R. H. Garnett, an 1842 graduate of the university and rising star on the political stage who was soon to be elected to the House of Representatives, stood before the crowd to offer a simple message: the University of Virginia was meant to defend the institution of slavery from all who would see it abolished. Far too many southerners, he proclaimed, were being educated at northern colleges, where they became sympathetic to the scourge of abolitionism. Those educated in the North had joined, said Garnett, "an out-cry against Southern indolence, and its fancied cause, Southern Slavery; they pointed us to Northern opulence and the growth of Northern cities . . . as examples of their superior enterprise and industry." These charges against slavery and the South were made so often that "we began to believe, what was so often dinned into our ears, that slavery was the moral, social, and political evil they pretended." Then, he made a surprising claim about the origins of the university: "Mr. Jefferson saw this danger, and designed the University to avert it."[1]

In the 1850s many justified southern universities—and especially the University of Virginia—because they defended slavery as a core part of southern values. If Garnett was right about Jefferson's original intentions, the University of Virginia certainly now fulfilled his intended purpose, for by the time he delivered his speech in the midst of a brewing national crisis, UVA had become an important center for proslavery thought. The university's faculty, students, and alumni sought to justify and preserve slavery by extending Jefferson's own arguments about the inferiority of the black race as well as the nature of Union into their own day and age. Their thinking increasingly followed proslavery positions: they wrote and spoke about the centrality of slavery to human history, the economic and moral benefits it conferred on the enslaved as well as the slaveowners, and the hierarchy inherent in human society that made slavery, in their minds, not just good but indispensable. Their vision for the United States was based on a hierarchy of race that spanned economics, history, sociology, and law. Slavery was, to them, consistent with republican government, if not a necessary part of it.

Interestingly, their thinking was often pro-Union in that they saw the Constitution the ultimate protector of slavery and discussed the benefits of slavery to the United States as a whole. In fact, many Virginia students opposed disunion until the nation was on the brink of a Civil War that they knew would amount to a rejection of the state's political legacy and would almost surely spell the end for slavery.[2] Nonetheless, the arguments at the university were increasingly sectional, as students and faculty articulated a vision of southern nationalism. In the words of historian Elizabeth Varon, "from the very founding of the United States, the 'question of Union or Disunion' was inseparable from the issue of slavery's destiny," and the discourse that occurred at the University of Virginia is no exception.[3]

Garnett's address highlighted one important feature of the many goals Jefferson had for the University of Virginia: his desire that the university educate young men in the values of the southern political and social order, and defend them against the corrupting influence of northern institutions. The rich proslavery thought that emerged at the university from its founding until the Civil War is an important part of its history, and helps us understand how students and faculty understood and justified the slave society in which they lived and how they treated the enslaved people who lived and worked at the university. In the hands of a faculty comprised of some of the leading proslavery voices in the South, the education that students received at UVA increasingly reinforced the values of a slaveholding society, creating the foundation for a nearly universal and deeply held proslavery ideology ingrained in the very character of the institution itself.

JEFFERSON ON SLAVERY

As his contemporaries noted, there were at least two Jeffersons on the topic of slavery. First was the idealistic Jefferson, the author of the Declaration of Independence who set the moral course of the Revolution and later our nation on the principle that all humans are created equal. Then came the more pragmatic, less utopian Jefferson who wrote about racial hierarchy in frightening terms. His 1787 *Notes on the State of Virginia* reveal Jefferson's uneasy relationship with slavery and mastery, from which one must conclude that at best

Jefferson found slavery to be a necessary evil.[4] There is a third, even darker portrait of Jefferson that emerges in parts of the *Notes,* revealing his belief in the inferiority of people of African ancestry.[5] In Query XIV, Jefferson discusses at length a "difference of race" that he believed manifested in physical, emotional, and moral deficiencies in the black race. He describes the sexual preferences of black men as animalistic, and observes an "immovable veil of black which covers all the emotions of the other race." Jefferson found blacks inferior to whites "in reason" and "in the endowments of both body and mind."[6] Shocking to modern eyes, these deeply held ideas represented a nearly insurmountable barrier between the idealistic Jefferson and emancipation.

The idealistic Jefferson fought against his pragmatism and racism in *Notes on the State of Virginia,* for instance, where he observed that God's "justice cannot sleep forever" in regard to slavery.[7] This internal conflict was borne out in his support of the American Colonization Society (ACS), an organization that proposed to move free blacks to Africa.[8] One of the central missions of the ACS was removal of people of African descent from the United States. Even though its antislavery mission was subordinated to racial separation, still in many places in the South it offered the only form of acceptable solution to the question of slavery. ACS supporters included the two other former presidents who joined Jefferson on the Board of Visitors, James Madison and James Monroe (fig. 6.1). Many of its supporters were conservative proponents of a racially pure United States, although on occasion it had supporters like James Birney who after leaving the colonization movement subsequently was a vocal proponent of abolitionism and ran for president of the United States on the Liberty Party ticket in 1844. The brand of mild critique of slavery proposed by the ACS appealed to Jefferson's ideology—subscribed to by a great many in his time—that white and black people could not live in harmony, and that termination of slavery would only be feasible were it accompanied by the removal of members of the black race from the United States entirely. They believed any alternative would surely lead to social dysfunction and great violence.

Despite his support for colonization, Jefferson's conception of Union was one that worked to protect slavery. Jefferson envisioned an empire of states stretching across the continent, bound by shared interests, equal in their standing and free from the undue "metropolitan" influence of an overly strong national government.[9] Together, he and Madison gave eloquent voice to this vision in the Virginia and Kentucky Resolutions of 1798, which in response

FIG. 6.1. Certificate of membership, American Colonization Society.

to the Alien and Sedition Acts asserted the right of a state to judge the constitutionality of federal law. Union was "conducive to the liberty and happiness of the several states," but "if those who administer the general government be permitted to transgress the limits fixed by that compact," the inevitable result would be the "annihilation of the state governments."[10] In 1820, Jefferson's harmonious vision for a union of free and equal states came under attack again when the Missouri Crisis rang like a "fire bell in the night" to the aged statesman.[11] The compromise sought to resolve the brewing controversy over slavery by prohibiting slavery in territories north of Missouri's southern border and permitting it below that line. Already slavery was driving a wedge between North and South, dividing their interests, undermining hopes for a peaceful coexistence, and raising the specter of sectional divisions.[12]

"THE FLAVOR OF THE OLD CASK": A SOUTHERN INSTITUTION

Jefferson clearly recognized later in his life that the interests of the North and South were diverging, and he felt strongly that the University of Virginia should provide an education that trained students, "especially of the South and West," in his vision for an agrarian society, emphasizing the principles of state sovereignty, and supportive of the institution of slavery. Jefferson had lamented the prominence of northern colleges to James Breckenridge in 1821: "We are now trusting to those who are against us in position and principle, to fashion to their own form the minds & affections of our youth.... This canker is eating on the vitals of our existence, and if not arrested at once will be beyond remedy."[13] For Jefferson, northern schools made "fanatics and tories" out of young men, and only a University of Virginia could provide the education that southern youth needed.[14] At no point during the antebellum years were there more than a small handful of students enrolled from outside of the South.[15]

Students who attended UVA in the early years were drawn in large part from the ranks of Virginia's elite planter class and prominent southern slaveholding families, who often rejected a northern education in favor of a southern one. Matriculation was almost entirely the province of the wealthy. The cost of attendance in the 1840s was routinely over $400 for a single term, which approached twice the price of elite northern universities.[16] A sample of thirty of the families from Virginia counties who sent students to UVA in 1830 reveals that more than 80 percent owned at least ten slaves. All but one family owned at least one slave. By 1850 that percentage had dropped slightly: 48 percent of a sample of thirty-one families owned more than ten slaves, but more than 80 percent of families still owned at least one slave. This in comparison to the fact that in 1850, only 35 percent of all families in Virginia owned even a single slave.[17]

Ideas about slavery were in constant circulation at the university. Members of the faculty wrote about and discussed slavery, and surely taught about it. Students also found numerous opportunities to discuss the issue outside of the classroom. They heard about slavery from public figures who came to the university to address them at annual celebrations, debated about it in student-organized literary societies, and sometimes put their thoughts on slavery to paper in the university's literary magazines. The constant presence of enslaved people in their daily lives ensured that slavery, its moral and political foundations and its economic ramifications were inescapable to anyone on the Grounds. We find that the ideas in circulation on the Grounds correlate with the ideas about slavery held in the larger Virginia society.

Despite being drawn from elite slaveholding families, a group of students educated in the first decade of the university were at least open to the idea of ending slavery, in large part as supporters of the American Colonization Society. These early students were, like many in Virginia, skeptical of the economic and moral benefits of slavery. Among them, Henry Tutwiler, perhaps one of the most intellectually accomplished early graduates of UVA, called slavery the source of "almost all moral and political evil in this state."[18] A student during the first five sessions, Tutwiler had graduated in 1830 from an unprecedented five schools at the university. The following year he became the professor of ancient languages at the University of Alabama, where he was so revered that one student called him "a whole faculty within himself."[19] Recruited to Alabama by the abolitionist James Birney, the two worked together to establish the ACS in Tuscaloosa. Likewise, the support ACS enjoyed at UVA and in Charlottesville was broad: in 1830, women at the university sponsored a fair "for the benefit of the Colonization Society," which was attended by Tutwiler's friend, UVA graduate and new professor Gessner Harrison, along with several other faculty and students.[20]

AN EMERGING PROSLAVERY THOUGHT

For two brief weeks in early 1832, in the aftermath of Nat Turner's Rebellion, it seemed as though Virginia might embrace Jefferson's vision for colonization and embark down a path of gradual abolition (fig. 6.2). At the urging of Jefferson's grandson Thomas Jefferson Randolph and others in the House of Delegates, the legislature considered resolutions that echoed proposals of the ACS, freeing slaves when they reached a certain age and removing them from Virginia. While the legislature narrowly rejected Randolph's proposed gradual abolition plan, the debates illuminate the breadth of attitudes in Virginia at the time regarding the desirability of slavery. Even among the advocates of gradual abolition, however, the safety and security of the white race dominated the debate at the expense of any moral obligation to end slavery.[21] The antislavery cause appealed—unsuccessfully—to white self-interest. Over time, however, the economic benefits of slavery seem to have bent attitudes in its favor, and no scheme of abolition received serious consideration in Virginia again.

Several years later, a student writing in the student-published *Jefferson Monument Magazine* looked back on the 1832 legislative session, analyzing the differences between northern abolitionists and the efforts of Virginians to end slavery in their state. He thought that the abolitionist message encouraged slaves to rebel, making antislavery advocacy tantamount to inciting violence. As long as white and black people were to coexist, slavery was the necessary ordering of society. Thus, he argued:

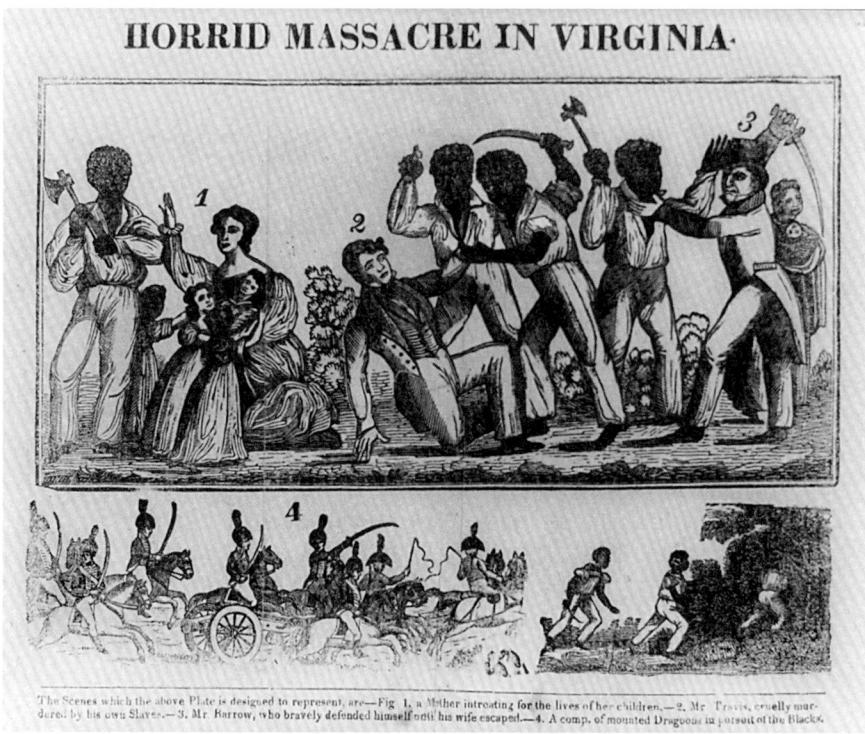

Fig. 6.2. "Horrid Massacre in Virginia" block print illustrating Nat Turner's Rebellion.

The Northern and Southern abolitionist were essentially different and incapable of co-operation. One addressed the slave, the other addressed the master. One involved "insurrection, rapine and murder," the other firmly supported law and order. . . . Let abolition come from the slave and it destroys all institutions, social and political. But if it come from the master, the supremacy of the law is maintained, and public tranquility preserved.—This was seen by Southern emancipationists. They felt that self-preservation required them to resist the Northern abolitionists, and that this can only be done by cutting off from the slave all hope of freedom. Like good citizens they sacrificed their wishes to the public good, and abandoned a measure which they could no longer advocate with safety to the country.[22]

To this student, the northern abolitionist values of freedom would encourage murder and rebellion. Such values were incompatible with southern society and threatened slavery in Virginia. Were abolition to occur in a measured, gradual way that favored the interests of whites, it might well be possible. But the immediate abolition proposed by the likes of William Lloyd Garrison would result in chaos, violence, and, if imposed from the outside, would amount to a rejection of Virginia's sovereignty.

As abolitionists became more vocal throughout the 1830s, a countervailing reaction emerged to defend slavery against its attacks. Just a few months before his election as Speaker of the United States House of Representatives, UVA alumnus Robert M. T. Hunter spoke before students and alumni on July 4, 1839. In the face of increasing abolitionist fervor, he believed it fell to Virginia to preserve the Union: "We can only acquit ourselves of this responsibility by the successful execution of the experiment, which our fathers have instituted. And if the true theory of our system has been this day developed, our success will depend upon that of the political school founded in Virginia."[23]

Hunter appealed to Jefferson's vision for a Union held together by shared interests, even as those interests were threatened by northern abolitionists: "We have already seen associations formed in our country . . . unmindful of the kindly associations of the past, of the fraternal bond of union, and of the solemn covenants of the Federal compact, threatening to move upon our domestic institutions in the storm of civil war, and revolutionize the order of the household government itself, which is the basis of every human society."[24] Hunter also drew on Jefferson's belief that it was impossible for the black and white races to coexist peacefully in a single free society. To emancipate slaves without granting them political rights would risk worsening their condition and would increase the burden they placed on society, while granting them political rights would lead inevitable violent conflict. Hunter warned against the dangers of abolition:

> Success in their schemes would only serve to injure the condition of both races. They forget, that on the one hand to emancipate the Negro without property or political privilege, would be to make him a slave of society—a condition infinitely worse than his who was bound to an individual master, not only by the ties of interest, but by those of personal sympathy and kindly association: Whilst on the other, to free him with his privileges, to place him in active collision with another race, without hope of union between them, would [cause great violence].[25]

Faced with this seeming paradox, slavery was, to Hunter, the only way forward. Not only would it allow both races to continue a peaceful coexistence, but it would also continue the positive benefits that he perceived arose from the institution of slavery for the enslaved. Jefferson's thinking clearly influenced Hunter, who may have even met him while a student. The enslaved, Hunter argued, were being civilized "under the discipline of its circumstances, and the dominion of the white race in the South," and slavery was "the only relation in which the two races can coexist in harmony, and operate for the mutual benefit of both."[26]

LESSONS INSIDE AND OUTSIDE OF THE CLASSROOM

The education that students at the University of Virginia received consistently reinforced the values of a slave society, both in the formal curriculum and in the students' activities outside of the classroom, where they constantly encountered proslavery rhetoric in speech, debate, and writing. The importance of this education extended into the sphere of civil society, where graduates (like Hunter) in important state and federal positions implemented a worldview shaped during their college years, relying on their education to articulate a prosouthern, proslavery, and uniquely Virginian position. Historians of the antebellum South have emphasized the vital society building that universities played in training the rising generation of leaders and reinforcing the political order. Lorri Glover, for example, has examined how "southern sons" grew into elite southern gentlemen: "Universities served a vital social function for southern elites: they were the setting for young men to begin the arduous, practiced process of acquiring the reputation of gentlemen."[27] The world of slavery and the politics of Virginia society found confirmation in what students discussed in their classrooms, literary societies, and boardinghouses.

The curriculum of the University of Virginia was one of its great innovations. Rather than require students to follow a strictly prescribed set of coursework, Jefferson devised an elective system where students could take courses in one or more schools, taught by an individual professor.[28] This unique ability for students to choose their own course of study at UVA was an exercise in controlling their own position in a social order defined first and foremost by perception.[29]

Although there was probably little explicitly proslavery material in the curriculum, in the hands of proslavery faculty members the curriculum reinforced compatible values. Ancient authors were generally slaveholders and aristocrats, and their social order was one built on hierarchies of race, economics, and social standing.[30] Students were likely to have encountered Thucydides' "Melian Dialogue," a discourse on power that held "Right, as the world goes, is only in question between equals in power, while the strong do what they can and the weak suffer what they must."[31] Those who studied the law in addition to these foundational subjects were taught the Constitution with a strong gloss of Jeffersonian states' rights, and put the ideals they learned in other courses into practice by safeguarding interests in property and the legal order of southern slave society.

Not every student, however, was receptive to this Jeffersonian view of constitutional law. Henry Winter Davis, a future antislavery congressman from Maryland who had completed his undergraduate studies at Kenyon College in Ohio, was a law student during the 1840–1841 session. Returning South, he found that "Jefferson's political ideas permeated the whole body of the students and infected the whole atmosphere of the slave States."[32] He recalled the overt emphasis on state sovereignty that law professor John A. G. Davis placed on the Constitution, and the sympathy in which most students held that view:

> I had sat at the feet of Clay and Webster as the rest had of Jefferson and Calhoun; the war was waged fiercely during my year at the University. There was, however, then still a great body of dissenters from the Jeffersonian theories in the University, as in the slave States—but always a minority on the defensive and gradually driven to occupy or concede more and more of the ground of their adversaries—till finally their opposition was a protest without principle, and the admission was universal, either tacitly or expressly, that the slavery interest found its only secure bulwark in the supremacy of the States, the right of nullification or secession, or the denial or limitation of every attribute of sovereignty of the United States.[33]

Davis knew that his position was unpopular. He recalled, "I was always on the other side, as well in theory as in practice, and was vigorously denounced for a Federalist."[34] Though he came from a slaveholding family (his father had been a supporter of the ACS in Maryland) and saw himself as a southerner, Davis's views on slavery placed him in the minority at UVA:

On my return I remember I was struck with a sort of revulsion of feeling at the aspect of slavery which I certainly had not carried with me to the West. But with the great mass of students it was the natural, the only tolerable or possible state of the negro. It was not frequently the theme of discussion, though sometimes its relation to the principles of freedom were looked in the face, and then it was generally admitted to be at once irreconcilable and irredeemable.[35]

Davis felt that his classmates had been schooled to become leaders who defended southern interests. From their law classes at the university, "the young men went home sufficiently instructed to make the rebellion, for it is that generation of students who have prepared, organized and led the rebellion. R. M. T. Hunter and [James Alexander] Seddon had just left the University a year or two when I got there. Mr. [Joseph] Orr, of South Carolina, and [Clement] Clay, of Alabama, were there during my year."[36] All four would go on to hold positions in the Confederate government.

Students at the University of Virginia like Hunter and Seddon also enjoyed a vibrant extracurricular life, which was another important way they controlled and structured their own social order and personal reputation. These pursuits, in conjunction with the formal curriculum, were part of a quest to attain what Timothy Williams calls "intellectual manhood." Students actively aspired to (but did not always attain) values of restraint, perseverance, and industry, while forming their own opinions and personal identity. They developed a strong proslavery and prosouthern bias in the process.[37]

In pursuit of this end, students formed literary societies, formal organizations where they debated, spoke, and engaged in political contests with their peers.[38] The Jefferson Society was formed just days after the first students arrived on the Grounds in 1825. It soon grew to be the most important and storied student organization at the university, and began holding its meetings in Hotel C, a vibrant hub of activity in Jefferson's Academical Village (fig. 6.3).[39] Its members sought to emulate the statesmanship of Jefferson, Madison, and Monroe; they elected all three to honorary membership.[40] Many of the university's most prominent graduates from the early years counted themselves as members, including Edgar Allan Poe, Robert M. T. Hunter, Robert Toombs, and Alexander H. H. Stuart, along with countless other governors, senators, and representatives, as well as future members of the faculty like James P. Holcombe.

FIG. 6.3. Hotel C, meeting place of the Jefferson Society.

In 1831 students formed a friendly rival, the Washington Society. The two societies created a lively literary culture at the university, debating against each other, hosting public celebrations for the university, and supporting literary publications. Nearly every student during the antebellum years counted himself a member of one or the other. They were a natural extension of the formal curriculum.[41] Ultimately, they were an important venue for the exposition of proslavery thought at the university, and, by allowing students to structure a significant portion of their own world, they played a crucial role in reinforcing the values of a slaveholding society.

The first crucially important function of the literary societies was to provide a forum for students to practice oratory.[42] Addresses delivered by students and visiting orators open an important window on the ideas students heard outside of the classroom. They were often reflective of larger political conversations, and they frequently turned to the subject of slavery. For example, when the Jefferson Society selected a student member, Merritt Robinson, to speak at a public celebration in 1832, he delivered a controversial speech on the immorality of slavery as he advocated for emancipation. Delivered only one year after Henry Tutwiler had graduated from the university, Robinson's speech reflected the political discourse of the time, particularly among students. But his remarks enraged the faculty, and even caused the Board of Visitors to ban student public speaking for a short time.[43] Likewise, addresses delivered by visiting dignitaries invited by the literary societies—like Garnett and Hunter above—were major events in the life of the university. They were well attended, and particularly well-received orations were published in pamphlet form. They provide an important view into the orators' social and political world, and were quite often ardently proslavery.[44]

The literary societies also sponsored debates. While precious few records from actual debates survive from before the Civil War, students often turned to questions of slavery, as they routinely did at other schools such as Washington College, Hampden-Sydney, Wake Forest, and William & Mary.[45] On the evening he joined the Jefferson Society, Louis Wigfall, later a zealously proslavery and prosecession United States senator from Texas, "joined in the debate with a good deal of ardor; and plunged headlong into nullification and secession at the bare mention of S. Carolina's course in 1832."[46] Another student, Robert G. H. Kean, wrote in 1853 that the Jefferson Society had engaged in a heated debate over slavery.[47]

Finally, the literary societies frequently supported the publication of literary magazines (fig. 6.4). Published monthly, the magazines featured poetry, fiction writing, satire, and essays composed and edited by students.[48] Like oratory, composition was an important part of a college education for the most part unavailable in the classroom. According to the editors of the *Collegian*, "Both of these branches of education, so indispensably necessary to every accomplished American, are entirely disregarded in the exercises of this Institution."[49] As such, the student magazines are a fascinating source, both as artifacts showing how students spent their time and for the glimpse into student thinking the articles provide. Affectionately known to students as "the Mag," several different iterations circulated among the students, including the *Collegian*, the *University Literary Magazine*, the *Jefferson Monument Magazine*, and finally the *Virginia University Magazine*, which survived to become a fixture on the Grounds for nearly a century.[50]

The *Magazine* offers a penetrating window into the social and political thought of students, who often concluded their articles with a call to action. Much of their writing was characterized by sectional animus, despite periodic commitments on the part of the editors not to publish pieces of a "sectarian" character.[51] In parallel with the distinctively southern education they were receiving at the university, the students felt quite strongly that the

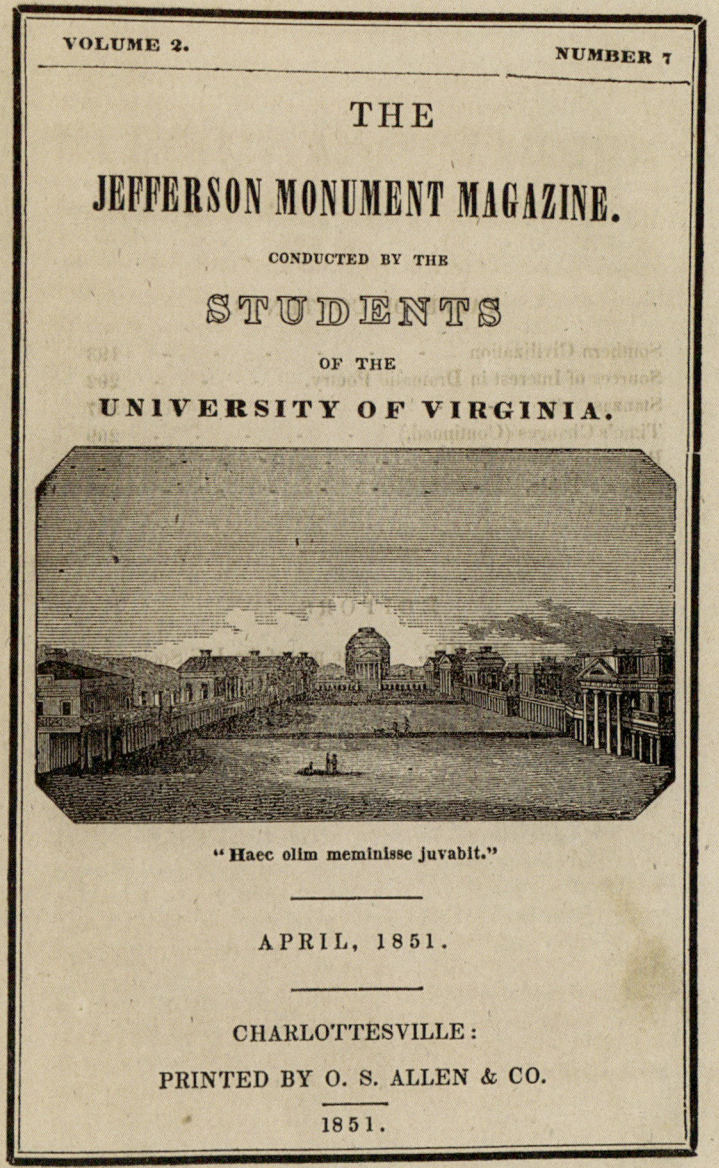

FIG. 6.4. Cover page of the *Jefferson Monument Magazine*, April 1851.

South should develop its own distinct regional literature, often defining their publication in opposing terms to similar northern publications like Princeton's *Nassau Literary Review*. In 1840, the editors of the *Collegian* invoked regional identity when calling for submissions and subscribers: "We appeal to your pride. Similar Periodicals are sustained at many of the Colleges of our country. Shall we fail, where they have succeeded? Shall it be said that a plant like this droops and dies in the sunny soil of the South, while it grows and is green on the bleak hills of the North?"[52]

SLAVERY AND SECTIONALISM TAKE CENTER STAGE

The year 1850 marked a turning point at the University of Virginia, as in the United States. In February, the sectional rhetoric in an editorial from the *Jefferson Monument Magazine* presaged the intense debate that captured the nation's attention over the Compromise of 1850 by imploring students to exhibit more southern pride and support the magazine:

> Will you let it be said that *by three hundred and fifty-five* SOUTHERN STUDENTS at the University of Virginia a monthly Magazine of 32 pages octavo *could not be supported*? Have you no more sectional pride than this? Are YOU *the southern sons, of southern sires,* and permit this, when you see your Northern brethren sending out, from almost every college north of Mason's and Dixon's line, a worthy periodical? *Will you,* CAN YOU as SOUTHERNERS yield the palm of literary attainment without a struggle? We know that there is not one true son of the South from whom the *indignant* NO does not all at once come.[53]

But soon the debates on the Grounds extended beyond support for a literary magazine. As Congress debated the Compromise of 1850, momentarily settling political conflicts over slavery, student authors at UVA revealed their increasingly sectional attitudes. In the *Jefferson Monument Magazine*, a student pointed out the chasm dividing North and South, voicing renewed concern that the different sections of the country would not be able to reconcile their differences:

> It cannot be denied that difficulties of a most serious nature exist between the two great sections of our country, difficulties which must occasion the deepest solicitude and most serious apprehensions to every public mind. The flames of Northern fanaticism have kindled a confla-

gration which seems likely to consume the ties of amity which bind us, and to destroy that sacred gift of our Fathers, the Union itself. Apathetic and indifferent, the South has permitted herself to be surpassed in all the elements of greatness, but with characteristic credulity has listened only to be deceived by the honeyed words of those who have attempted to rob her of her rights, and to interfere with her domestic institutions.[54]

By 1859 sectional pride had grown into overt animosity. Students at Yale had invited the University of Virginia to join them in the publication of a national literary magazine to be called the *Undergraduate Quarterly*. Not wanting to be associated with any degree of antislavery or abolitionist thinking, the Virginia literary societies insisted they could agree only "on condition that all institutions of learning which practically ignore the distinction between the white and black races, shall be excluded from the association."[55]

Section animosity was, of course, not limited to students. Muscoe Garnett, whose 1850 address introduced this chapter, expressed the concern of many of his contemporaries that sectional tensions would divide the country. He saw the university as playing an important role in the defense of the South, saying "there devolves upon us, gentlemen, as foster sons of this great University of Virginia, no light duty in the army for the defense of civilization. We owe no small debt to the good old Commonwealth, who here unrolled to our eager gaze, 'the ample page of knowledge, rich with the spoils of time.'"[56] Garnett identified slavery as a necessary precondition to the existence of an advanced society, providing a litany of examples of slave societies across history and their achievements in the realms of science, literature, and government. His message was simple: "We see that a truly democratic republic is impossible without some such institutions as ours, and we are convinced that African slavery is the fruitful source of moral and political, social and economical blessings to both parties."[57]

Slavery could be preserved, felt Garnett, by adhering to a view of a government of limited, decentralized powers, much in the school of Jeffersonian thought. Just as slavery could promote democracy, so could democracy protect slavery.

Perhaps heeding Garnett's call, in 1850 students embraced the idea of a southern nation by establishing a Southern Rights' Association. One hundred twenty-one of the 374 students that session joined an outcry over "the war which is now being waged against the rights and honor of the South."

Slavery was under attack, and this group of students advocated "state action" to keep the power of the North in check. "From the entire North has gone forth the fiat, that the area of African slavery shall never be extended," read their published address, "the people and institutions of the South have been excluded from a region of country, acquired by the common exertions and common sacrifices of the whole nation." The students called on the North to cease their attacks on slavery, or "the price of further aggressions on their part will be the dissolution of that Union."[58]

Even amid such strident sectional rhetoric, however, most Virginians remained emotionally tied the Union. William Roane Aylett, an 1854 graduate who had joined the Southern Rights' Association as a student, left extensive writings from his days at a student through his service in the Civil War, to a reunion at Gettysburg many years later. His writings allow us to see that some UVA students "reconcile[d] . . . seemingly contradictory claims of allegiance to the Old Dominion, the Union, and the South." Aylett saw the Union as a way of protecting southern interests, but as the 1850s wore on, many began to see the world differently. While many at the university clung to Union, others expressed more support for a separate, southern nation. The students became increasingly conservative, increasingly proslavery, and increasingly they calculated the value of Union and found it less than the value of secession.[59]

Articles that appeared in student publications reflect these opposing attitudes as well. When they put their pen to paper, students were far from unified in prosecession attitudes. In a number of articles running from the late 1840s to the mid 1850s,[60] students pled the case for Union, the value of the Union to the North and the South, and wrote of the importance of the Constitution and the economic and political benefits it conferred on American citizens. In late 1850 and early 1851, a comprehensive four-part series of articles examined aspects of "the Union," including its government, history and expansion, industry, and regional differences. The authors speculated on the effects that dissolution would have on the different sections of the country, warning that without the conservative influence of southern slavery, the North would slide into anarchy and despotism. Ultimately, however, they concluded "that each and every portion has so deep a stake in the perpetuity of our present system that a voluntary and unprovoked withdrawal by any member would be an act of madness and folly which it is impossible to conceive."[61] It took a long time for students to turn to the idea of secession, though they did in 1861.⁶² This mirrors other schools, where the ideas on campus supported the Union, even refused to enter into considerations of the value and costs of the Union, until the late 1850s.

THE PROSLAVERY VANGUARD

By the 1850s, the faculty at UVA was also serving the role that Garnett envisioned for the school: supporting proslavery values.⁶³ In fact, they developed an extensive body of scholarship that supported slavery. The best-known faculty member who wrote in defense of slavery was a professor of mathematics, Albert Taylor Bledsoe, whose 1856 book *Liberty and Slavery* built a political theory to sustain the idea that slavery was the natural state of humans. In critique of Jefferson's Declaration, Bledsoe wrote that people are not born equal, but unequal. He used that inherent inequality to argue that people are entitled only to the amount of freedom consistent with their station in life. And, perhaps most importantly, Bledsoe turned on its head Jean-Jacques Rousseau's theory that liberty was greatest in a state of nature. He argued that there must be restraints on individuals to preserve order in society. Far from being a restraint on liberty, society's regulations facilitate ordered liberty. Liberty for some, for those whom Bledsoe believed were entitled to it, was preserved by enslaving others.⁶⁴

Yet, significantly, not all the UVA faculty followed Bledsoe's proslavery ideas. In fact, one was downright critical of it. Engineering professor Charles Shaw responded to Bledsoe with a book called *Is Slavery a Blessing?* The book, whose thesis was also its title, was published in Boston by the house that had published Harriet Beecher Stowe's *Uncle Tom's Cabin* in 1852. Slavery was not, in Shaw's mind, fit for the progressive era of the 1850s. In short, the enormous cost of slavery was not worth its benefits to order.⁶⁵

Despite Shaw's important and underappreciated volume, the center of balance at UVA leaned decidedly in favor of slavery. Professor of history and literature George Frederick Holmes published an extensive article on natural law and slavery in Aristotle's *Politics*.⁶⁶ Shortly afterward he published a critique of *Uncle Tom's Cabin,* which focused on how Stowe's emphasis on humane sentiments for the slave rather than cold logical reasoning about the property rights of slaveowners "strikes at . . . the foundations of law, order, and government." It was a straightforward defense of slavery and hierarchy.⁶⁷

Perhaps the most strident proslavery thinker on the UVA faculty was law professor James Philemon Holcombe. Holcombe was a broad thinker and teacher, whose work spanned esoteric areas of commercial law through constitutional law and history. He likely honed his ideas about constitutional history and slave law with his students and his colleagues at UVA. Holcombe gave three important proslavery addresses in the 1850s. The first was an 1853 address to the UVA Society of Alumni that echoed Muscoe Garnett's 1850 address to the same body, as it justified the university in part because of its role in producing scholarship in defense of southern institutions.[68] The second, in 1856 at the Virginia Historical Society in Richmond, focused on Virginia's role in the American Revolution. Holcombe argued that slavery made freedom more salient to white Virginians. Slaveowners could see the value of liberty and could achieve it because of the wealth produced by slavery. Holcombe argued that Massachusetts antislavery advocates had strayed far from the colonial cooperation of the Revolution, forsaking the very liberty it made possible.[69] Holcombe's third and most important speech was his 1858 address to the state agricultural society in Petersburg, entitled "Is Slavery Consistent with Natural Law?" It built on Bledsoe's theory—and also on law professor Henry St. George Tucker, whose lectures argued that slavery was consistent with natural law.[70] Holcombe presented a world defined by racial hierarchy. He claimed that the Anglo-Saxon race was entitled to freedom and that people of African descent were not. An examination of millennia of world history suggested to him that slavery was Africans' natural condition. Holcombe reversed Thomas Jefferson's statement in the Declaration of Independence that slavery was inconsistent with natural law. Holcombe's final argument was that because slavery is consistent with natural law, the North should tolerate slavery and stop trying to abolish it.[71]

While it is difficult to know exactly how the faculty incorporated their scholarship into their daily lectures, professors almost certainly presented elements of their proslavery thinking in the classroom. That students were exposed to their ideas, however, is apparent in their writing in the literary magazines. Just as articles reflected students' attitudes toward Union, they also demonstrated their ideas about slavery. But even where there was surprisingly strong support for Union in the *Magazine,* articles were consistently proslavery. There were defenses based on the Bible's seeming support of slavery,[72] the economic necessity of slavery,[73] and the threat to safety of slaveowners if slavery ended.[74] The theme they developed most fully was that slavery reflected the hierarchy that is inherent in nature, harking back to Jefferson's ideas about race. Students wove together threads of "science"

Fig. 6.5. Unknown photographer, photograph of Public Hall in the Rotunda Annex, 1867.

claiming the supposed inferiority of people of African descent with social explanations for why slaves were not yet ready for freedom, let alone citizenship.[75] The political theory of hierarchy they developed in articles mirrored what they were hearing from faculty like Albert Taylor Bledsoe and James P. Holcombe.[76] It was a powerful explanation for why some people rightfully ruled over others; and it directly challenged abolitionist images of virtuous and humble enslaved people who were citizens in waiting.[77]

THE GATHERING STORM

The crisis of 1850 seems not to have weakened the attachments of Virginians to the Union, however, at least not for the time being. In 1855, naval engineer Matthew Fontaine Maury spoke to the literary societies at UVA on the progress and internal development of Virginia, lauding the South for achieving more than any society before it, largely as a result of slave labor. But he was careful to emphasize that North and South were both equally industrious, and that their efforts were inseparable: "The southern enterprise of this country has done more than the spirit of man has ever before accomplished in the same climates and between the same parallels of latitude," he said. But "northern enterprise and southern enterprise taken together, have effected the greatest achievements that human energies have ever accomplished."[78]

Two years later, in 1857, Joseph Hodgson, the student elected as the Jefferson Society's orator at Final Exercises, appealed to the Constitution as the ultimate defense against whatever differences might exist between North and South in an address delivered in UVA's Public Hall (fig. 6.5). Of the Constitution, he said:

> It has not failed us in former exigencies, and it will not fail us. When confusion and lowering tenants darken our political and moral horizon; when civil war threatens us with its direful train of evils; when fraternity seems but to exist in name; and when fanaticism seems ready to plunge us into the gulf where lies the wreck of empires, conservatism, with healing on its wing, ever leaps up from the fearful din to guide and guard us safely.[79]

Slavery, to Hodgson, was protected by the Constitution from whatever attacks might be leveled at it, in no small part because he, like Muscoe Garnett before him, felt that slavery was supported by American democratic values: "Frantic *philanthropists* may endeavor to solve by the law of expediency what they cannot prove by the law of justice; they may argue by all the niceties of rhetoric, and all the sophistry of logic, that our fathers and we are tyrannical monsters, yet America, true to her character of law-giver, has ever denounced at the ballot box these pitiful discovers of new morality."[80] Union, then, even in 1857, was to Virginians the ultimate protector of slavery: "Secede! And why? Have you so soon forgotten the lesson of history, the frailties and fanaticism of human nature? You cannot let our Union fall."[81]

Yet amid these rhetorical paeans to sectional harmony, cracks had begun to show in the patina of Union. On May 22, 1856, tempers reached a boiling point in the halls of Congress in the aftermath of the Kansas and Nebraska crisis. Preston Brooks, a representative from South Carolina, brandished his cane and beat Senator Charles Sumner of Massachusetts within an inch of his life on the floor of the United States Senate (fig. 6.6). In the process Brooks shattered his cane, and students at the university elected to send him a replacement in a show of support. They "fully approved the course of Mr. Brooks," and decided to purchase him a "splendid cane . . . to be suitably inscribed, and also bear upon it a device of the human head, badly cracked and broken."⁸² They chose for the inscription a line from Brooks's letter to his brother the day after the incident: "Every Southern man sustains me," wherein he also likened abolitionists to a "hive of disturbed bees."⁸³ Students lauded Brooks for his actions, and defended the existence of slavery in Kansas. "The chivalry of the South, it seems," read the *Richmond Enquirer,* "has been thoroughly aroused."⁸⁴

By 1859 students were openly discussing disunion. John Brown's raid on Harpers Ferry, only 100 miles away, is often cited as a key turning point for the South. It was for the students at UVA as well, it seems. The *Yale Literary Magazine* ran a story that mocked the University of Virginia students who went to Charleston to see John Brown's execution. It jokingly suggested that the UVA students ran home when they heard the rumor that Yale students were on the way to rescue Brown. The *Virginia University Magazine* editors saw no humor in this (fig. 6.7). They aggressively responded that while UVA students "sometimes run, it is always with their face towards the enemy."⁸⁵

In 1859, the Washington Society voted twelve to four that states had the right to secede.⁸⁶ And the situation was worsening heading into the election of 1860. In January, law professor James Holcombe addressed Albemarle County voters and warned of the dangers if a "Black Republican" were to be elected president.⁸⁷ Accordingly, Virginia hitched its star to Unionist Party

FIG. 6.6. "Southern Chivalry—Argument versus Club's" showing the caning of Charles Sumner by Preston Brooks, May 22, 1856 after Sumner's Rape of Kansas speech.

As before, we have been compelled to italicize. Note the withering sarcasm of that last sentence!!

 "The students of Virginia University having gone to Charlestown to prevent a rescue, this is a view of the manner in which they defended that city, when they heard that Yale College were coming to rescue " John Brown." It is said that they were so frightened that they *walked* right home, and have not been heard from since."

Here the wit being too profoundly obscured for even Yale penetration, the editors themselves kindly pointed it out. We hope their readers see it, and enjoy the fun, as also the very modest compliment to their valiant heroism.

Next follows a picture of the execution—too disgusting to be transferred to our columns.

We confess that our obtuseness is too great to discover whether the remarks accompanying it, were intended as wit, humor or sarcasm.

The other cuts are very much of a piece with those we have given.

Now these pitiful engravings and the liquorish remarks explaining them, are a disgrace to the periodical in which they appear. If gotten up by children, we would be disposed to laugh,—if by idiots, we could smile,—if for money, we could pity the poor mercenary souls of their authors; but when they appear in the third number of the twenty-fifth volume of the Yale Literary Magazine, they excite our profoundest disgust.

Oh, men of Yale, for shame! Forget not your high position, and stain not the purity of your calling! Let drunken politicians view with complacency the Sabbath-midnight murder of peaceful citizens, and treat it as but a jest; let *Weakly Pictorials* clutch the auspicious moment to heap up ill-gotten gains by pandering to a vitiated taste; but oh, let not the pages of college literature be stained with blots so foul!

One word more. Those students, of the University of Virginia, who went to Charlestown, needed but an opportunity to prove that, though they may sometimes run, yet it is always with their faces towards the enemy. Should the necessity arise—which may heaven forbid!—we'll march in a body to the defense of our border, whether against the raids of professional horse-thieves and assassins, or the attacks of more reputable assailants. And if, on the other hand, a *Hartford Convention* should ever assemble in our vicinity, or armed bands congregate in our midst for the purpose of wickedly invading northern soil and stirring up internecine strife amongst our peaceful neighbors, we'll capture the offenders and hang them as high as Haman!

Contrast this sentiment with that which prompted the silly and shameful article which we have been noticing!

FIG. 6.7. Page from the *Yale Literary Magazine* that discusses conflicts between northern and southern students after John Brown's raid seemed to confirm southerners' fears that there was widespread support for violent abolition among northerners.

candidate John Bell. Students gathered on the steps of the Rotunda some days before the election to cast mock ballots, and there was a "tremendous hurrah for Bell" when he garnered a majority.[88] Their preference aligned with the rest of Virginia, one of three states Bell carried in the Electoral College. But he lost to Abraham Lincoln, the personification of the fears harbored by Holcombe and others like him. Almost immediately, the call to secession sounded across the South.

Slavery remained at the forefront as alumni of the university advocated for secession in several states across the South in 1860 and 1861. United States Senator Robert Toombs, who had studied law at UVA, led the charge in his home state of Georgia. Toombs left no doubt that his goal was to protect the institution of slavery. In his farewell speech to the Senate on January 7, 1861, he proclaimed, "We want no negro equality, no negro citizenship; we want no negro race to degrade our own; and as one man [we] would meet you upon the border with the sword in one hand and the torch in the other."[89]

Virginia's convention to consider secession met in Richmond on February 13, 1861, with James P. Holcombe having taken leave of the faculty to serve as a delegate. In a fiery speech delivered over the course of two days, March 20–21, he persistently invoked the benefits of slavery, its moral rightness, and the dangers posed by abolition. He warned that if the South did not take affirmative action, slavery would be driven out:

> The institution of slavery is so indissolubly interwoven with the whole framework of society in a large portion of our State, and constitutes so immense an element of material wealth and political power to the whole Commonwealth, that its subversion through the operation of any unfriendly policy on the part of the Federal Government, whether that operation is extended over a long or short period of time, would, of necessity, dry up the very fountains of the public strength, change the whole frame of our civilization, and inflict a mortal wound upon our liberties.[90]

Back in Charlottesville, the students had left no doubt where their sentiments lay. In early morning hours of March 16, 1861, a group of students broke into the Rotunda and hoisted the Confederate flag. Randolph H. McKim, who was among the young secessionists, recalled: "a sudden explosion of excitement . . . Shouts and cheers are heard from various precincts . . . all eyes turned to the dome of the rotunda from whose summit the Secession flag is seen waving."[91] The students rallied around the flag the following day, forsaking their classes to lend their voices to the Confederate cause. The chairman of the faculty, Socrates Maupin, ordered the flag taken down, as Virginia had not yet seceded.[92] But by midday, "a great throng of students [were] assembled on the lawn in front of the lofty flight of steps leading up to the rotunda, and one after another of the leaders the young men mounts the steps and harangues the crowd in favor of the Southern Confederacy, and the Southern flag waving proudly up there."[93] Though Union was still an open question in Richmond, the ardor of secession had caught fire at the University of Virginia.

NOTES

1. Muscoe R. H. Garnett, *An Address Delivered before the Society of Alumni of the University of Virginia, at Its Annual Meeting: Held in the Rotunda on the 29th of June, 1850* (Charlottesville, VA: O. S. Allen, 1850), 27.

2. See Peter Carmichael, *The Last Generation: Young Virginians in War, Peace, and Reunion* (Chapel Hill: University of North Carolina Press, 2005).

3. Elizabeth Varon, *Disunion! The Coming of the American Civil War, 1789–1859* (Chapel Hill: University of North Carolina Press, 2008), 337.

4. Annette Gordon-Reed and Peter S. Onuf, *The Most Blessed of the Patriarchs* (New York: Liveright, 2016), 59–61.

5. Peter S. Onuf, *Jefferson's Empire: The Language of American Nationhood* (Charlottesville: University Press of Virginia, 2000), 147–51, 174–82.

6. Thomas Jefferson, *Notes on the State of Virginia,* Query XIV, *The Papers of Thomas Jefferson*, 1787, Albert and Shirley Small Special Collections Library, University of Virginia.

7. Ibid., Query XVIII.

8. Jefferson wrote to Edward Coles, "I have seen no proposition so expedient on the whole, as that as emancipation of those born after a given day, and of their education and expatriation after a given age." Thomas Jefferson to Edward Coles, August 25, 1814, http://founders.archives.gov/documents/Jefferson/03-07-02-0439.

9. Onuf, *Jefferson's Empire,* 113–46.

10. "The Kentucky Resolutions of 1798," in *The Papers of Thomas Jefferson,* vol. 30: *1 January 1798 to 31 January 1799* (Princeton, NJ: Princeton University Press, 2003), 529–56.

11. Thomas Jefferson to John Holmes, April 22, 1820, https://founders.archives.gov/about/Jefferson/.

12. Varon, *Disunion!,* 48.

13. Thomas Jefferson to James Breckenridge, February 15, 1821, https://founders.archives.gov/about/Jefferson/.

14. Thomas Jefferson to Joseph Cabell, January 22, 1820, https://founders.archives.gov/about/Jefferson/.

15. Each year the university published "Catalogue of the Officers and Students of the University of Virginia," which lists each student's hometown or home state if they were not from Virginia.

16. Yale, Princeton, and Harvard cost $195, $226, and $245, respectively. Charles Coleman Wall, "Student Life at the University of Virginia, 1825–1861" (PhD diss., University of Virginia, 1978), 66.

17. Ibid., 48. The authors are indebted to Wall for his thorough work examining tax records of the families who sent students to the university in 1830 and 1850. Wall divided the class into families from counties in Virginia and cities in Virginia: his statistics cover the whole entering class with available records in 1830, but only a representative sample of the entering class in 1850. The proportions of slaveholding families referenced above are only for families from Virginia counties, more likely to own slaves than urban families. The drop in the percentage is probably due in large part because beginning in 1847, the university enacted a statewide scholarship program, bringing some students without means to the university. There was one state scholar, as they were called, per senatorial district.

18. Henry Tutwiler to James Birney, August 20, 1832, in *Letters of James Gillespie Birney, 1831–1857*, vol. 1, ed. Dwight Lowell Dumond (New York: D. Appleton-Century, 1938), 17.

19. Thomas Chalmers McCorvey, "Henry Tutwiler and Influence of the University of Virginia on Education in Alabama," *Alumni Bulletin of the University of Virginia* 10, no. 3 (July 1917): 278.

20. Gessner Harrison to Peachy Harrison, May 13, 1830, Harrison, Smith and Tucker Family Papers, 1790–1936, Accession #3825, Albert and Shirley Small Special Collections Library, University of Virginia.

21. Thomas R. Dew's contemporaneous commentary on the Virginia debates of 1831–1832 won him notoriety as a proslavery intellectual. For more on the debates, see Alison Goodyear Freehling, *Drift toward Dissolution: The Virginia Slavery Debate of 1831–1832* (Baton Rouge: Louisiana State University Press, 1982); and Erik S. Root, *Sons of the Fathers: The Virginia Slavery Debates of 1831–1832* (Lanham, MD: Lexington Books, 2010). See also Varon, *Disunion!*, 78–85.

22. "Northern and Southern Abolition," *Jefferson Monument Magazine* 1, no. 5 (February 1850): 154–59.

23. Robert M. T. Hunter, "An Address Delivered before the Society of the Alumni of the University of Virginia, at Its Second Annual Meeting, Held in the Rotunda, on the 4th of July, 1839," p. 23, Albert and Shirley Small Special Collections Library, University of Virginia.

24. Ibid., 23–24.

25. Ibid., 24.

26. Ibid., 25.

27. Lorri Glover, *Southern Sons: Becoming Men in the New Nation* (Baltimore: Johns

Hopkins University Press, 2007), 27, 51, 83. John Thelin tells us that by the middle part of the nineteenth century, the University of Virginia had become particularly "successful at transmitting the distinctive code and culture of the nineteenth-century Virginia gentleman to its students and the South's future leadership." John Thelin, *A History of American Higher Education* (Baltimore: Johns Hopkins University Press, 2011), 52, 63. See also Jennifer Green, *Military Education and the Emerging Middle Class in the Old South* (Cambridge: Cambridge University Press, 2008); and Timothy Williams, *Intellectual Manhood: University, Self, and Society in the Antebellum South* (Chapel Hill: University of North Carolina Press, 2015).

28. See Darren Staloff, "The Politics of Pedagogy: Thomas Jefferson and the Education of a Democratic Citizenry," in *The Cambridge Companion to Thomas Jefferson,* ed. Frank Shuffelton (Cambridge: Cambridge University Press, 2009), 127–39; and Virginius Dabney, *Mr. Jefferson's University* (Charlottesville: University Press of Virginia, 1981), 1–15.

29. Glover, *Southern Sons,* 83.

30. Williams, *Intellectual Manhood,* 48, 70–74.

31. Thucydides, "Melian Dialogue," in *The Landmark Thucydides: A Comprehensive Guide to the Peloponnesian War,* trans. Richard Crawley, ed. Robert B. Strassler (New York: Free Press, 1996), 352. Students were required to read Thucydides for the final examination in Ancient Languages. Minutes of the Faculty of the University of Virginia, 1825–1856, April 5, 1828, http://juel.iath.virginia.edu/resources.

32. Henry Winter Davis, *The Life and Times of Henry Winter Davis,* ed. Bernard C. Steiner (Baltimore: John Murphy, 1916), 49.

33. Ibid., 50–51.

34. Ibid., 51.

35. Ibid., 50.

36. Ibid., 51.

37. Williams, *Intellectual Manhood,* 8–9, 18–20.

38. In the words of historian James McLachlan, they were "in effect, colleges within colleges. They enrolled most of the students, constructed—and taught—their own curricula, granted their own diplomas, selected and bought their own books, operated their own libraries, developed and enforced elaborate codes of conduct among their members, and set the personal goals and ideological tone for a majority of the student body." James McLachlan, "'The Choice of Hercules': American Student Societies in the Early Nineteenth Century," in *The University in Society,* ed. Lawrence Stone (Princeton, NJ: Princeton University Press, 1974), 472.

39. Board of Visitors Minutes, 1817–2007, July 18, 1831, http://juel.iath.virginia.edu/resources. See also John Shelton Patton, *Jefferson, Cabell, and the University of Virginia* (Washington, DC: Neal Publishing, 1906), 46; and Philip Alexander Bruce, *History of the University of Virginia, 1819–1919: The Lengthened Shadow of One Man,* 5 vols. (New York: Macmillan, 1921), 2: 359; 3: 171.

40. Jefferson declined to avoid the impression of bias, but Madison and Monroe both accepted the honor.

41. Williams, *Intellectual Manhood,* 39.

42. Oratory "was the public display of a superior personality" and allowed gentlemen to display their "superior intelligence and virtue." Kenneth S. Greenberg, *Masters and Statesmen: The Political Culture of American Slavery* (Baltimore: Johns Hopkins University Press, 1985), 12.

43. "Editor's Table," *Collegian* 1, no. 9 (June 1839): 346–47; Bruce, *History of the University,* 2: 358; Wall, "Student Life at the University of Virginia, 1825–1861," 138.

44. For a study of similar addresses delivered at the University of North Carolina, the ideas in which largely paralleled those at the University of Virginia, see Alfred L. Brophy, "The Republics of Liberty and Letters: Progress, Union, and Constitutionalism at Graduation Addresses at the Antebellum University of North Carolina," *North Carolina Law Review* (2011): 1881–964.

45. Students in similar organizations, particularly at universities across the South, debated questions of slavery and secession with increasing frequency as the Civil War approached. Thomas S. Harding, *College Literary Societies: Their Contribution to Higher Education in the United States, 1815–1876* (New York: Pageant Press International, 1971), 192–215.

46. Charles Ellis Jr., A Student's Diary, 1835–36, April 4, 1835, http://juel.iath.virginia.edu/resources.

47. Student Diary of Robert Garlick Hill Kean, Kean family papers, 1859–1951, Accession #1331-c, Albert and Shirley Small Special Collections Library, University of Virginia.

48. Harding, *College Literary Societies,* 59.

49. "Editor's Table: Address to the Literary Association," *Collegian* 4, no. 1 (October 1841): 31.

50. For more of the magazines, see Wall, "Student Life at the University of Virginia, 1825–1861," 141n13. See also Bruce, *History of the University of Virginia,* 2: 350–53 and 3: 106–11; and Patton, *Jefferson, Cabell, and the University,* 254–59.

51. "Prospectus," *University Literary Magazine* 2, no. 1 (January 1858): back cover.

52. "Editor's Table," *Collegian* 3, no. 1 (October 1840): 27.

53. "Editorial," *Jefferson Monument Magazine* 2, no. 3 (December 1850): 95.

54. "The Present Crisis," *Jefferson Monument Magazine* 1, no. 5 (February 1850): 146.

55. Minutebook of the Washington Society, 1859–68, p. 19, Papers of the Washington Literary Society and Debating Union, 1859–1924, Accession #1780-a, Albert and Shirley Small Special Collections Library, University of Virginia. The *Undergraduate Quarterly* was in fact published in 1860 and 1861, though after the first issue under the name the *University Quarterly*. It was administered by a group of mostly northern schools, with some participation from midwestern and European universities, and none from the South. No mention of UVA's refusal to participate appears in its pages.

56. Garnett, *An Address Delivered before the Society of Alumni of the University of Virginia*, 3–4.

57. Ibid., 30.

58. *The Address of the Southern Rights' Association, of the University of Virginia, to the Young Men of the South* (Charlottesville, VA: James Alexander, 1851); *Catalogue of the University of Virginia, Session of 1850–51* (Richmond, VA: H. K. Ellyson), 1851.

59. Carmichael, *The Last Generation*, 90.

60. See, e.g., "Our Union," *Jefferson Monument Magazine* 1, no. 4 (January 1850): 121–23; "The Present Crisis," *Jefferson Monument Magazine* 1, no. 5 (February 1850): 146–49 (pleading for Union and urging caution because of the potential costs of disunion); "A Plea for the Union," *University Literary Magazine* 1, no. 7 (October 1857): 289–96.

61. See "The Union," pts. 1–4, *Jefferson Monument Magazine* 1, nos. 3–6 (December 1850–March 1851): 70–76, 106–13, 129–37, 177–85. Quote appears in pt. 1, 76.

62. See, e.g., "Reply to the Rev. Charles Hodge, D.D., 'On the State of the Country,'" *Virginia University Magazine* 5, no. 6 (March 1861): 265–95 (arguing that the Missouri Compromise was unconstitutional and supporting secession).

63. Carmichael, *The Last Generation*, 82.

64. Albert Taylor Bledsoe, *An Essay on Liberty and Slavery* (Philadelphia: J. B. Lippincott, 1856).

65. A Citizen of the South [Charles Shaw], *Is Slavery a Blessing? A Reply to Prof. Bledsoe's Essay on Liberty and Slavery: With Remarks on Slavery as It Is* (Boston: Jewett, 1857).

66. George Frederick Holmes, "Some Observations on a Passage from Aristotle," *Southern Literary Messenger* 16 (1850): 193.

67. George Frederick Holmes, "Uncle Tom's Cabin," *Southern Literary Messenger* 18 (1852): 721.

68. James P. Holcombe, *An Address Delivered before the Society of Alumni, of the University of Virginia, at Its Annual Meeting* (Charlottesville, VA: Macfarlane & Fergusson, 1853).

69. James P. Holcombe, *Sketches of the Political Issues and Controversies of the Revolution: A Discourse Delivered before the Virginia Historical Society, at Their Ninth Annual Meeting, January 17, 1856* (Richmond, VA: The Society, 1856).

70. See Henry St. George Tucker, *Lectures on Constitutional Law, for the Use of the Law Class at the University of Virginia* (Richmond, VA: Shepherd & Colin, 1843); Henry St. George Tucker, *A Few Lectures on Natural Law* (Charlottesville, VA: J. Alexander, 1844).

71. James P. Holcombe, "Is Slavery Consistent with Natural Law?" *Southern Literary Messenger* 27 (1858): 401–21.

72. "Is Slavery a Moral Evil?" *Virginia University Magazine* 5, no. 7 (April 1861): 363–70.

73. "The Utility of Slavery Discussion," *University Literary Magazine* 1, no. 1 (December 1856): 25–30.

74. "Reply to the Rev. Charles Hodge, D.D., 'On the State of the Country'"; "The Unity of Mankind," *Virginia University Magazine* 3, no. 4 (January 1859): 165–71.

75. "The Unity of Mankind."

76. "Government a Divine Institution," *Virginia University Magazine* 3, no. 6 (March 1860): 326–29.

77. "The Unity of Mankind," 170 (portraying slaves as menacing rather than the peaceful citizens depicted by abolitionists).

78. Matthew Fontaine Maury, *Address Delivered before the Literary Societies of the University of Virginia, on the 28th June, 1855* (Richmond, VA: H. K. Ellyson's Steam Press, 1855), 19.

79. Joseph Hodgson, *An Address Delivered before the Jefferson Society of the University of Virginia: At Its Anniversary Celebration, Held in the Public Hall, April 13, 1857* (Richmond, VA: J. D. Hammersley, 1857): 14.

80. Ibid.

81. Ibid., 16.

82. "Another Cane for Mr. Brooks," *Richmond Enquirer,* May 30, 1856, Library of Virginia, Richmond, VA.

83. Preston S. Brooks to J. H. Brooks, May 23, 1856, quoted in Chauncey Samuel Boucher, "South Carolina and the South on the Eve of Secession, 1852 to 1860," *Washington University Studies* 6, no. 2 (April 1919): 115.

84. "Another Cane for Mr. Brooks."

85. "Editor's Table," *Virginia University Magazine* 4, no. 4 (January 1860): 208.

86. Minutebook of the Washington Society, 1859–1868, p. 19.

87. James P. Holcombe, *The Election of a Black Republican President: An Overt Act of Aggression on the Right of Property in Slaves: The South Urged to Adopt Concerted Action for Future Safety* (Richmond, VA: Thomas Whyte, 1860).

88. Alexander Fleet to Benny, October 29, 1860, in *Green Mount: A Virginia Plantation Family during the Civil War: Being the Journal of Benjamin Robert Fleet and Letters of His Family,* ed. Betsy Fleet and John D. P. Fuller (Lexington: University of Kentucky Press, 1962), 38.

89. Quoted in Adam Goodheart, *1861: The Civil War Awakening* (New York: Alfred A. Knopf, 2011), 77.

90. George H. Reese, ed., *Proceedings of the Virginia State Convention of 1861* (Richmond: Virginia State Library, 1965), 76. Holcombe's full speech, one of the most important at the convention, appears on 75–101.

91. Randolph H. McKim, *A Soldier's Recollections: Leaves from the Diary of a Young Confederate* (New York: Longmans, Green, 1910), 1.

92. Journals of the Chairman of the Faculty, 1827–1864, March 16, 1861, http://juel.iath.virginia.edu/resources.

93. Ibid.

7

ANATOMICAL THEATER

Kirt von Daacke

Early on the morning of December 10, 1834, James Oldham, who had been a contractor for the University of Virginia during its construction and now owned a small plantation nearby, heard his dogs barking. He whistled for them, grabbed his gun, and headed out into the brightly moonlit night to see what was causing the commotion. He and two friends headed in the direction of the barking, toward a burial plot on his property where an enslaved person had recently been interred. As he approached the gravesite, he found a group of five men busy digging up the recent burial. Oldham was furious at the trespassing grave robbers. He yelled, "We will come on and blow your brains out!" The grave-robbing party quickly dispersed, with three men running away. Two, however, were caught in the midst of digging up the body, and did not immediately leave. Oldham continued to advance—when he got closer, he yelled: "Go off my land!" One of the grave robbers responded by asking if they could not have a word with Mr. Oldham. Oldham, visibly angry, refused as the two grave robbers stopped digging and prepared to leave. Oldham, then within twenty yards of the remaining two grave robbers, fired his gun at them, striking one in the back, as they fled.[1]

The next day, university student Hudson S. Garland, himself likely one of the grave robbers, met with Albemarle County Justice of the Peace James R. Watson and filed a complaint. That same day, Watson issued a warrant for Oldham's arrest, charging him with "feloniously, voluntarily, maliciously and of purpose shoot[ing] and maim[ing]" university student Archibald F. E. Robertson.[2] Fellow medical student Archibald Cary wrote to Thomas Jefferson's granddaughter Septimia Randolph (then living in Washington, DC) on December 14 about the incident: "Your acquaintance, A.F.E. Robertson (the young man you saw at Davis and thought so handsome), was shot in the back by an old fellow whilst endeavoring to take a dead negro for our anatomical dissections. He is recovering and the old [coot?] will be sent to the Penitentiary."³ On December 16, Robertson himself gave a statement to the court and explained that on the evening that Oldham shot him, he and four others visited Oldham's plantation in "search of a[n] [anatomical] subject."⁴ Upon finding the burial plot, Robertson and the other students began uncovering the grave, attempting to dig it up and retrieve the body.

Several months later, in May 1835, an Albemarle Grand Jury decided not to indict Oldham, so he was ultimately not prosecuted for shooting the trespassing student.⁵ Another student, Charles Ellis, wrote in his diary that same day after attending the grand jury's impaneling at the Charlottesville Courthouse. Ellis was shocked by the decision not to indict Oldham and sought to explain why there would be no trial. He wrote that "there is so much prejudice against the Students, among the county people, and citizens of Charlottesville that there would have been some disturbance between the Students and them if the trial had have gone against Oldham." It is telling that Ellis saw the local population as "ignorant countrymen" who could not understand that the grave-robbing students were acting as modern, scientifically minded disciples of medical inquiry. He said the locals "imagine us cannibals, or something worse, who can take up the bodies of dead persons, and cut them to pieces; thus it is that Superstition ever combats against Learning, and Science."⁶ Ellis's characterization of locals as "ignorant countrymen" fit perfectly with emerging medical views at the time: "Even as Americans took elaborate pains to defend the bodies of their dead, physicians sought to discredit the resistance. In the nineteenth century, the medical profession typically dismissed opposition to dissection as the relic of a bygone primitive age when the 'prevalent [was] that the touch of a dead body communicated a moral pollution.'"⁷

To appreciate the context of this bizarre incident fully, we need to return to Thomas Jefferson and the founding of the University of Virginia. As early at 1778, Jefferson was aware of the importance of anatomical subjects for scientific investigation and displayed few qualms about how schools or scientists might procure those cadavers. In that year, Jefferson wrote "A Bill for Proportioning Crimes and Punishments." The bill specifically stipulated that "if any person commit Petty treason, or a husband murder his wife, a parent his child, or a child his parent, he shall suffer death by hanging, and his body be delivered to Anatomists to be dissected."⁸

In his 1784 *Notes on the State of Virginia,* Jefferson discussed what he saw as black inferiority: "The first difference which strikes us is that of colour . . . the difference is fixed in nature & is real . . . & is this difference of no importance? Is it not the foundation of a greater or less share of beauty between the two races?" As he continued, he even compared a supposed desire of great apes to mate with black women to African Americans' mythical desire to mate with whites, terming the problem an interspecies one. He further argued that blacks "secrete less by the kidneys, & more by glands of the skin. . . . Perhaps too a difference of structure in the pulmonary apparatus." For Jefferson, this "difference of race" was one that almost always favored whites and one that was rooted in a form of speciation. Thus, as early as the 1780s, Jefferson articulated a white supremacist understanding of racial difference and racial hierarchy (one where white always ruled over black), and one that was rooted in an understanding of white and black as basically different species. He was speculating on a proto-biologic explanation for racial difference. Jefferson had quite a bit more to say about African Americans: "Blacks are in reason much inferior . . . & in imagination they are dull, tasteless, & anomalous . . . never yet could I find that a black had uttered a thought above the level of plain narration." Jefferson ended this line of thought with a slight equivocation: "The opinion, that they are inferior in the faculties of reason & imagination, must be hazarded with great diffidence." So, Jefferson briefly acknowledged that he might be wrong, but ever dedicated to reason, imagined that racial difference was a suitable subject for scientific investigation. He thought scientists in the future would answer the race question and likely discover a biologic basis for white superiority. Jefferson even had an idea about how they would investigate: racial difference and black inferiority "requires many observations, even where the subject may be submitted to the Anatomical knife."[9] That very research, submitted to the anatomist's knife, would begin at the University of Virginia.

Decades after writing *Notes,* at that point in time long thinking about how to create in Virginia a university "so broad & liberal & *modern,*" [10] Jefferson corresponded with Dr. John Crawford and discussed disease, natural history, medicine, and scientific investigation. Jefferson was imagining a fully modern university that included the most up-to-date scientific pursuits. He told Crawford that "while Surgery is seated in temple of the exact sciences, medicine has scarcely entered it's threshold." Jefferson would come to see his anticipated public university in Virginia as helping to change that—medicine and medical inquiry could also enter the scientific temple, but only through understanding past "fatal errors . . . recorded in the necrology of man."[11] Thus, clinical study and dissection would augment the university's theoretical focus on medicine and materia medica (the forerunner of pharmacology). Dr. Thomas Cooper, corresponding with Jefferson about the new school in 1818, urged him "to look forward to making your university a medical school. For this purpose, a Hospital will be absolutely necessary; not merely on account of clinical lectures . . . but of subjects for dissection."[12] Unsurprisingly, the professors and doctors who would teach at the university would spend decades dissecting largely black bodies in an effort to prove Jefferson's racial theories.

By 1819, when the state chartered the already under construction University of Virginia, Jefferson expected the institution to offer courses of instruction in the foundational branches of medicine, including anatomy and surgery. His vision for a school of medicine at his newly chartered university dovetailed neatly with an emerging national trend in higher education. Up to 1820, there were only ten medical schools established in the United States since 1768. By 1860, an additional fifty-two would be established, with Jefferson's University of Virginia an early trendsetter (founded in 1819 and opening in 1825).[13]

This was also part of a shift in the focus of medical training, generally away from stressing materia medica and therapeutics and instead toward anatomical dissection of corpses and clinical examination of live patients.[14] Jefferson's university, despite his insistence on theoretical learning, was no different—a professor of anatomy was included as one of the original eight professorships as early as 1824. Later that same year, Francis Walker Gilmer, dispatched to Europe by Jefferson to track down quality professors, wrote back approvingly of Robley Dunglison as a person "of considerable eminence on various medical and anatomical subjects." Largely because the university was not located in an urban area, there were no initial plans prior to 1824 to create an actual hospital with a clinical school of medicine.[15] Jefferson nonetheless saw anatomy as vital, for it "promised to serve as the vehicle whereby medicine . . . could remake itself into a reliable science, via a commitment to empirical investigation. Anatomy was a privileged mediator between mind and body, a middle way. To know anatomy one had to read learned texts *and* get one's hand bloody."[16]

Thus, Jefferson's plans for the university by 1825 included a separate Anatomical Hall where professors would perform cadaver dissections while students watched.[17] Writing to Joseph Carrington Cabell in January 1825, Jefferson argued: "There cannot be a single dissection until a proper theatre is prepared giving an advantageous view of the operation to those within, and effectually excluding observation from without."[18] The building, designed by Jefferson, included a dissection theater with tiered seating, at least one lecture room, and initially, a faculty apartment (figs. 7.1, 7.2, 7.3). Students, as part of their medical training, would afterward perform their own dissections on cadavers and cadaver parts. The plan for medical education privileged anatomical dissection and investigation and was part of Jefferson's emerging plan to create a special southern institution that catered to southern interests, because the North was a place "against us in position and principle."[19] In

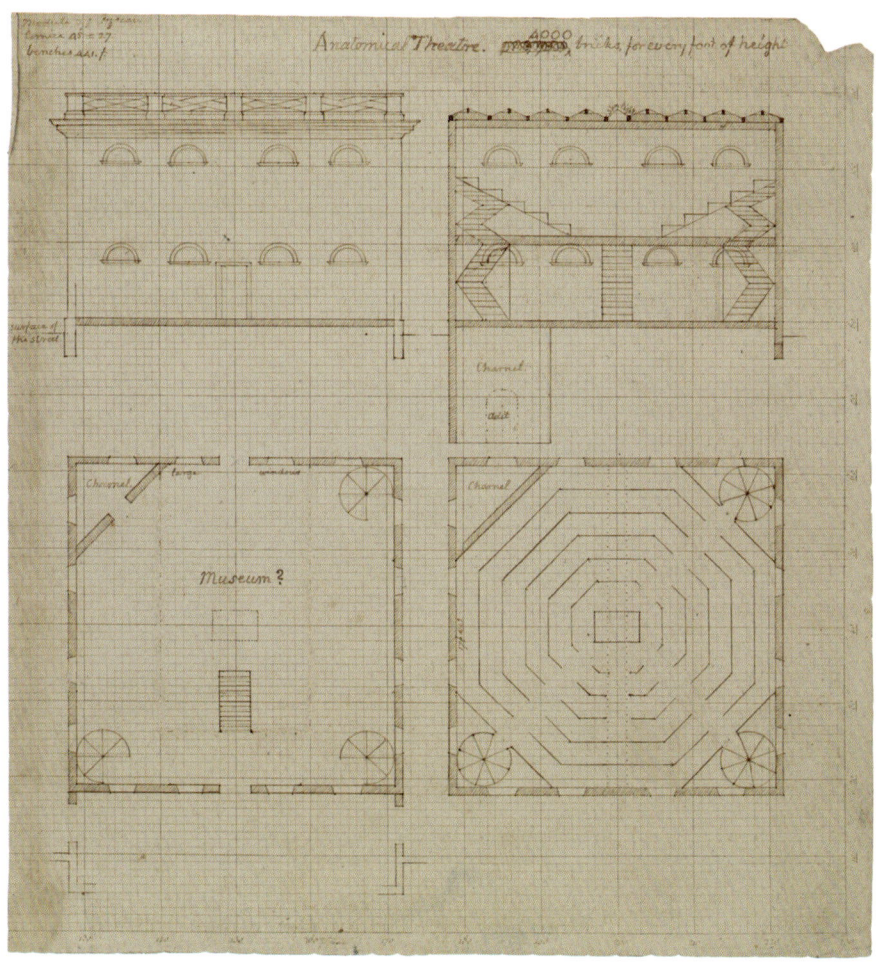

FIG. 7.1. Thomas Jefferson, study for Anatomical Theater, ca. February 1825.

FIG. 7.2. Detail of Anatomical Theater from Edward Sachse, *View of the University of Virginia, Charlottesville and Monticello taken from Lewis Mountain*, 1856.

FIG. 7.3. Anatomical Theater from the JUEL digital reconstruction of the Academical Village.

1827, the school included three separate faculty positions in the department of medicine—professors of medicine, anatomy and surgery, and a demonstrator of anatomy and surgery who would conduct "dissections and demonstrations." The Board of Visitors, anticipating the completion of the Anatomical Hall, set aside an apartment in the building for the demonstrator.[20] The building of a separate Anatomical Hall for dissection, the hiring of Robley Dunglison in 1825 as professor of medicine, the hiring of Thomas Johnson in 1827 as demonstrator of anatomy and surgery, and the 1833 building of a separate dissecting hall for students set the stage for decades of grave-robbing that specifically targeted African American burial sites and for that late-night shooting of student Archibald Robertson in 1834.

In 1827, the university had been open for almost two years and construction on the Anatomical Hall was "so far advanced" that the building was essentially ready to use—it would be open for instructional purposes in September. All that awaited was the July hiring of Thomas Johnson as the first demonstrator of anatomy and surgery (he would be promoted to professor in 1831).[21] By November 1827, the Anatomical Hall was clearly being used for cadaver dissections. In that month, John M. Perry's enslaved woman Prudence was paid by the university for washing linens used in demonstrations. In 1829, at the behest of Thomas Johnson, a student named Miller approached the chairman of the faculty "to know whether the Chairman had any objections to dissections going on in the Anatomical Theatre." Unsurprisingly, the chairman replied that "so far from having an objection . . . [I] strongly encourage it."[22] The race to procure fresh cadavers, driven by the rising popularity of "clinic-based scientific medicine" was officially under way.[23]

The university's records first reference paying for corpses for dissection purposes in a proctor's draft for "expenses for procuring a subject for demonstration, $14.50," in September 1829.[24] In the university's first few years, there was no official school plan or fund for getting anatomical subjects for demonstration—instead it was left to individual professors and medical students themselves to find bodies by robbing graves (what they termed anatomical excursions or anatomical expeditions). Student Henry M. Beatley, charged by the faculty with a breach of the school's uniform law in October 1830, explained that he "had injured his uniform, by an anatomical excursion, and was obliged to send it to the tailor's to be repaired. The same reason forced him to be at lecture, out of uniform, several times."[25] A year later, university faculty approved a leave of absence for six medical students "for the purpose of their going to Prince George County, on an anatomical expedition," nearly one hundred miles away. Historian Philip Alexander Bruce noted that "those picked up were generally the corpses of negro slaves, and in many instances had been snatched away by students under the blanket of darkness."[26]

This was not surprising and fit with a general national trend that had emerged alongside the American adoption of hands-on dissection as a focus of medical education in the late eighteenth century. As one New Yorker commented in 1788, "I rather believe that the only subjects procured for dissection are the productions of Africa or their descendants . . . and if those characters are the only subjects of dissection, surely no person can object."[27] African Americans in nineteenth-century America essentially had no rights any white person was bound to respect—this extreme vulnerability extended beyond life. As one scholar has noted, "The intimate relationship between enslavers, physicians, and human property shows just how commodification—the act of being treated as a commodity—touched every facet of enslaved people's births, lives, and afterlives."[28] Faculty and students alike pursued grave-robbing—not illegal at that time but nonetheless an activity that would come to provoke public outrage—as a way of procuring dissection material. As one scholar has argued, doctors and anatomy students had great "power to deny the social nature of the corpse" and African Americans understood it and "wondered how God would recognize the believer if her body did not appear intact on Judgment Day."[29] Unique to the University of Virginia (and perhaps other southern schools), however, was a focus on whenever possible securing African American bodies for dissection as part of an emerging race science project, one Jefferson had anticipated decades before the university opened its doors to students.

Charles Christian Wertenbaker, an 1853 UVA alumnus and son of the long-time university librarian, wrote in 1897 that "in old times, the University [enslaved] servants were buried on the north side of the cemetery, just outside the wall." Those burials may have fallen prey to faculty or students seeking cadavers. Wertenbaker remembered that at the enslaved burial ground, "many of the bodies were only log of wood or stones, for the fear of having their dead taken up by the medical class (then entirely dependent on their own enterprise for subjects), caused the negroes to inter their dead secretly, and hold the usual ceremonies over the dummy."[30] Wertenbaker's 1897 memories were clearly firsthand ones—in 1859 he and a medical professor had corresponded about getting the bodies of prisoners who had been executed in Charles Town.

By 1832, the ad hoc system for procuring anatomical subjects had proved insufficient to the demands of both students and faculty. The Board of Visitors responded by creating a $100 annual fund for the purpose of procuring subjects. Faculty contacted hospitals and magistrates across the region, paying for corpses in distant locations including Baltimore, Maryland. Students continued local anatomical expeditions, and the Anatomical Hall's dissecting facilities were visited with heavier and heavier use. By 1833, the same year that a separate student dissecting hall opened (dubbed "Stiff" Hall by students), an anatomical subject was found in the university ice pond (visible on the Pratt Plan, fig. 2.26 on page 64) apparently sunk there by students for the purpose of bleaching. The professor of anatomy and surgery by that time had appropriated "the small brick building in the Valley below the Theatre, as a boiling house and receptacle for subjects immediately after dissection," and people regularly filed complaints about the "extremely offensive" odors emanating from the Anatomical Hall (fig. 7.4).[31] Even that annual $100 appro-

FIG. 7.4. A 1910 photograph of the Anatomical Laboratory (wryly called "Stiff" Hall by the students) built behind the theater to provide more laboratory space for the preservation, dissection, and disposal of anatomical subjects.

priation proved insufficient to meet the demands of faculty and students for more bodies. In August 1837, the Board of Visitors levied a five-dollar dissecting fee on each student taking anatomy and surgery courses. With thirty-two students enrolled that year, this amounted to an additional $160–$260 or more yearly to pay for anatomical subjects.[32]

The birth and evolution of medical training at the University of Virginia had a profound impact upon enslaved families and perpetuated a form of violence against the bodies of the enslaved. This violence was not confined to enslaved people who lived near the university: enslaved people—Prudence, Simpson, Lucy, Jack, Jack Wilson, James Smith, Lewis, a "coloured man," other unnamed "servants," and many more—cleaned the Anatomical Hall, washed the bloody surgical linens, cleaned the waste pit of human remains, kept the building heated in cold weather, prepared cadavers for dissection, cleaned up after dissection demonstrations, and boiled down whatever was left after dissections. The work was at times highly technical. In 1890, a student wrote that the Anatomical Hall attendant "received the subjects or 'stiffs' as they are professionally termed, washes them, inserts the embalming fluid into the blood vessels and otherwise prepares them for use in the hall. The Doctor has the source of a large revenue in the bones of the 'stiffs' which [the anatomical hall attendant] boils free of all flesh" so the doctor can sell the bony remains to students.[33] The medical school had two sessions each academic year. By 1837, it hoped to get four or five cadavers from Richmond, Baltimore, Norfolk, or Alexandria weekly during both sessions just for professorial demonstrations. The students as well continued to go out on their own anatomical expeditions. The corpses were almost certainly overwhelmingly African American. This followed a trend seen at other southern schools. Eighty percent of the cadavers dissected at Kentucky's Transylvania University in the 1830s and 1840s were African American. The percentage was similar at the Medical College of Georgia. That nineteenth-century medical training focus on dissection, however, appears at the University of Virginia to have implicitly focused on developing a race science that proved white superiority and black difference. It also meant that the search for cadavers would have an impact that stretched well beyond the university community and fell upon enslaved people across an entire region.[34]

Enslaved African Americans at the university and elsewhere were typical nineteenth-century Americans who cared deeply about how loved ones were handled and interred after death and who also understood that to touch the dead was to be poisoned by moral pollution. African American neighborhoods in Virginia were often quite aware of the prevalence of grave-robbing and went to great lengths to hinder grave robbers' efforts. Some families built elaborate "sculptures" on top of burials in hopes of deterring a grave robber. The enslaved community at the university, according to a handful of white recollections, clearly saw the Anatomical Hall attendant—Lewis—as polluted in powerful ways. Lewis, who became known at the university as "Anatomical Lewis" for his work, was reported to be "an object of fear to the negroes," and "from the nature of his avocations was regarded by the children very much an ogre."[35] He reportedly lived alone in the garden space behind Pavilion VII, what was then known as the wood yard. The work in the Anatomical Hall shaped the lives of the enslaved at the university in powerful ways.

Thus, that moonlit night when James Oldham found five students digging up a recently buried enslaved African American represents just one vivid episode in a decades-long expansion of medical training at the University of Virginia. Oldham's response, outrage at the desecration of a burial plot, was typical of white Virginians when confronted by this macabre medical practice. By late 1834, there were nearly three dozen students taking anatomy and those numbers would continue to grow over the next quarter century. Medical faculty also expanded from one professor in 1825, to two in 1827, and three in 1845. James L. Cabell's hiring in 1837 as the professor of anatomy and surgery would inaugurate decades of medical school growth. Cabell himself was a product of the university's emerging race science–based medical education, having graduated in 1833 with a master of arts degree that included graduating at the top of his anatomy class with Dr. Johnson.[36] Cabell would complete his MD a year later at the University of Maryland, where his professor was Dr. Robley Dunglison, the first professor of anatomy and surgery at UVA (and someone Cabell had likely studied with while at UVA).

Cabell's return to the University of Virginia in 1837 inaugurated decades of more intense focus on anatomy, surgery, and dissection. Cabell's expansions and reorganizations by 1861 had created five separate medical professorships as well as a number of subordinate faculty demonstrator positions. All that growth meant more demand for anatomical subjects and thus more pressure on African American burial grounds, which were the preferred target for anatomical expeditions by students, faculty, and professional grave robbers. As Harriet Martineau observed in 1838, "The bodies of coloured people exclusively are taken for dissection 'because whites do not like it, and the coloured people cannot resist.'"[37] For both free and enslaved African Americans in Virginia, "anatomical dissection meant even more: it was an extension of slavery into eternity, because it represented a profound level of white control over their bodies, illustrating that they were not free even in death."[38] Cabell would come to dispute Harvard University professor Louis Agassiz's anti-evolutionary and polygenist understanding of race, humanity, and hierarchy. Instead, Cabell would argue for monogenesis, the "specific unity and common origins of all varieties of man," followed by separate evolutionary development resulting in contemporary white European superiority.[39] His conclusions undoubtedly grew out of his medical training at both UVA and Maryland, his reshaping of medical pedagogy at the university, and his own dissections of African American bodies.

The practice of grave-robbing and the specific targeting of African American graves were undoubtedly routine at the school. UVA student Philip Claiborne Gooch on October 11, 1844, referenced the practice when he wrote that while on his way to the anatomy lecture (by Professor James Lawrence Cabell), he "smelled something *queer*—the first reflection suggested a body for dissection. . . . I saw something covered with a black cloth & my nose told me what before Dr. Cabell did." The bodies often arrived in active decay, so teaching schedules, as they did that day, shifted to accommodate arrivals of "a couple of subjects which arrived last night unexpectedly & we had to stop acting on the bones & c to go immediately into the subject." Cabell divided the class into dissection companies and then drew lots for the subjects, but Gooch indicated "my class did not get it, the other was so old that it cd [could] not be used." Gooch also remarked on just how common the grave-robbing must have been and indicated that the one good body that day was "an old negro woman who came from Richmond."[40]

Gooch's memories also suggest that student grave-robbing was in no way secretive. Just four days after the classroom dissection of that woman, Gooch recollected that "2 fellows called me, (who were Garnett & Lewis). . . they told me that McKenney had informed them of a good piece of 'fresh meat' . . . a man [who had] fell ill in the road and died drunk." The students then borrowed a local merchant's (Clement McKennie's) cart and enslaved driver, went to the coroner's house, snuck in, and stole the body. Gooch noted that "we took him out and cut stick for the cart . . . he was very heavy (170 lbs I guess) but we shot slapped him in cart . . . we all take big rock and place them in well [in the now empty coffin] and fix on the lid." The students, after stealing the body, weighted down the coffin so no one would notice the body's absence. When Gooch and the other students returned to UVA with the stolen corpse, Professor Howard "impressed us of the *very great* importance of *never* revealing the circumstances" of how they stole the body lest they damage the coroner's reputation.[41]

"Anatomical Lewis," the enslaved man rented yearly from George W. Spooner who was forced to work as the Anatomical Hall attendant, was likely part of Gooch's anatomical expedition and would have prepared the stolen body for dissection. Gooch remembered that the next day, he "came to the college & went to see our fresh meat which [Anatomical] Lewis had striped—went to Dr. Cabell's lecture—then saw him surprised and delighted him by telling him our adventure." Just about a week later, Gooch noted that he "dissected a little—6 or 8 of us tried all morning to get out the viscera but nobody knew how—Dr. Cabell laughed heartily when he heard that we asked *Lewis* (the old negro) to aid us."[42] Gooch's diary entries are dotted with references to grave-robbing and dissection, the memories shared as casually as were those of sleeping, eating, and visiting friends. To white medical students and professors, the practice was completely unremarkable. Only a couple days after that conversation with Professor Cabell, Gooch "was informed by Lewis that the Sick negro at Verulam was to be buried this morning and also one at Dr. Woods, so we made arrangements to go out." Once again, the desired corpses were of people of color. That same night, the students went out to attempt to dig up the bodies, but were deterred by the sound of men's voices as they approached the grave.[43]

In the 1840s, the University of Virginia found itself in competition with two other medical schools—Winchester Medical College and Hampden-Sydney College's Medical School in Richmond (which would later become the Medical College of Virginia)—all in need of anatomical subjects. This competition drove up prices for subjects from twelve to fifteen dollars in the early 1830s to twenty dollars or more at times a decade later. It also specifically pitted UVA against Hampden-Sydney's medical school in Richmond in the race for subjects because Richmond and nearby Petersburg had large urban black populations and several African American burial grounds that professional grave robbers known as resurrectionists could plunder (fig. 7.5). Hampden-Sydney promoted its school in Richmond, reminding anyone who would listen that "from the peculiarity of our institutions [white rule and slavery], materials [anatomical subjects] can be obtained in abundance,

Fig. 7.5. Nineteenth-century print of grave robbers.

and we believe are not surpassed if equaled by any city in our country."[44] In 1845, the University of Virginia hired John Staige Davis as a demonstrator of anatomy. Davis, an 1841 graduate of Cabell's medical program at UVA and later a doctor in Winchester, had personal connections to the other medical schools.[45]

The Virginia General Assembly in 1848, almost certainly responding to public outcry, legislated against "violation of the sepulture," decreeing that "any free person who shall without authority wilfully disinter, remove or convey away a human body, or the remains thereof, shall be punished by confinement in the jail not more than twelve months and by fine not exceeding five hundred dollars."[46] The law, passed largely in response to the state's medical schools' poorly concealed and endless pursuit of bodies, was merely a parchment barrier to continuing dissection at medical schools. It is doubtful that enforcement was robust statewide and was nearly nonexistent when African American burial grounds were the targets of resurrectionists. That fact, however, did not mean that most Virginians accepted the practice when confronted directly with it.

By 1849, Professor Davis was working closely with former classmates and former students then working at other medical schools in Virginia, hoping to create at least a multiyear contract with a resurrectionist promising a steady supply of cadavers, or even a sharing agreement among two or more schools. These plans arose in response to the 1848 outlawing of grave-robbing. In August 1849, Richmond doctor Howell Lewis Thomas, an 1848 graduate in Anatomy & Surgery from UVA, wrote to his former professor Davis about the "criminal" grave-robbing resurrectionists in Richmond, the difficulties of finding "reliable material," and ironing out something close to a contract: "it would be better if you would state how many subjects you would want at a time, and at what intervals, for though a contract of this sort could not be followed utterally, owning to *indicents* of the trade."[47]

Thomas wrote again the following week regarding a conversation with a white resurrectionist named Charles J. Miller, "an old trafficker" and teamster whose brother-in-law was fellow Richmond resurrectionist John Vest. According to Thomas, Miller had "agreed to let [Davis] enjoy a monopoly of the trade . . . and to have nothing to do with the Richmond College, but claims Preemptorily $25 apiece . . . good fresh subjects well packed, delivered at the Richmond Depot . . . or at the University by his own conveyance" for thirty dollars. That represented a significant increase in price from the corpses earlier procured for the university by Bob Saunders, a white resurrectionist in Richmond.[48] Thomas explained that the Hampden-Sydney medical faculty had "sworn that no [anatomical subject] shall be carried from Richmond this winter."[49] This push for fresh corpses clearly targeted African Americans. Thomas wrote to Davis in November 1849, explaining that the recent lack of suitable subjects was because "the subjects are all in incipient putrefaction when buried" thanks to some very warm weather and because there had been a recent paucity in "colored burial[s]." Thomas, however, was listening and searching for potential cadavers. He told Davis that "I heard the darkies talking of a funeral tomorrow; if there be anything to it, I will watch and endeavor to secure the commodity for you."[50] Faculty communications such as these confirm that the University of Virginia, along with other southern medical colleges, assumed that the illicit traffic in corpses would target African American burial grounds. Competition for black bodies was intense indeed.

By 1850, the university's appetite for anatomical subjects had not diminished and in fact continued to grow, but Professor Davis's efforts to work out a deal with Hampden-Sydney faculty appeared to be bearing fruit. On July 1, 1850, Hampden-Sydney demonstrator of anatomy Arthur E. Peticolas wrote to Davis acknowledging the receipt of a check for one hundred dollars for subjects.[51] Although the university had begun to work with Hampden-Sydney in Richmond to share the corpses resurrectionists robbed from graveyards and delivered to them, Davis continued to pursue corpses in other locales independently. In September 1850, Lewis W. Minor, then a doctor in the U.S. Navy serving on the U.S.S. *Pennsylvania* stationed in Portsmouth, Virginia, wrote to Davis shortly after Davis had returned from a visit with Lewis in Norfolk. Minor "held a conference with Thomas White, the body snatcher . . . who agreed to furnish you in liquor or oil barrels, well secured," a variety of anatomical subjects ranging in price from four dollars for a child under eight years old to fifteen dollars for a mother and infant. Later that month, Davis had Minor write up an agreement with Thomas White of Norfolk and by early October the university, with a check from the university account with the Farmer's Bank of Virginia signed by the proctor, deposited one hundred dollars with Minor to pay White for cadavers as they were delivered.[52]

The system was rather elaborate—Davis and the university sent money to Minor, who paid White to find subjects, pack them in bran in barrels, and ship them via steamboat to a man named J. W. Brockenbrough in Richmond, who would then arrange for the cadavers to be shipped to the university via freight train to "McIntire Charlottesville" (fig. 7.6). The new agreement produced two subjects—a women of about thirty-five years and a child of about four—by early November. Minor paid White sixteen dollars. Davis also made regular arrangements with a shipping company regarding delivering the barrels to J. W. Brockenbrough in Richmond. The complicated system was not without its problems. On November 15, 1850, Lewis W. Minor wrote to Davis regarding complications with the shipping plan. Apparently, a barrel containing a corpse did not quite make it to the university and was discovered by some unassuming train station agent, who opened the barrel in hopes of figuring out where it was to go. His macabre discovery apparently received

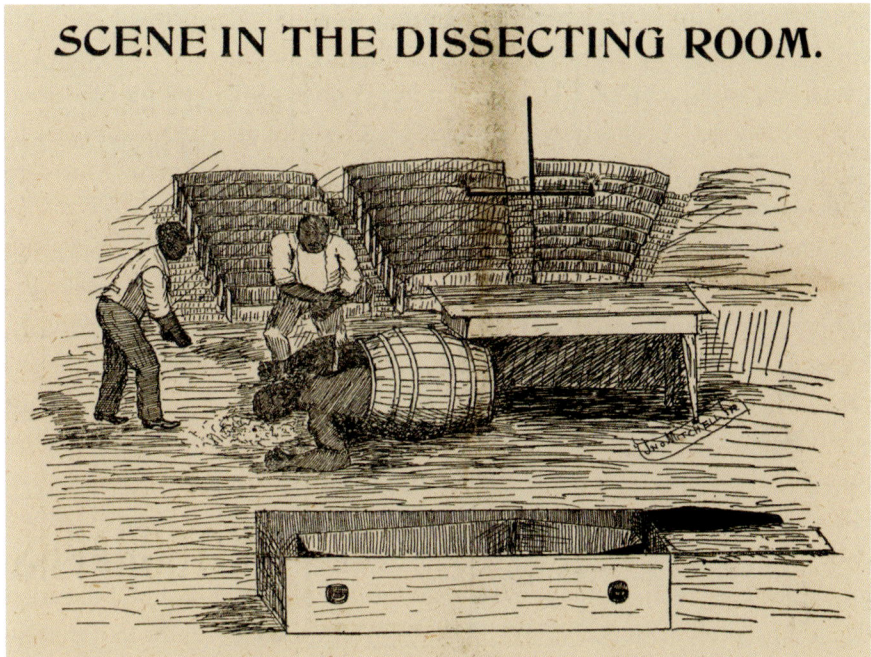

FIG. 7.6. "Scene in the Dissecting Room," *Richmond Dispatch*, August 1, 1896. The illustration shows a body spilling out of a barrel after shipping to a dissecting room at the Medical College of Virginia.

fevered news coverage. Minor reported: "The papers this morning state that *the barrel* was addressed to 'McIntire Charlottesville' and was 'large enough to contain your favorite article of trade, and addressed as above, will in future be closely scrutinized.'" Minor further suggested that in the future steps be taken to mask what was in the barrel, who sent it, and who was supposed to receive it.[53]

By the end of the month, Davis began to amend plans so that the shipping of the bodies would be more discreet. He wrote to Thomas White, instructing him no longer to address barrels to J. W. Brockenbrough in Richmond and instead address them to "McIntire Charlottesville." Apparently, Brockenbrough would be on the watch for barrels addressed that way. Despite those difficulties, the bodies kept coming. White shipped two adults and two children in late November—the charge was thirty-two dollars. Lewis W. Minor, trying his best to manage the complicated shipping arrangement from his end in Portsmouth, asked Davis to send him "a statement of the dates at which you have received each barrel and its contents—whether it contained adults, their sex; or children, their age & sex." Minor also ordered White to "in the future mark on the barrels the date of burial & of shipment," one date on one end of the barrel, the other date on the other end.[54]

Minor and Davis continued to correspond almost weekly, discussing repeatedly the possible locations of bodies suitable for anatomical dissection in great detail. Davis was working on multiple fronts simultaneously, engaging resurrectionists to grave-rob in Richmond, Norfolk, and Alexandria. On November 30, 1850, Minor wrote to Davis regarding a "prime subject [at Woodville, the Ivy, Virginia, depot] to be buried tomorrow, who died the day before yesterday of mania, and is, I understand, perfectly emaciated. It is a coloured woman." He also mentioned "a newborn child found dead at a door in N[orfolk] some two days since which I was very anxious to send you for exhibiting foetal circulation, but cannot do so, as it would be too much decomposed by Friday next." At that time, Thomas White indicated that he could average twelve subjects a month.[55]

Richmond, however, remained the best place to procure anatomical subjects, as it had a large African American population, many cemeteries, was linked to Charlottesville via rail, and was the closest urban area to the university. University Professor of Comparative Anatomy, Physiology, and Surgery James L. Cabell by 1851 cautioned Davis about the likelihood of ironing out an agreement with Hampden-Sydney. Cabell reminded Davis that he "had for a series of years . . . extreme difficulty . . . in processing a very moderate supply [of anatomical subjects] for a class of only forty or fifty students at the enormous price of thirty dollars a barrel."[56] Davis continued to work on a sharing agreement with Hampden-Sydney College's medical school and in July 1851 finally succeeded. In that month, Davis and Dr. Chapman Johnson of Hampden-Sydney came to terms. Davis and UVA would "no longer employ a Resurrectionist in Richmond, but that all of the Subjects in the City afforded shall be taken to the [Hampden-Sydney] College, where any that were unsuitable for dissection should be rejected, and of the remainder the College should retain two-thirds (⅔) & send me the residue."[57] Professor Cabell consented and instructed Davis that "acceptance . . . does not preclude any attempt on our part to get an additional supply, if necessary, from

Norfolk, [and elsewhere] but it does forbid any competition in the Richmond market."[58]

Although both universities worked to move illegally obtained cadavers as discreetly as possible, the business was not entirely secret. Professor Davis worked directly with the railroads to set up transport agreements. Davis also worked out an arrangement whereby anatomical subjects packed in barrels in Richmond would be sent to Charlottesville via the Virginia Central Railroad on freight trains or in a separate freight car attached to a passenger train. This was because the railroad "concluded that it would not be proper to take subjects for dissection in the baggage car of a passenger train."[59] The railroad scheduled regular freight runs between Richmond and the university, with trains running through Charlottesville at least twice a week. For the medical school, this meant that they "would always be able to get subjects for dissection without much delay."[60]

Railroad President E. F. Fontaine knew that the university was transporting stolen corpses, so he required that Davis ensure an "agent" of the university "shall always in person apprise the Depot agent what the article is" as a way to avoid further public outrage.[61] And public scrutiny was a real concern. One scholar has argued that "from the late-eighteenth century to the late-nineteenth century, medical grave robbery was a common occurrence in America, and the fear of body snatching and consequent anatomical dissection was widespread in any area within reach of anatomists or their agents."[62]

In January 1852, Hampden-Sydney anatomy professor Arthur E. Peticolas wrote to Davis predicting "much difficulty . . . in procuring material from" Richmond for the remainder of the spring session because "soon after the Christmas vacation the resurrectionist [Gennet] was arrested and brought before the Mayor." Peticolas continued, explaining that the arrests had "directed public attention to the *guarding* of the pauper and negro burial places, and as a consequence, our man [another resurrectionist], has since, found but little opportunity for the exercise of his talent."[63] According to House of Delegates records, Gennet, a white resident of Richmond, "was tried . . . for having on the night of the first of January 1852, assisted in disinterring a dead (colored) body," found guilty and "sentenced to pay a fine of five dollars, and to imprisonment in the jail three months."[64] Despite the momentary public uproar about grave-robbing in Richmond, Gennet's conviction was overturned when he was pardoned a month later. Governor

Joseph Johnson, in pardoning Gennet in March, described him as "a very poor and *ignorant* man, with a wife and children . . . [who had lost] one of his arms by amputation." He would quickly return to work as a resurrectionist.[65]

Notwithstanding the numerous resurrectionists available for hire by universities seeking anatomical subjects, schools often struggled to keep one in their employ and routinely sought more cadavers than they were supplied with. In 1856, Hampden-Sydney anatomy professor Arthur E. Peticolas wrote to Professor Davis at UVA, explaining that for two months, their resurrectionist had vanished, refusing to continue grave-robbing. Peticolas, frustrated by the dearth of anatomical subjects, "was forced to play resurrectionist" himself, and, much like students at both schools, go grave-robbing in the evening.[66] At the University of Virginia, the body-sharing agreement with Hampden-Sydney, contracts with resurrectionists in Norfolk and Alexandria, and also routine local student anatomical excursions still did not bring the medical school the large and regular supply of corpses they demanded.

By the late 1850s, if not earlier, the medical school also targeted the criminal justice system, chasing bodies of the executed statewide. In 1856, Prince William County slaveowner George E. Green was murdered by those he enslaved. They were charged with insurrection, tried, convicted, and sentenced to death, with the execution scheduled to take place in Brentsville, Virginia, on January 18, 1857.[67] Four days before the scheduled execution, someone calling himself "T. R. Roberts," whose letter implies he may have been (or was pretending to be) a medical student, wrote to Governor Henry A. Wise as a representative of the University of Virginia's medical school. No one by that name or initials ever appears in university records as a student or faculty in that era, so "T. R. Roberts" may in fact be a pseudonym. Regardless, someone from the university, possibly a student, wrote the governor, reminding Mr. Wise that "to study Anatomy without subjects for demonstration is as fruitless as Geometry without diagrams. . . . There has been an unusual dearth of medical subjects this session both here & in Richmond." "Mr. Roberts" also inquired whether or not the governor might give the university "an order for the bodies of some negroes who will be hung on the 18th prox. in Pr. Wm. County Va." Roberts continued, assuring Mr. Wise that he had "the hearty cooperation of our whole class . . . if we obtain your permission the bodies will be brought either by a committee of Medical Students or some one whom we can trust."[68]

It appears that Mr. Roberts's plea had no effect—the students were not successful in securing the bodies of those executed. Professor Davis also sought out the bodies of slaves executed in Prince William County. On March 5, 1857, Dr. T. C. Brown of Alexandria wrote back to Davis regarding Brown's efforts with resurrectionists in Alexandria. They had sent seven anatomical subjects from Alexandria to the Gordonsville Depot for UVA. Brown also commented, "I thought those negroes at Brentsville were to be executed the last day of Feby & by mistake failed to make the effort to get them." This would not be the last time that the university, voracious for cadavers suitable for dissection, sought out the bodies of executed African Americans.[69] In fall 1859, as the trials of those involved in John Brown's raid on Harpers Ferry ended and those convicted headed to the gallows in Charles Town, Virginia, Davis and Cabell again sought the bodies of those executed. The first three people to hang were runaway enslaved man Shields Green, free man of color John A. Copeland, and a young white man. On December 8, 1859, Davis wrote to Charles Christian Wertenbaker (an 1853 alumnus of UVA) in Charles Town regarding "the convicts awaiting execution & to the chance of procuring one or more of their bodies for dissection in my department." The university would be unsuccessful, as nearby Winchester Medical College managed to get two of the bodies first (the white man's body was not sent for dissection—he was properly buried—yet more evidence that black bodies were preferred).[70]

Professor Davis continued to work with doctors in Richmond, Norfolk, and Alexandria regarding hiring resurrectionists and having cadavers shipped back to Charlottesville. The one hundred dollars appropriated by the Board of Visitors for anatomical subjects back in 1832 had long since proven to be insufficient to meet the demands of both faculty and students for dissection materials. By 1837, with the addition of the dissecting fees, the university set aside at least $260 annually for cadavers. By the 1850s, extant correspondence between university professors and doctors in Richmond, Alexandria, and Portsmouth/Norfolk indicate that much more money may have been allocated to procuring anatomical subjects. For example, in 1850, Professor Davis sent at least $100 to Richmond and $100 to Tidewater. In 1856, he sent at least $226 to Richmond alone. In 1857, $150 was directed to resurrectionists in Alexandria. In 1859, a stunning $450 was sent to Richmond for cadavers.[71] With cadaver prices fluctuating month to month and running the gamut from four dollars to thirty dollars, it is hard to estimate just how many stolen bodies the university paid for, but most often the price hovered between twelve and twenty dollars per adult body.

By 1837, the university hoped to get four or five a week, which over the course of five or six months (the fall and spring sessions) could have amounted to as many as one hundred bodies. By 1850, resurrectionist Thomas White in Norfolk was promising twelve subjects monthly—if he fulfilled the promise, sixty or more bodies would have come from that city alone during the academic year. This number by the 1850s may have been realized at the university. Between November 19, 1858, and January 13, 1859, Dr. Davis received a total of thirteen subjects from Richmond alone. In February 1860, Davis told Arthur E. Peticolas that the university had received another body the day before, making it a total of twenty-two received so far that session. Davis indicated they would need five more before the session ended in March.[72] That number, twenty-seven subjects per session or fifty-four per year, would have included only the bodies paid for by university funds. Medical students, following in Archibald Robertson's footsteps, continued to independently grave-rob locally on their own.

This race to find bodies whenever and wherever they were recently interred clearly had a profound effect on African American communities across the state. Before 1865, at any one point in time, there were as many as five different medical schools in the state who were actively pursuing bodies by scouting local burials and using professional grave robbers in Richmond, Petersburg, Norfolk, and Alexandria. The demand from those schools alone meant that hundreds of recently buried African Americans in Virginia each year faced a real threat of being stolen from the ground under cover of night and delivered to one of those schools. There is even some evidence that the grave-robbing for anatomical subjects business was so brisk at that time that resurrectionists may have "regularly shipped the bodies of southern blacks to northern medical schools."[73] That reality surely created a palpable fear for both enslaved families and the families of free people of color. Winchester Medical College student Robert Christies bragged about "his midnight raids on the graves of his black neighbors" and remembered the palpable fear local African Americans had about grave-robbing doctors.[74] Jim Burrell, the African American janitor at Jefferson Medical College in Philadelphia, reflecting on his work there, stated "it makes me feel very bad when I think of the way the graves of my race have been desecrated."[75]

The grisly business of cadaver procurement continued largely unabated after the Civil War started. In November 1861, Professor Davis wrote to Dr. Isaiah White, stating that he "would like to purchase several dead bodies for practice in Operative Surgery." Davis again requested "another subject" in February 1862. The demand for anatomical subjects may have declined briefly in 1863 and 1864 as the Civil War reduced the university to about fifty students in total (most of them wounded Confederate soldiers) and eventually turned Charlottesville and the university into a series of crude hospitals tending to Confederate wounded. The end of hostilities in 1865, however, brought a quick return of demand for cadavers. In December 1865, a doctor in Richmond wrote to Professor Davis he had just sent "per National Express two subjects and shipped two" other bodies a couple days earlier. Davis received a similar note in January 1866 regarding the shipment of two subjects. It would continue in this fashion for another several decades.

Jefferson's interest in scientifically proving white supremacy and black difference, James Lawrence Cabell's similar desires and the expansion of race science–based medical training at the university, and decades of black cadaver dissections set the stage for the rise of eugenics at the school in the early twentieth century. Dr. Paul Barringer, who earned his MD from Cabell's program in 1877, would return to UVA in 1889 and in 1913 directed the founding of the first university hospital. UVA for decades afterward would be a center of eugenics research. Those later developments, beyond the scope of this chapter, nonetheless had their genesis in both Jefferson's ideas and in medical and scientific education at the University of Virginia from 1825 to 1865. Even the end of slavery did not divert the university's focus on medical pedagogies supporting white supremacy through dissection of black bodies.[76]

NOTES

1. "John F. Peebles' Witness Statement," December 16, 1834, Albemarle County Criminal Cases, Box 21, Ref. 1594, Microfilm Reel 260, Library of Virginia, Richmond, VA.

2. "Warrant for Arrest of James Oldham," December 11, 1834, Albemarle County Criminal Cases, Box 21, Ref. 1594, Microfilm Reel 260, Library of Virginia, Richmond, VA.

3. Archibald Cary to Septimia Randolph, December 15, 1834, Randolph-Meikleham Family Papers, 1792–1882, Albert and Shirley Small Special Collections Library, University of Virginia.

4. "Archibald F. E. Robertson's Witness Statement," December 16, 1834, Albemarle County Criminal Cases, Box 21, Ref. 1594. Microfilm Reel 260, Library of Virginia, Richmond, VA.

5. *Albemarle County Law Order Book 1831–1837—May Term 1835,* p. 271, Albemarle County Court Clerk Records Room, Charlottesville, VA.

6. Ronald B. Head, ed., "The Student Diary of Charles Ellis Jr., March 10–June 25, 1835," *Magazine of Albemarle County History* 35–36 (1977–1978): 94.

7. Michael Sappol, *A Traffic of Dead Bodies: Anatomy and Embodied Social Identity in Nineteenth-Century America* (Princeton, NJ: Princeton University Press, 2002), 14.

8. Thomas Jefferson, "A Bill for Proportioning Crimes and Punishments," in *The Founders' Constitution,* vol. 5, Amendment VIII, Document 10, http://press-pubs.uchicago.edu/founders/documents/amendVIIIs10.html, accessed May 25, 2017. According to one account, the bill failed to pass by a single vote. See Newell Martin, ed., *Johns Hopkins University Studies from the Biological Laboratory*, vol. 2 (Baltimore: Johns Hopkins University, 1883), 83.

9. Thomas Jefferson, *Notes on the State of Virginia,* Query XIV, http://web.archive.org/web/20080914030942/http://etext.lib.virginia.edu:80/toc/modeng/public/JefVirg.html

10. Thomas Jefferson to Joseph Priestley, January 18, 1800, https://founders.archives.gov/about/Jefferson.

11. Thomas Jefferson to John Crawford, January 2, 1812, https://founders.archives.gov/about/Jefferson.

12. Thomas Cooper to Thomas Jefferson, April 19, 1818, *The Papers of Thomas Jefferson, Retirement Series* vol. 12, *1 September 1817 to 21 April 1818*, ed. J. Jefferson Looney (Princeton, NJ: Princeton University Press, 2014), 647–48.

13. James O. Breeden, "Body Snatchers and Anatomy Professors: Medical Education in Nineteenth-Century Virginia," *Virginia Magazine of History and Biography* 93, no. 3 (July 1975): 325.

14. Wyndham B. Blanton, *Medicine in Virginia in the Nineteenth Century* (Richmond, VA: Garrett & Massie, 1933), 12.

15. John S. Patton, *Jefferson, Cabell, and the University of Virginia* (New York: Neale Publishing, 1906), 100–101. See also Philip Alexander Bruce, *History of the University of Virginia, 1819–1919: The Lengthened Shadow of One Man,* 5 vols. (New York: Macmillan, 1920), 2: 107 for Jefferson's musings about how Norfolk, Virginia, might be a perfectly suitable location for an anticipated University of Virginia medical school because the "promiscuous and vagabond population of a seaport would furnish a plenitude of anatomical subjects for dissection."

16. Quoted in Michael Sappol, *A Traffic of Dead Bodies: Anatomy and Embodied Social Identity in Nineteenth-Century America* (Princeton, NJ: Princeton University Press, 2002), 54.

17. Board of Visitors Minutes, 1817–2007, March 4, 1825, http://juel.iath.virginia.edu/resources (hereafter cited as Board of Visitors Minutes).

18. Thomas Jefferson to Joseph Carrington Cabell, January 11, 1825, https://founders.archives.gov/about/Jefferson.

19. Thomas Jefferson to James Breckenridge, February 15, 1821, https://founders.archives.gov/about/Jefferson.

20. Board of Visitors Minutes, July 10, 1827, http://juel.iath.virginia.edu/resources.

21. Board of Visitors Minutes, October 2, 1826, and July 10, 1827, http://juel.iath.virginia.edu/resources.

22. Papers of the Proctor, Box 19, Bills and Accounts, November 24, 1827, and September 16, 1829, Albert and Shirley Small Special Collections Library, University of Virginia (hereafter as Proctor's Papers); Journals of the Chairman of the Faculty, 1827–1864, April 1, 1829, http://juel.iath.virginia.edu/resources (hereafter cited as Chairman's Journals).

23. Harriet A. Washington, *Medical Apartheid: The Dark History of Medical Experimentation on Black Americans from Colonial Times to the Present* (New York: Anchor Books, 2006), 123.

24. Proctor's Papers, Box 19, January–June 1829, Bills and Accounts, September 16, 1829.

25. Chairman's Journals, October 18, 1830, http://juel.iath.virginia.edu/resources.

26. Bruce, *History of the University,* 1: 110–11.

27. Quoted in Steven Robert Wilf, "Anatomy and Punishment in Late Eighteenth-Century New York," *Journal of Social History* 22, no. 3 (Spring 1989): 511.

28. Daina Ramey Berry, *The Price for Their Pound of Flesh: The Value of the Enslaved from Womb to Grave, in the Building of a Nation* (Boston: Beacon Press, 2017), 2.

29. Franny Nudelman, *John Brown's Body: Slavery, Violence, and the Culture of War* (Chapel Hill: University of North Carolina Press, 2004), 41.

30. Charles Christian Wertenbaker, "Letter in Response to Query by Professor James Albert Harrison, March 29, 1897," *Alumni Bulletin of the University of Virginia* (1898):, 112.

31. Board of Visitors Minutes, July 10, 1832, http://juel.iath.virginia.edu/resources; Chairman's Journals, November 15, 1834; April 5, 1833; May 14, 1833; and May 14, 1834, http://juel.iath.virginia.edu/resources; Board of Visitors Minutes, July 10, 1833, http://juel.iath.virginia.edu/resources.

32. Board of Visitors Minutes, August 17, 1837, http://juel.iath.virginia.edu/resources.

33. Anonymous, "Dr. Fawcett," in *Corks and Curls* (Charlottesville: University of Virginia, 1890), 130. This post–Civil War description of Anatomical Hall attendant Fawcett's (an African American man) duties probably included very similar work to that done by Jack/Jack Wilson from 1830 to 1836 and Lewis from 1839 to 1857; Robert L. Blakely and Judith M. Harrington, eds., *Bones in the Basement: Postmortem Racism in Nineteenth-Century Medical Training* (Washington, DC: Smithsonian Institution Press, 1997), 163, 175.

34. Proctor's Papers, Box 19, November 24, 1827, and September 16, 1829; Proctor's Papers, Box 8, November 28, 1832, and December 26, 1832; Proctor's Papers, Box 9, January 19, 1833; Journals of Business Transactions of Central College, vol. 1, 1819–1828,

and its successor, the University of Virginia (hereafter cited as Proctor's Journals), vol. 4, 1832–1844, December 31, 1833, p. 84, Albert and Shirley Small Special Collections Library, University of Virginia; Proctor's Journals, September 16, 1834, p. 114; January 2, 1836, p. 135; November 1839, p. 195; and November 1840, p. 207; Chairman's Journals, November 15, 1834, http://juel.iath.virginia.edu/resources; Bruce, *History of the University*, 2: 112–13; *Report of the Rector & Visitors to the President and Directors of the Literary Fund*, March 1838, pp. 16, 21, and January 19, 1846, pp. 14, 16, Albert and Shirley Small Special Collections Library, University of Virginia.

35. Charles C. Wertenbaker, "Early Days of the University," *Alumni Bulletin* 4, no. 1 (May 1897): 21–25, 112; D.C.T. Davis, "Old Times at the University," *Alumni Bulletin* 4, no. 4 (February 1898): 115–17.

36. Minutes of the Faculty of the University of Virginia, 1825–1856, July 15, 1833, http://juel.iath.virginia.edu/resources.

37. Harriet Martineau, *Retrospect of Western Travel*, vol. 1 (London: Saunders and Otley, 1838), 140.

38. Washington, *Medical Apartheid*, 125.

39. James Lawrence Cabell, *The Testimony of Modern Science: Being a Summary of the Conclusions Announced by the Highest Authorities in the Several Departments of Physiology, Zoölogy, and Comparative Philology in Favor of the Specific Unity and Common Origin of All the Varieties of Man* (New York: Robert Carter & Brothers, 1859).

40. Commonplace Book and Diary of Philip Claiborne Gooch, 1839–1846, pp. 187–91, Virginia Historical Society, Richmond, VA. Thanks to Joshua Morrison, a UVA graduate student, for sharing this revealing set of diary entries with me.

41. Ibid.,189–190.

42. Ibid., 191–93.

43. Ibid.,193–94.

44. "An Address to the Public in Regard to the Affairs of the Medical Department of Hampden-Sydney College. By several physicians of the City of Richmond, 1853, Appendix I." Quoted in Blanton, *Medicine in Virginia*, 38–39.

45. Board of Visitors Minutes, July 1, 1845, http://juel.iath.virginia.edu/resources; Breeden, "Body Snatchers," 326; Carter P. Johnson to John Staige Davis, December 19, 1847, Papers of John Staige Davis, Albert and Shirley Small Special Collections Library, University of Virginia.

46. *Acts of the General Assembly: Passed at the Session Commencing December 6, 1847, and Ending April 5, 1848* (Richmond, VA: Samuel Shepherd, 1848), 111–12.

47. Howell Lewis Thomas to John Staige Davis, August 31, 1849, Albert and Shirley Small Special Collections Library, University of Virginia.

48. Thomas to Davis, September 5, 1849. For Howell and Vest, see *Census, Population Statistics, Richmond, Albemarle County, Virginia, 1870 United States*, Schedule 1, p. 17. Other resurrections included "booty men" English, Gennett, and Thacker. See Thomas to Davis, November 27, 1849.

49. Thomas to Davis, September 12, 1849.

50. Thomas to Davis, November 3, 1849.

51. Arthur E. Peticolas to John Staige Davis, July 1, 1850, Albert and Shirley Small Special Collections Library, University of Virginia.

52. Lewis W. Minor to John Staige Davis, September 19, 30, October 16, 17, 26, 1850, Albert and Shirley Small Special Collections Library, University of Virginia.

53. Robert O. Scott to John Staige Davis, November 9, 1850, Albert and Shirley Small Special Collections Library, University of Virginia; Minor to Davis, November 15, 1850.

54. Minor to Davis, November 15 and 27, 1850.

55. Minor to Davis, November 30, 1850.

56. James L. Cabell to John Staige Davis, July 23, 1851, Albert and Shirley Small Special Collections Library, University of Virginia.

57. John Staige Davis to Dr. Isaiah White, November 6, 1867 (Letterpress book, p. 437), Albert and Shirley Small Special Collections Library, University of Virginia.

58. Cabell to Davis, July 23, 1851.

59. E. F. Fontaine to John Staige Davis, January 1, 1857, Albert and Shirley Small Special Collections Library, University of Virginia.

60. Fontaine to Davis, January 16, 1857.

61. Fontaine to Davis, October 24, 1851.

62. Sappol, *Traffic of Dead Bodies*, 13.

63. Peticolas to Davis, January 26, 1852.

64. *Journal of the House of Delegate of the State of Virginia for the Session of 1852* (Richmond, VA: William F. Ritchie, 1852), 265–66.

65. Ibid.; Carter P. Johnson to John Staige Davis, March 22, 1852, Albert and Shirley Small Special Collections Library, University of Virginia.

66. Peticolas to Davis, January 21, 1856.

67. Prince William County Clerk's Loose Papers (coroner inquest, statements of accused), December 26, 1856, Albert and Shirley Small Special Collections Library, University of Virginia.

68. T. R. Roberts to Governor Henry A. Wise, January 14, 1857, Virginia Governors Papers—Henry A. Wise, Box #6, Albert and Shirley Small Special Collections Library, University of Virginia.

69. T. C. Brown to John Staige Davis, March 5, 1857, Albert and Shirley Small Special Collections Library, University of Virginia.

70. John Staige Davis to _____, December 8, 1859, Albert and Shirley Small Special Collections Library, University of Virginia. See also Berry, *The Price for Their Pound of Flesh*, 120–26.

71. Bruce, *History of the University*, 2: 112–13; Peticolas to Davis, July 1, 1850; Minor to Davis, October 26, 1850; Peticolas to Davis, January 30, 1856; Statement of Account, Peticolas to Davis, October 6, 1856; Brown to Davis, March 5, 1857; Peticolas to Davis, January 1, 1859; Davis to Peticolas, February 8, 1859.

72. Minor to Davis, November 27, 1850; Davis to Peticolas, January 17, 1859; Davis to Arthur E. Peticolas, February 3, 1860.

73. Blakely and Harrington, eds., *Bones in the Basement,* 163.

74. Nudelman, *John Brown's Body,* 41.

75. "Jim's Revelations: Threatened by Students, Be Prepared to Resign," *Philadelphia Press,* December 8, 1882, quoted in Berry, *The Price for Their Pound of Flesh,* 148.

76. Gregory Michael Dorr, "Assuring America's Place in the Sun: Ivey Foreman Lewis and the Teaching of Eugenics at the University of Virginia, 1915–1953," *Journal of Southern History* 66, no. 2 (May 2000): 257–96; Gregory Michael Dorr, *Segregation's Science: Eugenics and Society in Virginia* (Charlottesville: University of Virginia Press, 2008).

8

FREE PEOPLE OF COLOR

Kirt von Daacke

On October 6, 1832, the University of Virginia paid four dollars to "Col'd woman Kitty Foster" for clothes washing.[1] Less than two years later, in May 1834, Faculty Chairman Charles Bonnycastle "received information that on the night of the 22nd inst. a party of students, four or five in number, had visited several houses in the neighbourhood, where they had conducted themselves in a disorderly manner." Bonnycastle explained that the students "had thrown down several flower pots at Foster's" and attempted to enter her home forcibly. At that time, Katherine "Kitty" Foster owned a house with 2⅛ acres of land immediately south of the university (figs. 8.1, 8.2). The chairman's investigation led to student Thomas L. Patterson, who admitted that "the party [of students] went from Kitty Foster's where they had upset some boxes containing dirt and they had knocked at her door" before continuing on to a cockfight behind the university stable.[2] Three years after that incident, Faculty Chairman John A. G. Davis, responding to noise complaints, noted that "almost every evening, and sometimes for an hour or more at a time, students are in the practice of firing pistols across the road south of the University and just out of the precincts, with pistols they allege they keep out of the precincts." Davis continued, saying that the students were "violating no law" because everything took place away from the school. Davis also indicated that students did not keep their guns on campus: "The place of deposit is, I understand, the house of Kitty Foster." Certainly, Foster charged for this service.

Just what was going on here? How could a free woman of color, denied full citizenship rights both as a woman and as a member of a tiny marginalized population in a slaveholding state, come to own real property and run a gun storage facility? She had come to the area drawn by the promise of economic advancement. Once there, she indeed found economic opportunity working as a laundress, but also a powerful white hostility to her presence, as

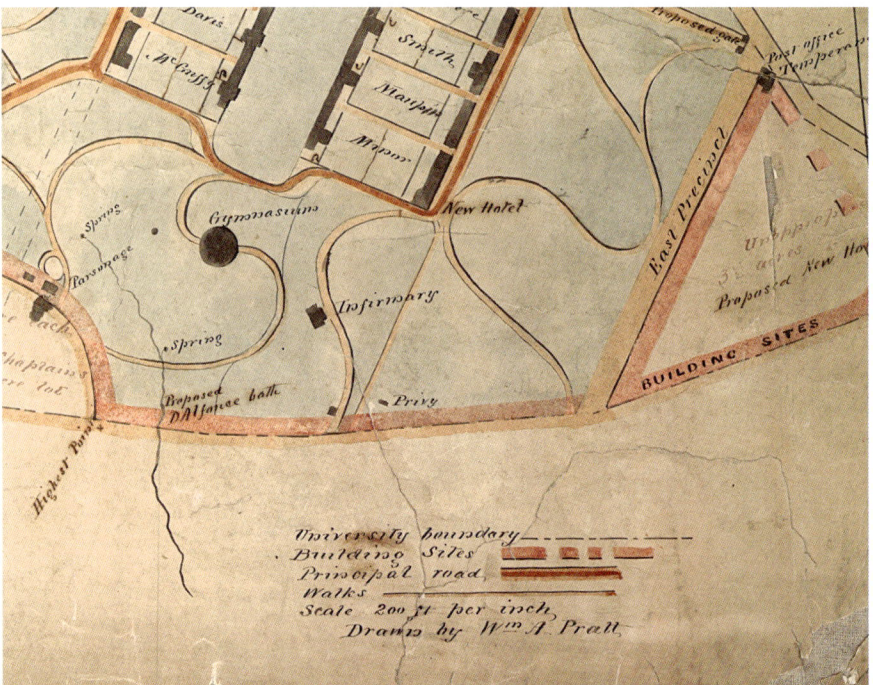

Fig. 8.1. William A. Pratt, "Plan of University Cleared Land," 1858; the legend is approximately the location of the Kitty Foster residence.

the mob violence at her property attests. Those three events involving Katherine "Kitty" Foster capture the complexities of race that the all-white, male school's birth created in the years after it opened. The university offered to free people of color desperate for opportunities to earn a living both great promise and significant peril. The history of their interactions with students, faculty, and administrators there captures the power of both the neighborly face-to-face relationships the rural area was built on and the outright hostility directed at free blacks.[3]

Built in Virginia's Central Piedmont—a rural plantation district encompassing several counties east of the Blue Ridge Mountains—the University of Virginia created one of the first significant urban centers the area had ever seen (Scottsville, some twenty miles south of the university, was a booming river town ca. 1820–1840). Over half of the twenty thousand people living in Albemarle County (where UVA was located) were held in human bondage when the school opened, with a significant portion of white adult male heads of household owning at least one slave. The county was also home at

FIG. 8.2. Steel framework that marks the site and scale of Kitty Foster's house adjacent to the South Lawn project.

that time to a few hundred free people of color, representing approximately 3 percent of the African American population and 1.5 percent of the total population. Legally free, they were nonetheless denied in law and custom the full fruits of that freedom. A body of state laws, growing in fits since 1806, denied them voting and office-holding rights, required them to register their emancipation with the court and renew the certificates every three years, and barred them from owning or possessing firearms.

Free people of color were routinely subjected to intense scrutiny by magistrates and slave patrollers who often assumed any African American person was enslaved. They also lived in a rural farming community among many white neighbors who saw them as inferior and troublesome. That meant free blacks had to carefully navigate a social world that privileged face-to-face interactions—people knew one another, knew their neighbors, whether black or white. They also resided in a locale where over half the population and almost all people of color were enslaved. Simply put, there were very limited economic opportunities for free black people. Free people of color in Virginia, as a result, were typically very poor and had little opportunity for economic advancement. Nonetheless, they strove for success and found ways to finesse that highly personal culture to their own advantage.

The university would subtly but powerfully alter that universe in Albemarle County, creating in the middle of a plantation district an urban landscape filled with the promise of employment opportunity, more regular pay, and even skill development. Thus, free people of color gravitated to the university in search of jobs. They often found work, at times developed close relationships with white neighbors and white people at the university (just as they did elsewhere in the county and central Virginia), but also viscerally bore the brunt of the white supremacist violence directed at people of color. The underfunded and brand-new university needed labor and gladly paid free people of color low wages to do anything and everything. But the school, peopled by white men steeped in the politics, economics, and culture of slaveholding society, simultaneously sought to control tightly the black presence on campus and to eliminate unknown or uninvited people of color from the school precincts. Unsurprisingly, university administrators did little to curb violence directed at black Virginians, including free people of color.

When construction began in 1817, the region's free people of color who lived in Albemarle County were drawn to the urban employment opportunities the school offered. For instance, in October 1819, the university paid free woman of color Fanny Barnett ten dollars for washing clothes for Italian stonemasons, brothers Michele and Giacomo Raggi, who had been hired by Thomas Jefferson to carve the capitals of the Rotunda. Less than a month later, the university would again pay her an additional five dollars for more washing. Over the course of the next year, she would continue to wash clothes for the Italians, commencing a decades-long shift as free people of color gravitated toward the university in search of economic opportunity.[4]

Despite the very real opportunities for employment provided by the university, the potential for violence, especially gender-based violence against women, was quite palpable at the school. Students most frequently attacked the enslaved at the university, but free people of color living or working near the university were also at risk. That night in May 1834 when intoxicated students smashed flowerpots and "knocked" on Katherine Foster's door may well have been sexual violence in the making.[5] One Wednesday night in April 1837, a free woman of color living about a half mile from the university along the road to Charlottesville found her home under siege. Four or five students who had been drinking "committed an outrage upon the house," breaking windows, pounding on the front door, and ultimately knocking it down. On a Sunday afternoon in February 1839, a group of university students came upon what they later described as "a large and disorderly assemblage of negroes in the street" and "some ways down the road to Charlottesville." According to one student, "two of them [the free blacks in the street] were engaged in a fight," and the white students endeavored to "drive away the crowd of negroes gathered about," including the two fighting free men of color. Other students, some passing by on a carriage, jumped down to join the attack on the free blacks. The student's mob violence against the free men of color was ultimately redirected at Fielding, an enslaved man owned by Professor Bonnycastle, who intervened, telling the mob of white students that the African American men gathered on the street "were free and should not be parted."[6] The students, however, did not see those free men of color as really free or worthy of treating as if free and independent.

Free people of color may have seen the potential for harassment and violence at the school as worth the risk—the employment opportunities were simply so much better than what the rural county had offered before. In April 1820, free man of color Stephen Bowles, after hauling coal for the university, earned $1.43 for his work. That same month, the university paid free woman of color Milley four dollars for "one munt [month] work" and five dollars "hand hire to Milley for cooking."[7] A month later, the university paid free man of color William Barnett nearly ten dollars for his labor. At that time, William Barnett was the twenty-one-year-old son of Fanny Barnett, who did clothes washing for the school. Barnett had recently come of age and completed an Overseers of the Poor–mandated apprenticeship, but one in which his mother appears to have had some control as to where and to whom her son was apprenticed.[8] Fanny Barnett's efforts on behalf of her son were almost certainly part of a calculated strategy to prepare William for independent adulthood while connecting him to potential white employers at the university. Fanny, meanwhile, continued to work for the university, earning nearly four dollars for washing for the Raggi brothers. That same month, she washed "6 dozen and 3/9 pr dozen 22s/6d" for the stonemasons.[9] For the remainder of the year, free people of color Milley (also known as Milly King), Stephen Bowles, Fanny Barnett, and William Barnett continued to work for the university hauling coal, washing clothes, cooking, performing manual labor, and even selling corn to the school.[10] In 1823 and 1824 at the height of construction activity, the university paid free woman of color Dolly Battles, the daughter of free man and Revolutionary War veteran Shadrach Battles, for making clothes for the enslaved people the university had rented.[11] In 1824, William

Barnett sold beef to the university, earning twelve dollars for his family.[12] Those five free people of color were not the only ones drawn to employment opportunities offered by the fledgling university. In 1821, the university paid free man of color King Pharo six dollars for "1 monts work" as a laborer.[13]

While the majority of the work during construction was performed by enslaved people rented by the university, all the major construction projects were awarded to white artisans, contractors, and builders. Local whites and contractors who came to build the university bought or rented property near the school—some did so in the area just south of the university. These included carpenters George W. Spooner and James W. Widderfield. Charlottesville merchant Nimrod Branham also owned land at that time that stretched from this neighborhood toward the village of Charlottesville. Since much of this area was not considered to be prime farming land, it quickly developed as a residential neighborhood with landowners subdividing properties and renting out housing and small farm plots. Free people of color, seeking employment and opportunity, would come to represent the single largest group of renters in the residential neighborhoods adjacent to the university. These neighborhoods included the one immediately south of the university that by the Civil War era would be known as "Canada," the name a direct reference to the free people of color living there. Another neighborhood arose across the main road north of the Rotunda (which we now know as Carr's Hill), and a third more dispersed area of settlement arced to the east of the university and toward Charlottesville along and south of the main road.[14]

One of those renters was William Spinner, a free man of color and son of free black Revolutionary War veteran Richard Spinner. In April 1825, the university hired William, "as a person of good character," as the school's first janitor. Spinner at the young age of twenty-four had purchased a half-acre lot in Charlottesville back in 1819 and took full possession of the title in 1822 after paying a debt to University Bursar Alexander Garrett. That property had a simple house on it, but it is not clear if he lived there or rented the property out. It may have been Spinner's existing relationship with Garrett, one that Spinner had carefully cultivated for years, that led to his hiring as janitor. Technically, the university was supposed to provide Spinner a "room for lodging," but it is not clear if he ever lived on the campus. Instead, records indicated that he rented housing in the neighborhood just south of the school. Spinner was paid one hundred fifty dollars per year and began working on April 27, 1825. At that time, the university faculty may have seen the janitorial position as a menial one and thus appropriate for a free person of color. That would soon change, and not for the better for Spinner.[15] His employment history with the university is one that speaks powerfully to the world in which he lived—at once a rural farming community structured on face-to-face neighborly relationships and a small city where whites struggled to maintain what they saw as appropriate power and control over students, the enslaved, and free people of color.

With the arrival of students in fall 1825, the faculty's vision of the janitor's position evolved—as the reality of controlling nearly one hundred students dawned on the faculty, they came to demand that the janitor take on policing and inspection duties. In early 1826, Spinner "absented himself from the University for the space of a fortnight," refusing to work or spend time on the Grounds. Although the records remain silent as to why Spinner left work at the school, it seems clear that he may have found his new duties impossible to carry out—white students and faculty simply would not accept his oversight and he may have experienced harassment or violence. Even University Bursar Alexander Garrett's trust of Spinner as a hard-working person was not enough to overcome a generalized white hostility. Spinner, despite his best efforts, was still a free man of color in a society that coded all nonwhites as would-be slaves. The faculty paid Spinner for his services up to the time he quit and then hired a white man as his replacement, but the position now included clear supervisory and surveillance duties. The university in 1828 would even build a cottage on the campus for the white janitor (visible on the 1858 Pratt Plan, fig. 2.26 on page 64). Spinner and his family, however, did not leave the area. They continued to rent property south of the university and Spinner and his father Richard repeatedly found short-term contract employment on the Grounds digging and cleaning wells—work that did not demand regular interaction with students.[16]

After Thomas Jefferson died in 1826, some of the enslaved people he freed in his will, likely benefiting from their personal connection to the school's founder, sought employment at the university. Two weeks after Jefferson's death in July 1826, Burwell Colbert, in his forties at the time and described by John Hartwell Cocke as "the faithful servant of our late lamented Rector," was hired by the university to do painting and odd jobs. Colbert for a time lived in university-owned housing and worked at the school for years. It is not clear where the faculty may have let Colbert live, but it was in all likelihood a cellar space somewhere in the Academical Village. In 1828, Colbert earned fifty-two dollars for three-and-a-half-months' work painting. He paid the university twenty dollars during that time for boarding expenses.[17] Colbert successfully capitalized on his reputation—one closely connected to the university's founder and to his own reputation as a trustworthy worker—to find a measure of success and security at the school.

Even after marrying free woman of color Elizabeth "Betsy" Battles in 1834 and no longer living on the Grounds, Colbert would continue to do piecework for the school. His wife Betsy was part of the extended Battles family—people free since the eighteenth century who were often small propertyholders in and around Charlottesville. In 1836, he was paid twenty dollars for twenty days of painting buildings, and in 1837, he took on a major work project. In that year, the university paid him over one hundred eighty dollars for his services. Colbert's skills in painting helped to deliver to him the university's promise of economic security and opportunity. By living outside of the university precincts, performing services that demanded little or no interaction with students, and being known as Jefferson's "faithful servant," Colbert may have been able to shield himself to a degree from open white hostility and abuse that probably drove William Spinner from his janitor position.[18]

Similarly, Joseph Fossett, also freed by Thomas Jefferson's will, left Monticello after Jefferson's death and began working for the university, desperately trying to make enough money to purchase and free his wife and children, who were sold to several different people at Jefferson's estate dispersal sale in 1827 (fig. 8.3). Fossett, approaching fifty and trained as a blacksmith, would regularly do metalwork for the school. Almost immediately after he began life as a free man, Fossett found employment at the university. By early 1828, he was fabricating iron wagon wheels for the university. In 1829, Proctor Arthur S. Brockenbrough paid him fifty dollars "for one quarter's salary," probably as a university blacksmith. As with Colbert, his reputation as one of Jefferson's "faithful servants" may have protected him, and his metalwork may have meant he did not routinely interact with students, thereby insulating him to a degree from that pervasive climate of harassment African Americans experienced when forced to interact regularly with students.[19]

Joseph Fossett worked very hard at the university and elsewhere to earn enough money to begin purchasing his wife and children. Carpenter James Dinsmore, who had worked at Monticello during Jefferson's lifetime and was

FIG. 8.3. Photograph of Joseph Fossett, formerly enslaved blacksmith at Monticello who spent many years working to purchase the freedom of his wife and children.

also a contractor with the university, had purchased members of Fossett's family at the estate dispersal sale in February 1827. After Dinsmore died in 1830, Fossett, using money earned in part working as a blacksmith for the university, purchased family members, including his wife, Edy. He continued to work for the university as late as 1836, when the school paid him nearly sixty dollars for his work. A year later, the university again paid him twenty-six dollars as a blacksmith. By the time Fossett was preparing to move to the free state of Ohio, he had successfully purchased and freed several family members: his wife, Edy, and their children Elizabeth Ann, William, Daniel, Lucy, and Jesse, as well as Elizabeth Ann's children James, Joseph, Thomas, and Maria Elizabeth. In October 1837, all visited the courthouse to have their freedom certified. Meanwhile, Joseph Fossett continued to do blacksmith's work for the university. He was paid nineteen dollars in February 1838. Edy also sought employment at the university and was hired to work as a nurse in the infirmary in 1840. After that ten-dollar payment to Edy, the Fossetts ended their employment with the university and moved to Ohio. A combination of factors may have driven the Fossetts to Ohio: laws making it difficult for the recently emancipated to remain in Virginia, white Virginians' attitudes about and treatment of free people of color, and even perhaps Joseph and his family's experiences at UVA.[20]

Any free person of color who sought economic opportunity at the university would find an institution very willing to pay them low wages for work but, at the same time, wanting to ban people of color from the university and its neighborhood entirely. After construction at the school wound down in the late 1820s, the university continued to rent five to ten enslaved people yearly for ongoing work that required a daily presence on the Grounds. Faculty, administrators, and hotelkeepers hired or purchased enslaved people to supply their individual needs. For the remaining odd jobs and piecework, especially the kind of work that could be done off-campus, the university remained attracted to inexpensive and locally available labor, which free people of color could provide in relative abundance. For instance, free man of color Thomas Sturrs, who rented housing in the neighborhood near Katherine Foster south of the university, did occasional piecework for the school. At age forty-seven, Sturrs moved to the area in 1830 along with his family: wife Priscilla and their seven children. In 1833, the university paid him for making and mending shoes and described him as a "colored shoemaker who cannot write."[21] But those same faculty and administrators simultaneously saw free people of color as anomalous and inferior, a troublesome group that threatened to undermine slave discipline on the Grounds. As early as 1828, the faculty informed the proctor that they "disapprove of free Negroes being located within the University."[22] The university later sought to rid the areas adjacent to the school of much of the free black presence. In 1847, Proctor William Kemper, worried about "the evil resulting from the number of free Negroes, and those nominally so, hanging on about the University," tried to convince the faculty to stop hiring free people of color to do the washing and instead require hotelkeepers (or their enslaved laborers) to do it.[23]

Despite the persistent concerns of white administrators about the presence of free people of color at the university and the very real threat of harassment and violence, free African Americans continued to seek wage work there and the school continued to hire them. In April 1828, free man of color John Neale asked Proctor Arthur S. Brockenbrough if he could rent and occupy one of the vacant hotels. Brockenbrough took the request to the faculty, who responded in the negative: "The Faculty disapprove of free negroes permitted to reside within the University." They additionally ordered that John Neale "be removed from the University."[24] Again in 1833, Jack Kennedy, "a mulatto man," sought to move into "one of the cellar rooms for a barber's shop for the accommodation of students." The proctor brought the request to the faculty, and faculty wrestled with the request, because Jack Kennedy the barber was "such a person [that] was much wanted here, that the students might thus be prevented from going to Charlottesville so often."[25] They were attracted to the double usefulness of Kennedy's barbering—providing a much-needed service on campus and perhaps reducing the number of off-Grounds trips the students took—but they were also suspicious about the threat to slave discipline having a free black person live in the precincts posed.

White faculty and administrators associated the presence of free people of color with a breakdown in slave discipline and also with the prevalence of immoral student activities, so they often sought removal of free people of color from the campus and from nearby areas. On May 30, 1828, the faculty, this time concerned about "whether the house occupied by Phil a free man of colour, and a free white woman at the foot of the hill below the University is not reputed to be a house of evil fame" and worried that Phil's off-Grounds home was "injurious to the morals of the University," ordered that the proctor "consult as to any legal means which ought to be pursued to get rid of such disorderly neighbors."[26] Phil may have been running a bawdy house—a tavern providing alcohol, food, gaming, and prostitutes. His business was almost certainly located a short distance from Katherine Foster's house just south of the school. Phil's real crime, as far as university administrators were concerned, may have been that he lived openly with a white woman. In 1863, the faculty chairman ordered William Pratt, the superintendent of grounds and buildings, "to remove Jackson, a negro having a white wife, from the house he occupied on University Grounds." The records do not indicate in this instance exactly what precipitated the faculty decision, but the result was not surprising. Jackson and his wife were removed within a week.[27]

Some free people who moved near the university were ultimately successful in their quest to find continuing employment, build labor skills, and find a measure of economic security. For example, Elijah Battles Sr. found work with the university for decades. Elijah Sr., a carpenter by trade who regularly worked on outbuildings and fencing for many white landowners in the county, was first hired by the university in 1828 to help build a small observatory on a hill about a half mile west of the school (visible on the Pratt Plan, fig. 2.26 on page 64) and also to saw railings for use on the Grounds. His work that year cutting chestnut railings suggests that he was already a skilled carpenter.[28] In 1835, now working with friend and free man of color Thomas Farrow, Battles had picked up some plumbing, piping, and hydraulic engineering skills, as the two were paid nearly ten dollars for repairing a water pump.[29] Both men continued to do small carpentry jobs and work on the water system—this included the hydraulic pumps, the wooden pipe system, cisterns, and even pond floodgates—over the course of the next three decades. Their long-term success in working for the university was in part attributable to the kind of work they did—work that largely insulated them from daily contact with the students.[30] Their children, including James Franklin Battles, would continue to work for the school in similar capacities right through the Civil War. Starting in 1863, the younger Battles repaired and installed fencing almost everywhere on university property, continuing to do so at least through 1870.[31]

Free women of color also gravitated toward the university in search of employment. Fanny Barnett and Katherine Foster were just the first in a line of women who would cook, wash, or sew for the school. Less than three years after the university had opened its doors to the first class of students, the school paid free woman of color Sally Kinny seventy-five cents for "making two shirts & pr pantaloons for Henry a labourer at the university."[32] Similarly, free woman of color Keziah Davis was first paid by the university in 1828 for "making clothes" for the enslaved laborers rented by the school. At that time, Kinny made "2 shirts and pr trowsers for Zachariah." With up to fifty enslaved laborers living and working on construction projects, the university needed quite a bit of cooking, washing, and sewing—area free women of color took the work. These jobs, too, typically included a measure of independence from direct oversight by white managers and often did not involve significant interaction with students.

At the end of 1828, university Proctor Brockenbrough approached the faculty chairman and inquired "whether he would object to a decent free woman's occupying the house of the late Janitor and paying rent." This time, the plan was actually sanctioned and a free person of color was allowed to live at the university. Keziah Davis paid rent to the school for the first time on January 29, 1830. Through 1830, she lived at the university and continued to do piecework as a seamstress for the school.[33] Several months later, the faculty chairman complained "that a free black woman, named Keziah Fortune, of bad character, was living within the precincts without being under the control of any particular master." Again, white faculty associated free people of color with immoral student activities. In reality, it was often white students who sought out alcohol or gambling and actively demanded sex from the women of color in their midst, but the culture of slaveholding society dictated that blame rest with African Americans, not white enslavers.

In this particular situation, Keziah Davis may well have found herself accosted or threatened by white students knocking on her door at all hours of the day. As South Carolina slave Harry McMillan explained in 1863, if the son of a master (any UVA student) "wanted to have intercourse with the colored women, [tho' not technically at liberty to do so], they did it. There was a good deal of it . . . they would go wherever they could get it."[34] Even more problematic than university officials blaming Keziah Davis for student behavior was the fact that they appear not to have known her name, calling her Keziah Fortune. White men at the university who benefited from her labor as a clothes washer held a somewhat different view, valuing Davis solely for her labor. Hotelkeeper John Rose, who was paying Fortune/Davis to do washing, worried that "her immediate removal would cause him some very serious inconvenience." The matter was referred to the proctor. From that point through 1836, Keziah Davis continued to make clothes for the university, so she may not have been removed or, after forcing her to move off-Grounds, she was allowed to continue working for the school, but in a capacity that kept her away from the students.[35] Although the university indeed promised wages for work and thus economic opportunity, school officials also routinely sought to limit the free black presence on the Grounds because they saw free people of color as contaminating both the morals of students and the discipline of the enslaved.

Fanny Barnett, who had done washing for the university in the early years of construction, achieved some measure of economic success through that work. By 1832, Professor George Blaetterman's house on the hill north of the university was being rented to "free negroes," in all likelihood Fanny Barnett and her family. In that year, the proctor arranged to use Blaetterman's house "as a hospital if wanted" and "its present occupants—free negroes—had also agreed to act as nurses and attendants." Within a decade of washing clothing for the university, Fanny Barnett and her family had come to rent a house adjacent to the university and worked out arrangements with school administrators to work as nurses and attendants at a proposed infirmary. The promise of economic freedom the university offered free people of color was real enough, and Barnett's careful navigating of both the rural face-to-face neighborly culture and the quasi-urban university landscape played a key role in her family's success.[36]

Two years later in 1834, though, university records indicate that Fanny Barnett had clearly begun more enterprising arrangements at the house she rented north of the university. This, too, represented a series of active decisions by Barnett seeking economic success and security, but choices deeply shaped by the dictates of slave society and the specifically white male-dominated university context. In June, three students were brought before the faculty and questioned about what they had done the night of May 22. The three students indicated that "on the night in question, they came to the farm which lies north of the University and is the property of Professor Blaetterman: went to the house rented to Fanny Barnett, were intoxicated." Another witness to that evening, also questioned by the faculty chairman, was an unnamed free woman of color, who "described the establishment of Fanny Barnett as a brothel—students come there every night." That witness came forward despite students threatening her if she did not keep quiet about their extracurricular activities. By that time, Barnett was probably catering to demand from students, who routinely sought alcohol, better food, gambling, or sex when they left the university precincts.[37]

In fact, Fanny Barnett may have been working as a prostitute as far back as 1821, when she was also washing clothes for the university. This was in part a choice of the desperate and marginalized. Prostitution, although dangerous and degrading work, promised far greater economic gain than washing ever could. While Barnett was washing clothes for the university and working as a prostitute, probably in a bawdy house run by someone else and catering to the dozens of white and black men building the university, she proactively had the Overseers of the Poor apprentice her children so they could learn some basic skills, would be out of harm's way at the brothel, and could make connections to white employers and the larger white community in the area.[38] By 1828, she was no longer pushing her children into apprenticeship and had begun to run her own brothel (probably in the property she rented from Blaetterman) while remaining off-Grounds. This work put Barnett and other free women at risk of greater violence—working nights surrounded by often drunken young white men. In 1821, court documents described her as "not of good fame, nor honest conversation." Court documents charged that she, along with white woman Nancy Riley, "unlawfully and wickedly did keep and maintain . . . for filthy lucre and gain, divers and dissolute persons as with man as woman, both black and white, and whores."[39] In 1834, officials charged Barnett with "breach of the peace and unlawful and riotous assembly." She would be in and out of court repeatedly, almost always charged with or as the victim of physical assault. In 1845, she was found guilty of "keeping a bawdy house."[40] Despite all of that, Barnett managed to be successful, continuing to run a brothel, paying court fines when necessary, purchasing real estate, and continuing her decades-long effort to protect her family. By 1864, Fanny's daughters still lived in the area, had amassed quite a bit of real property, and successfully petitioned the court to be declared "not a negro."[41]

It seems likely that the university records barely capture the presence of free people of color working at the school. Some certainly worked directly for professors, administrators, and hotelkeepers. Many were married to or part of larger families that included those enslaved at the university or in the county. Sadly, personal records and papers for individual professors rarely make mention of such household arrangements. In at least one instance, however, extant letters leave clues. University librarian William Wertenbaker, whose wife, Louisa, was visiting family in Spotsylvania County during the summer months, wrote to her with household and university updates. In one letter in August 1830, Wertenbaker mentioned that their servant Harriett "was sick—she has been confined to her bed . . . it will be some time before she will be able to do any thing." Wertenbaker continued, saying that one of Harriett's friends, "a girl named Malinda French . . . has done Harriett's business" while she was sick. "Malinda" French was almost certainly a free woman of color who was more often known as Marinda or Varina. Even her surname varied—sometimes she was recorded as "French," others as "West." In the 1830s and 1840s, French lived and worked near the university and was well acquainted with other free people of color, including Fanny Barnett.[42] This one brief mention in a letter is the only document connecting French to the university.

Enslaved man James Munroe's life in the area, one that carried him from slavery to freedom, speaks to the complicated world both the enslaved and free people of color had to navigate. Munroe came to the University of Virginia from Amherst County circa 1829; he was rented to hotelkeeper John Rose by another Rose family member. Maria Rose and her husband, Erasmus, would soon move to Memphis, Tennessee, leaving James Munroe behind to continue working for hotelkeeper John Rose at the University of

Virginia. They had arranged a deal with Munroe whereby he would hire himself out, send payments to the Roses in Tennessee for his hire, and also work on his own time to purchase himself. By 1836, Munroe had married another enslaved woman, Evelina, who was owned by local merchant Opie Norris. It would take Munroe over a decade to purchase himself. In September 1847, still working in a university hotel as well as in hotels in Charlottesville and at professors' homes, Munroe made the last payment to the Roses and was manumitted. In freedom, he continued to work for wages at university hotels and also at a number of locations in town and elsewhere in the county. Munroe, ever busy, came to know almost everyone in the area. He was busy scraping and saving so he could purchase his wife and six children and free them.[43]

Desperately working at as many jobs as he could manage, Munroe worried that because he had been freed in 1847, he could be charged with violating the 1806 removal law, which stipulated that any enslaved person freed after May 1, 1806, would have to leave the state within twelve months unless granted permission to remain. By 1850, he had long been "residing at the University of Virginia in the capacity of dining room servant and attendant upon the students." His decades of work at the university and in town meant that he knew quite a few white men who could vouch for his industry, sobriety, and usefulness. So, he sent three separate petitions to the state legislature that included the signatures of over two hundred white Albemarle County residents. Several even wrote glowing affidavits. Among those supporting his petition to remain were university professors William McGuffey, St. George Tucker, and John B. Minor, who "unhesitatingly recommend him . . . as a suitable person to whom permission should be granted to remain."[44] Another university hotelkeeper, Addison Maupin, also supported Munroe's desire to remain in the area, as did Thomas Jefferson's grandson and eight other justices of the peace for the county. His initial success in garnering vocal public support for his desire to stay demonstrates clearly how he had successfully finessed that neighborly world in which face-to-face interactions powerfully shaped daily life.

Ever-present with that intimate, neighborly world was the reality of white domination and antipathy toward free people of color. James Munroe's petitions from 1847 to 1850 sparked a fevered response from a few dozen rabid proslavery Albemarle residents who saw free blacks—even the few hundred in the county—as dangerous anomalies whose continued residence in the area threatened the slave system and white rule. This group of local whites called on Munroe's residency petition to be rejected and fashioned him as "a slave who says he purchased his freedom."[45] Munroe continued to live and work in the area while he awaited a decision, but the heated sectional conflict over slavery prior to the Compromise of 1850 had a serious impact on Albemarle. Late in that year, the court filed charges against nearly one hundred free people of color, including James Munroe, for violating the 1806 removal law. Munroe would work feverishly over the next several years to earn enough money to purchase his family before he was arrested, deported, or sold back into slavery (all of which were possibilities in the new climate of the 1850s).

Munroe's reputation protected him for a few years, even after a warrant was issued for his arrest and a grand jury found him in violation of the removal law in 1851, but times had changed for the worse. In 1852, Munroe was still in the area, continuing to work at the university. He had saved up enough money (or perhaps taken donations or a loan from a white patron) to purchase part of his family. In July that year, Munroe paid $650 to purchase his wife and children Mary Ann and Thomas Jefferson Munroe from merchant Opie Norris, and two other children. Despite those successes, antipathy to free blacks was clearly on the rise in the 1850s, as was enforcement of the laws controlling them. He was not arrested, but this may be because so many justices of the peace had actually supported his residency. One of them scrawled "not known" on the back of the warrant. That magistrate falsely claimed he didn't know who Munroe was.[46] Munroe abandoned life in Albemarle sometime in 1854 and moved his family to Ohio, leaving behind two children still held in slavery. In August 1856, James Munroe wrote a letter from Cincinnati, Ohio, to professors John B. Minor and William McGuffey asking for help in purchasing his daughter Roseia. He indicated he was "getting very old now . . . and hardly able to take care of myself. . . . would very much like to have my Daughter along with me." Munroe asked them to offer "800—cash. . . . and not take 800—I will give 50—more" (fig. 8.4).[47] Records do not indicate whether the professors agreed to help or if Munroe successfully purchased Roseia and freed her. Four years later, he managed to purchase his son James Jr. from Albemarle attorney Egbert R. Watson for a stunning $1,200. The family would remain in Ohio until after the Civil War. It appears that after the war, Munroe returned to Charlottesville, perhaps to reunite his entire family. In 1868, he is listed as a resident of the "Canada" community, the one just south of the university where Katherine Foster had purchased land back in the early 1830s.

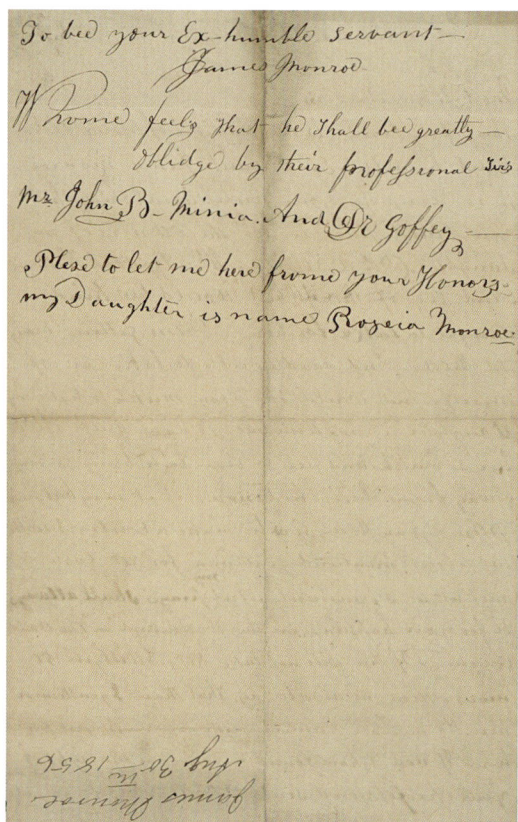

Fig. 8.4. An 1856 letter drafted by James Munroe asking for help in purchasing his daughter Roseia.

The economic promise of the university was real for free people of color. But their experiences living near the university highlight the challenges free people of color faced. Yes, the university represented employment opportunities and with them the promise of economic security. The university, however desirous for their labor, appears to have worked to minimize their visibility on the campus, regularly fretting about their presence both on the campus and in adjacent neighborhoods. White residents, whether affiliated with the university or not, routinely saw all people of color as slaves and were very willing to use violence, intimidation, or intense pressure to maintain white control.

From May to October 1823, free man of color Robert Battles, who already owned a small farm between the university and Charlottesville, hauled nearly

200,000 bricks from the brickyards and kilns that had popped up at various locations nearby. Many of those bricks were destined for the Rotunda. He also hauled several tons of sand, earning over one hundred sixty dollars.[48] In 1824, continuing to farm on his own land while working for the university, Battles sold a cow to James Brockman, the overseer hired by the university to manage and control the dozens of enslaved laborers working there.[49] Board of Visitors member John Hartwell Cocke of Fluvanna County spent years working with others at the university to pressure Robert Battles into selling his land and to remove both the Battles family and other free people of color living in the area. Cocke and his Charlottesville associates, all involved in the creation of the university, were explicitly speculating that land adjacent to the school would greatly increase in value in just a few years. As Alexander Garrett (the same man who knew William Spinner well) told Cocke in 1825, "nothing but the failure of the University can prevent my opinion of its [Battles's land] value then being realized and that in a very short time." Thus, speculating in land meant both profit and the removal of "the mulattos" from the vicinity of the school. Cocke's 1825 purchase of Robert Battles's farm succeeded in removing Battles and his family as well as free people of color Stephen Coram and William Burwell from property-owning in the vicinity. For this trouble, Battles netted a tidy profit, as Cocke paid him a total of two thousand dollars for the twenty-six-acre farm between 1825 and 1827.[50]

Stephen Byars, born enslaved in Albemarle County, purchased his own freedom from Joel W. Brown after years of living as if free and hiring himself out. Though he formed strong connections to many white people, they could not insulate him completely from the threat of removal from his home. Byars worked out a nonlegally binding term slavery agreement whereby he would pay Brown in installments to purchase his own freedom. Brown, in return for the payments, allowed Byars to live in the vicinity of Charlottesville and find his own work, most likely as a groom or stableman at taverns, inns, and boardinghouses near the university.[51] In 1835, when Byars sought permission from the county to remain in the Commonwealth, he sought recommendations from his white neighbors, including university postmaster and bookseller William Wertenbaker. In supporting Byars's request to remain in the county, Wertenbaker signed the petition and added: "for twenty years my friend." Although "friend" may have stretched the definition beyond what white Virginians would have understood at that time, Wertenbaker's choice of words evokes the strange world the university inhabited where promise and peril, black and white, racial animosity and intimacy lived uncomfortably together. When Byars made the last payment to Brown, Brown fulfilled his promise and formally manumitted Byars in 1837. At that time, Byars had been living and working near the university for close to two decades. Although he does not appear to have worked directly for the institution itself, he nonetheless made his living working for those, like Wertenbaker, who worked for the university. The university community, despite the desires of white administrators, included free people of color as employees, employers, and neighbors.[52]

Despite Byars's success in purchasing both his own and his wife Ginney's freedom and forging close personal relationships with white people near the university, Byars had not been granted permission to remain in Virginia in 1837 and probably remained worried that his freedom was quite insecure. So, he and his wife left the area and moved to Ohio. The move to a free state did not last long. By 1839, they had returned because, as Byars explained in a new residency petition, "he found after a trial of about six months' residence there, that so marked was the difference in the manners and habits of the people of Ohio that he would not remain amongst them with the least happiness or contentment." His request was supported by a number of white residents who had lived and worked with him in the vicinity of the university.[53] His return to Albemarle was in some ways risky—he had left the state and moved to a free state, meaning he could have been found in violation of an 1834 law banning the migration free people of color into the state. He still had not been granted permission by the county or state to remain. Four years later, he would actually be charged with illegally remaining in the Commonwealth, but the court would find him not guilty. However, some in the community continued to find his presence objectionable and sought his removal. He would be charged again in 1844—some whites in the area simply wanted Byars and other free blacks gone. Byars was again lucky—the case against him was dismissed the same day.[54]

Byars continued to work as a groom and stableman for taverns, hotels, and boardinghouses along the road from the university to Charlottesville. In June 1840, having saved enough money from all his wage work at those businesses, Byars purchased 2¼ acres of land along the Three Notched Road, the main road connecting Richmond to the Valley of Virginia. This road led directly from Charlottesville to the university, passing the Rotunda just to the north. He purchased the acreage for seven hundred dollars from white hatmaker Andrew McKee. Byars must have known McKee quite well, for McKee agreed to sell Byars the land over the course of seven years (Byars would make the last payment in 1846). This plot of land was a stone's throw from the university, bordering Professor George Blaetterman's property on the east. The Blaetterman property was the one rented by free woman of color Fanny Barnett and her family where she ran a bawdy house catering to students. Byars's land, where he would run his own stabling business, also shared a property line with a parcel owned by Clement McKinnie. McKinnie lived in a brick house on the property and ran a bookstore catering to university students.[55]

As they sought opportunity at the growing university, free people of color settled wherever they could purchase land or rent housing nearby. Most often, they chose areas close to roads connecting the school to the growing town of Charlottesville. Although many were successful in the pursuit of a measure of economic security, the move to the nearly all-white male world of the university brought with it some unique challenges. Free people of color in and around the university regularly faced intense harassment and white resistance to their visibility and presence. This abuse was particularly acute because the student population changed every year, limiting the development of the kinds of neighborly bonds that typically mitigated chronic abuse of free people. As a result, like janitor and well-cleaner William Spinner, many free people of color hired by the university only worked for the school in brief stints. Those who could do more skilled work that did not involve regular contact with students—painting, ironwork, carpentry, and the like—were more likely to work for the university long-term. Free people of color, in working at the university, had to chart an uneasy course toward opportunity that could not entirely avoid harassment, violence, and peril at the hands of the predominantly white male population at the school.

NOTES

1. Papers of the Proctor of the University of Virginia, Box 8, Bills and Accounts October 1832, October 6, 1832, Albert and Shirley Small Special Collections Library, University of Virginia (hereafter cited as Proctor's Papers).

2. Minutes of the Faculty of the University of Virginia, 1825–1856. May 31,1834, http://juel.iath.virginia.edu/resources (hereafter cited as Faculty Minutes).

3. For detailed examinations of free people of color in central Virginia, see Kirt

von Daacke, *Freedom Has a Face: Race, Identity, and Community in Jefferson's Virginia* (Charlottesville: University of Virginia Press, 2012); Melvin Patrick Ely, *Israel on the Appomattox: A Southern Experiment in Black Freedom from the 1790s through the Civil War* (New York: Alfred A. Knopf, 2004).

4. Journals of Business Transactions of Central College, vol. 1, 1819–1828, and its successor, the University of Virginia (hereafter cited as Proctor's Journals) October 5, 1819, p. 11, Albert and Shirley Small Special Collections Library, University of Virginia; Proctor's Journals, November 1, 1819, p. 9; Ledgers Maintained by the Proctor, 1817–1910, vol. 1, 1817–1822, p. 4, Albert and Shirley Small Special Collections Library, University of Virginia (hereafter cited as Proctor's Ledgers); Proctor's Ledgers, vol. 2, 1819–1825, p. 5.

5. Faculty Minutes, May 31, 1834, http://juel.iath.virginia.edu/resources.

6. Faculty Minutes, April 25, 1837, http://juel.iath.virginia.edu/resources (student attack on free people of color living in General Cocke's house in town); Journals of the Chairman of the Faculty of the University of Virginia, 1827–1864, February 25, 1839, http://juel.iath.virginia.edu/resources (hereafter cited as Chairman's Journals); Faculty Minutes, March 2, 1839, http://juel.iath.virginia.edu/resources.

7. Proctor's Journals, April 4, 1820, p. 16; Proctor's Papers, Box 17, Accounts January–June 1820 (the Milley named here may have been a free woman of color known as Milly King); Proctor's Journals, April 21, 1820, p. 19.

8. Proctor's Journals, May 2, 1820, pp. 19, 20; Proctor's Ledgers, vol. 1: 1817–1822, p. 24. Albemarle County Court Order Book 1821–1822, p. 24, Records Room, Albemarle County Courthouse, Charlottesville, VA; Albemarle County Court Order Book 1822–1823, p. 32.

9. Proctor's Journals, vol. 1: 1817–1822, May 15, 1820, p. 20, May 11, 1820, p. 21; Proctor's Ledgers, vol. 2: 1819–1825, May 15, 1820, p. 12; Proctor's Papers, Box 17, Accounts January–June 1820.

10. Proctor's Journals, vol. 1: 1817–1822, p. 38; Proctor's Ledgers, May 15, 1820, p. 26. Proctor's Papers, April 3, 1820; Proctor's Journals, April 4, 1820, p. 17, and April 8, 1820, p. 16; Proctor's Journals, May 11, 1820, p. 21, and May 15, 1820, p. 20; Proctor's Ledgers, May 15, 1820, p. 12; Proctor's Papers, May 15, 1820; Proctor's Journals, May 20, 1820, p. 21.

11. Proctor's Journals, July 26, 1824, pp. 282, 316; Proctor's Papers, Accounts July–December 1823, December 31, 1823. For more on Shadrach Battles, see von Daacke, *Freedom Has a Face,* 16–22.

12. Proctor's Journals, October 22, 1824, p. 336.

13. Proctor's Journals, September 27, 1821, p. 58; Proctor's Ledgers, vol. 2, 1819–1825, September 27, 1821, p. 208.

14. For more on the "Canada" neighborhood and the Foster family, see Benjamin P. Ford et al., *Phase III Data Recovery Investigations: The Foster Site: 44AB525* (Charlottesville: University of Virginia, 2008).

15. Faculty Minutes, April 27, 1825; Albemarle County Deed Book no. 22, December 7, 1819, p. 46; Albemarle County Deed Book no. 28, January 15, 1822, p. 169; Faculty

Minutes, February 3, 1826, http://juel.iath.virginia.edu/resources. See also von Daacke, *Freedom Has a Face*, 62, 63, 191, 192.

16. Proctor's Journals, vol. 2: 1820–1827, February 7, 1826, p. 412; Proctor's Journals, vol. 3: 1828–1832, September 11, 1830, p. 89; Proctor's Journals, vol. 4: 1832–1844, July 12, 1833, p. 77.

17. John H. Cocke to Arthur S. Brockenbrough, July 17, 1826, Proctor's Papers, Box 6, Folder 646; Albemarle County Will Book no. 8, p. 248; Albemarle County Court Order Book 1827, p. 223; Proctor's Papers, Box 18, Bills and Accounts, July–December 1826; Proctor's Papers, Box 19, Bills and Accounts, January–April 1828; Freedom Certificate for Burwell Colbert (age forty-eight, light complexion, five-feet ten-inches high), February 6, 1832, Library of Virginia Free Negro and Slave Records, Richmond, VA.

18. Albemarle County Marriage Register 1806–1868, December 5, 1834, p. 59; Proctor's Journals, vol. 4: 1832–1844, September 21, 1836, p. 141; Financial Records of the University of Virginia Patron, 1832–1833, Repairs and Improvements, December 1837, p. 160, and January 1838, p.168, Albert and Shirley Small Special Collections Library, University of Virginia.

19. Albemarle County Will Book no. 8, p. 24; Albemarle County Court Order Book 1827, August 6, 1827, p. 223; Ervin L. Jordan Jr., "'A Just and True Account': Two 1833 Parish Censuses of Albemarle County Free Blacks," *Magazine of Albemarle County History* 53 (1995): 125; Proctor's Papers, Box 19, Bills and Accounts, January–April 1828, February 2, 1828; Proctor's Papers, Box 16, Letters and Receipts, n.d.; Proctor's Papers, Box 19, Bills and Accounts, July–December 1829, December 12, 1829.

20. Albemarle County Will Book no. 10, p. 109; Albemarle County Will Book no. 11, pp. 72–76; Albemarle County Deed Book no. 34, p. 34; Albemarle County Deed Book no. 35, p. 219; Financial Records of the University of Virginia Patron, pp. 154, 157; Proctor's Journals, vol. 4: 1832–1844, May 1837, p. 152; Albemarle County Minute Book 1836–1838, October 1837, p. 259; Proctor's Journals, vol. 4: 1832–1844, February 1838, p. 168; Proctor's Journals, vol. 4, 1832–1844, August 1840, p. 204.

21. Jordan, "'A Just and True Account,'" 132; Proctor's Papers, Box 9, Bills and Accounts, January 1833; Proctor's Papers, Box 16, Letters and receipts, n.d.; Proctor's Papers, Box 9, Bills and Accounts, March 1833; Proctor's Papers, Box 10, Bills and Accounts, June 1833.

22. Proctor's Papers, Faculty Resolutions, Box 7, 1827–1828, April 23, 1828; Faculty Minutes, April 23, 1828, http://juel.iath.virginia.edu/resources.

23. Proctor's Papers, Box 15, 1843–1847; Proctor's Report, June 25, 1847.

24. Faculty Minutes, April 23, 1828, http://juel.iath.virginia.edu/resources.

25. Chairman's Journals, 1832–1833, May 6, 1833, pp. 66–67, http://juel.iath.virginia.edu/resources.

26. Faculty Minutes, May 26, 1828, http://juel.iath.virginia.edu/resources.

27. Chairman's Journals, October 5 and 10, 1863, http://juel.iath.virginia.edu/resources.

28. Proctor's Journals, vol. 3: 1828–1832, April 2, 1828, p. 1; Proctor's Papers, Box 19, Bills and Accounts, May–July 1828, May 17, 1828.

29. Proctor's Journals, vol. 4: 1832–1844, November 6, 1835, p. 129.

30. Proctor's Journals, vol. 4, 1832–1844, June 20, 1836, p. 137, September 21, 1836, p. 141, and December 1841, 218; Proctor's Journals, vol. 5, 1844–1851, November 1844, p. 4, April 1845, p. 9, November 5, 1845, p. 26, October 1, 1846, p. 44; Proctor's Papers, Box 15, Disbursements 1847, October 1, 1846; University of Virginia Bursar's Accounts, 1851–1860, March 23, 1854, pp. 54–55; Proctor's Ledgers, 1817–1910, vol. 1860–1861, October 17, 1860, pp. 713, 742; Proctor's Ledgers, vol. 1861–1865, February 1, 1862, p. 442, February 1, 1862, p. 555, September 15, 1863, p. 567.

31. Proctor's Ledgers, September 1865 June 1866, pp. 408–410, July 28, 1863, p. 565, July 2, 1863, p. 568, December 6, 1866, 576; Proctor's Ledgers, vol. 1866–1867, March 4, 1867, p. 580; Proctor's Ledgers, vol. 1869–1870, December 14, 1869, p. 717, May 16, 1870, p. 719, December 14, 1869, p. 737.

32. Proctor's Papers, Box 7, Folder 881. Sally Kinny is listed variously in the county and university records as Kinny, Kinney, Kenny, or Kenney. In 1828, she was in her early thirties and worked as a "taylorist." See Jordan, "'A Just and True Account,'" 130.

33. Proctor's Journals, vol. 3: 1828–1832, p. 15; Proctor's Papers, Box 7, Folder 881, Receipt, September 12, 1828; Proctor's Papers, Box 19, Bills and Accounts, January–June 1829; Proctor's Journals, vol. 3: 1828–1832, p. 30; Chairman's Journals, December 24, 1828, http://juel.iath.virginia.edu/resources; Proctor's Journals, vol. 3: 1828–1832, January 29, 1830, p. 63, and July 1, 1830 p. 81.

34. Harry McMillan, "American Freedman's Inquiry Commission Interview, 1863," in *Slave Testimony: Two Centuries of Letters, Speeches, Interviews, and Autobiographies*, ed. John W. Blassingame (Baton Rouge: Louisiana State University Press, 1977), 382.

35. Chairman's Journals, November 30, 1830, http://juel.iath.virginia.edu/resources; Proctor's Papers, Box 8, Estimates of Various Expenses, 1831, Labour account for last year ending 9 July 1831; Proctor's Journals, vol. 4: 1832–1844, July 6, 1833, p. 75, August 5, 1834, p. 117, January 1835, p. 121, December 11, 1835, p. 129, and August 15, 1836, p. 138.

36. Chairman's Journals, September 24, 1832, http://juel.iath.virginia.edu/resources.

37. Chairman's Journals, June 3, 1834, http://juel.iath.virginia.edu/resources.

38. Albemarle County Court Order Book 1822–23, p. 24; Old Papers Orphans' Indentures, August 20, 1822; Albemarle County Court Order Book 1823–1824, p. 42. She had children William, Jane, Betsy, Mary, and Estin apprenticed for several years. For more on apprenticeship as both a system of white social control and a system manipulated by free people of color for their own benefit, see Reginald D. Butler, "Evolution of a Rural Free Black Community: Goochland County, Virginia, 1728–1832" (PhD diss., Johns Hopkins University, 1989).

39. Albemarle County Commonwealth Causes, Box 13, October 13, 1823; von Daacke, *Freedom Has a Face*, 140.

40. Peace Recognizance of Fanny Barnett, Albemarle County Commonwealth

Causes, Box 12, July 9, 1821; Albemarle County Commonwealth Causes, Box 28, October 25 and November 2, 1841; Peace Recognizance of Fanny Barnett, Albemarle County Commonwealth Causes, Box 32, July 5, 1845; Albemarle County Commonwealth Causes, Box 34, May 5 and June 4, 1847; Albemarle County Minute Book 1845–1847, p. 412.

41. Von Daacke, *Freedom Has a Face*, 164. Certification as "not a negro" meant that the person involved was deemed by the court to be sufficiently white so as to no longer be subject to the legal disabilities imposed upon free people of color.

42. Letter to Louisa Wertenbaker from University of Virginia, August 20, 1830 (MSS 805), Albert and Shirley Small Special Collections Library, University of Virginia. For more on Malinda/Marinda French, see von Daacke, *Freedom Has a Face*, 142, 147, 149–50, 151, 153, 163.

43. Von Daacke, *Freedom Has a Face*, 84–94. For more on term slavery and self-hire, see T. Stephen Whitman, *The Price of Freedom: Slavery and Manumission in Baltimore and Early National Maryland* (Lexington: University Press of Kentucky, 1997); Jonathan D. Martin, *Divided Mastery: Slave Hiring in the American South* (Cambridge MA: Harvard University Press, 2004); and John Zaborney, *Slaves for Hire: Renting Enslaved Laborers in Antebellum Virginia* (Baton Rouge: Louisiana State University Press, 2012).

44. Von Daacke, *Freedom Has a Face*, 86–87.

45. Ibid., 90.

46. Ibid., 92–93.

47. James Munroe to Mr. John B. Minor and McGuffey, August 30, 1856, in Minor and Wilson Family Papers, Box 8, Albert and Shirley Small Special Collections Library, University of Virginia. Thanks to University of Virginia graduate research assistant Joshua Morrison for his work in faculty archival collections and his discovery of this important letter.

48. Proctor's Journals, vol. 2: 1819–1828, May 13, 1823, p. 215, May 26, 1823, p. 217, June 7, 1823, p. 224, June 12, 1823, p. 228, June 24, 1823, p. 231, July 3, 1823, p. 233, July 5, 1823, p. 235, July 10, 1823, p. 236, August 4, 1823, p. 244, August 18, 1823, p. 246, August 25, 1823, p. 248, September 17, 1823, p. 255, September 22, 1823, p. 256, and October 22, 1823, p. 272; Proctor's Papers, Box 18, Accounts February–June 1823 (June 13 and July 30, 1823), Accounts July–December 1823 (July 3, August 25, and September 3, 1823).

49. Proctor's Journals, vol. 2: 1819–1828, February 9, 1824, p. 286, July 26, 1824, p. 316, May 1, 1824, p. 301.

50. Alexander Garrett to John Hartwell Cocke, March 18, 1825, Papers of John Hartwell Cocke, Box 43, Albert and Shirley Small Special Collections Library, University of Virginia; Deed of Sale, March 22, 1825, Papers of John Hartwell Cocke, Box 43, Albert and Shirley Small Special Collections Library, University of Virginia.

51. Von Daacke, *Freedom Has a Face*, 98–107. For more on term slavery arrangements, see T. Stephen Whitman, *The Price of Freedom: Slavery and Manumission in Baltimore and Early National Maryland* (Lexington: University Press of Kentucky, 1997).

52. Albemarle County Legislative Petitions 1817–1836, Box 4, Folder 53, December 11, 1835; von Daacke, *Freedom Has a Face,* 100.

53. Albemarle County Legislative Petitions 1837–1848, Box 5, Folder 13, February 8 and 14, 1839.

54. Albemarle County Commonwealth Causes, Box 30, Indictment October 17, 1843, and Verdict October 21, 1843; Albemarle County Commonwealth Causes, Box 31, May 16, 1844.

55. Albemarle County Deed Book No. 38, Jun 15, 1840, p. 104; Mary Rawlings, ed., *Early Charlottesville: Recollections of James Alexander, 1828–1874* (Charlottesville, VA: Albemarle County Historical Society, 1942), 97; John Hammond Moore, *Albemarle: Jefferson's County 1727–1976* (Charlottesville, VA: Albemarle County Historical Society, 1976), 133.

9

THE AFRICAN AMERICAN BURIAL GROUND

Benjamin Ford

Only four years after the opening of the University of Virginia an enslaved man named Sebra, the property of white planter Joel Shiflett, spent the late summer of 1829 into the early winter of 1830 selecting, forming, and laying the stone in the wall that enclosed the university's new burial ground. The University Cemetery was a 150-foot square of sacred space carved out from heavily wooded lands located at the eastern base of what is now Observatory Mountain. Located only one-half mile west of the Rotunda, and standing just south of and overlooking the Meadow Creek drainage, the burying ground was established for the exclusive use of white residents of the Academical Village (fig. 9.1).

Sebra was not a stranger to the Academical Village. As a stonecutter Sebra was responsible for the cutting, shaping, and laying of stone. During the university's initial period of construction, Sebra assisted Samuel and Andrew Campbell in the stonework required for the Anatomical Theater. University records document that Joel Shiflett received a payment of $18.50 for stonework performed by Sebra "on the Anat. Hall."[1] When not laboring at the university, Sebra was part of a much larger community of thirty-two enslaved individuals residing with the Shifletts on their Albemarle County plantation. As human chattel, Sebra and his relations were owned by Joel Shiflett until his death in 1834; and then by Joel's widow Sarah Shiflett until her death in the mid-1840s. In an inventory and assessment of Joel Shiflett's estate Sebra was valued at $300. A decade later in 1845 Sebra was valued at $500.[2]

University records document that Joel Shiflett was paid for Sebra's labor on the graveyard wall between August 1829 and March 1830.[3] Unlike on other

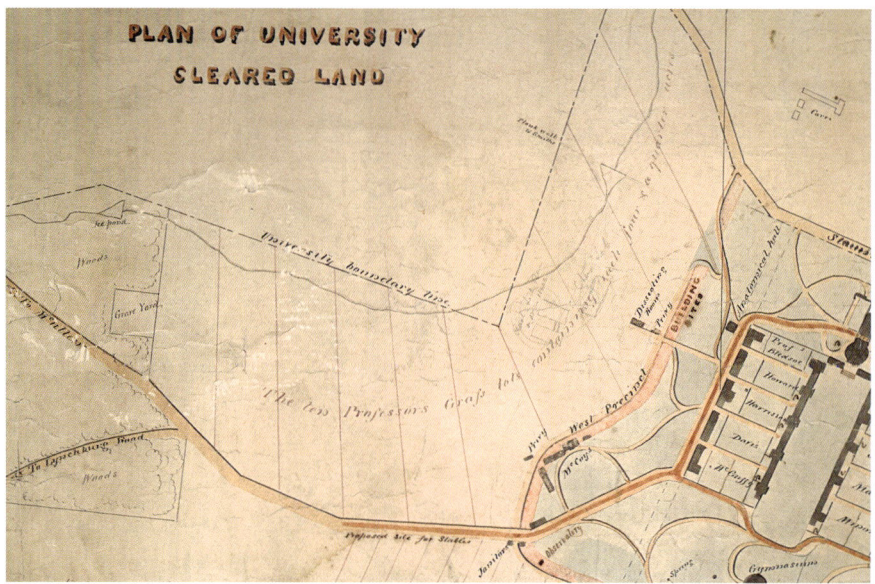

FIG. 9.1. William A. Pratt, "Plan of University Cleared Land," 1858, showing the location of the graveyard (inset square at center left).

major building construction projects, university records do not document that a white contractor was supervising the graveyard wall construction project.[4] Sebra therefore managed the project on his own, most likely supervising other enslaved laborers as needed. He would have selected the stone from the quarry, and once delivered to the site, formed and trimmed it to shape prior to constructing the enclosure. The stone used to create Sebra's wall was most likely taken from the university quarry, an outcropping of metamorphosed coarse sandstone called the Rockfish conglomerate located a quarter mile west of the University Cemetery where the university's Facilities Management buildings now sit (fig. 9.2).[5] Harry, also enslaved, worked with Sebra on the enclosure project. On November 21, 1829, the proctor recorded payment to Harry for his labor "hauling rock to grave yard." Harry was a wagoner who was owned by the estate of David Watts of Charlottesville, Virginia.[6] Despite their labor, when they died neither Sebra nor Harry would have been allowed to be buried inside these walls.

Like other markers of slave presence in the South, the university's cemetery reveals important new insights into the African Americans who lived and died at the University of Virginia. In this instance, the creation, maintenance, and expansion of the white cemetery, staked out on maps and in uni-

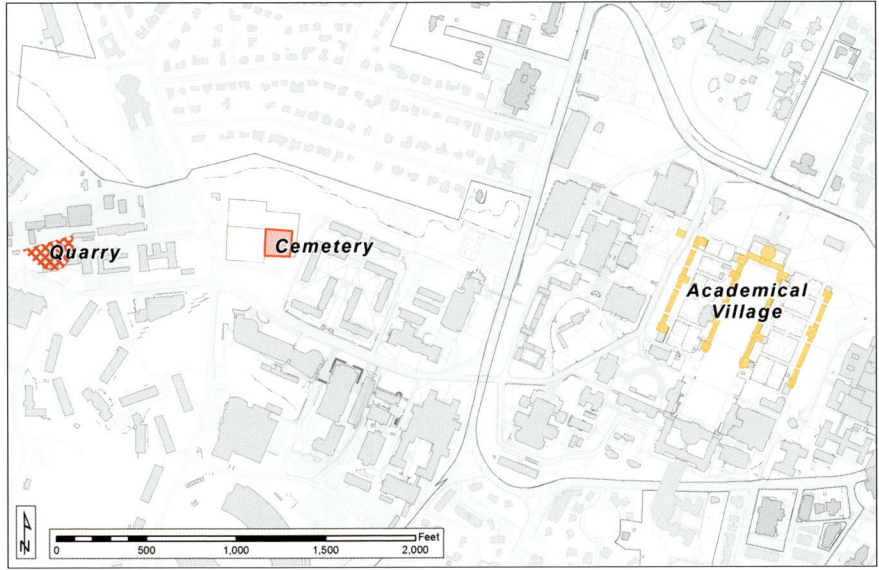

FIG. 9.2. Modern map of the university showing the location of the cemetery and the quarry.

versity records and with walls and gates on physical land, points to the adjacent slave cemetery through what it does not demarcate (fig. 9.3). Although never explicitly defined as such in past university records, nor demarcated as such on any known map, the portion of land that comprised the African American Burial Ground—an area directly north of and adjacent to the University Cemetery boundaries—was an anonymous-yet-sacred plot of land that existed and was only revealed incidentally in a planned expansion.[7]

ESTABLISHMENT OF THE UNIVERSITY CEMETERY

The establishment of pre-Emancipation cemeteries at southern universities was never a consistent practice, perhaps reflecting the unique circumstances surrounding the location and historic context of each academic institution. Although some pre-Emancipation southern universities established formal burial grounds, they were often jointly shared with adjacent towns and communities (University of North Carolina, ca. 1798; University of Georgia, ca. 1810; Emory University, ca. 1836). Other universities established formal burying grounds quite late in their history (College of William & Mary, 1859), or ignored the issue altogether.[8]

Although the University of Virginia's Board of Visitors had provided for

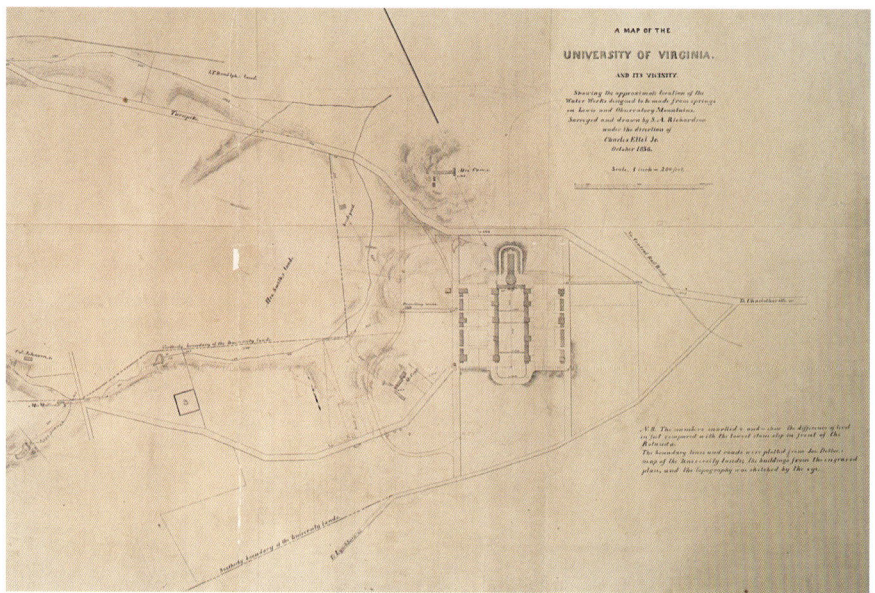

Fig. 9.3. An 1856 waterworks map of the university that locates the site of the university graveyard (inset square at center left, marked by a gravestone bearing a cross), but leaves blank the site of the African American cemetery.

the many needs of its white residents, a cemetery or burying ground was not conceived of as part of the original plan. The land containing what later became the University Cemetery was purchased in 1825 by Arthur S. Brockenbrough, proctor of the University of Virginia. The 132-acre parcel was acquired because of its access to reliable springs and woodlots, to protect the university's water supply, as well as to connect the university's two large parcels, the Academical Village and what is now Observatory Mountain.

Tradition states that the University Cemetery was established out of necessity, shortly after the death of Henry William Tucker, M.D., on January 28, 1828.[9] Just over a year after Tucker's death, Chairman of the Faculty Robley Dunglison asked Proctor Brockenbrough to enclose the cemetery, stating: "The Proctor was again spoken to on the subject of inclosing Burial Grounds." Despite repeated requests to undertake the same, the task appeared not to have the priority that Chairman Dunglison assigned it.[10] In early 1829, the university faced an epidemic of fevers (thought to be typhoid), thus simultaneously delaying attention to the cemetery as well as heightening the need for it.[11] Regardless, apparently fed up with the continued delay, the chairman finally sought and received permission from John H. Cocke.[12] It was Cocke, a

FIG. 9.4. The stone wall of the cemetery appears in the left background (between the two mountains) in Casimir Bohn, *View of the University of Virginia*, from the east, 1856.

member of the Board of Visitors, who approved the use of university funds to hire an outside contractor to enclose the burial ground.[13]

A mid-nineteenth-century image depicts what the original University Cemetery and vicinity may have looked like in its first few decades of operation (fig. 9.4). The image shows a small, square, walled enclosure. Enslaved laborers hired by the university would have cut the trees and cleared the small plot of land creating the new burial ground. This is where Sebra and Harry built the wall. The area surrounding the cemetery on its south, west, and north sides was heavily wooded and remained so for many decades. The contrast between the formal walled and gated but relatively open University Cemetery with the adjacent wooded area must have been great.

The University Cemetery was clearly built for the exclusive use of its white staff and students. No policy formalizing rules for burial was put in writing until the early twentieth century, and during the nineteenth century burial within the University Cemetery was a highly informal process. The chairman of the faculty appeared to be the individual who oversaw the maintenance and operation of the burial ground. Although interments were dominated

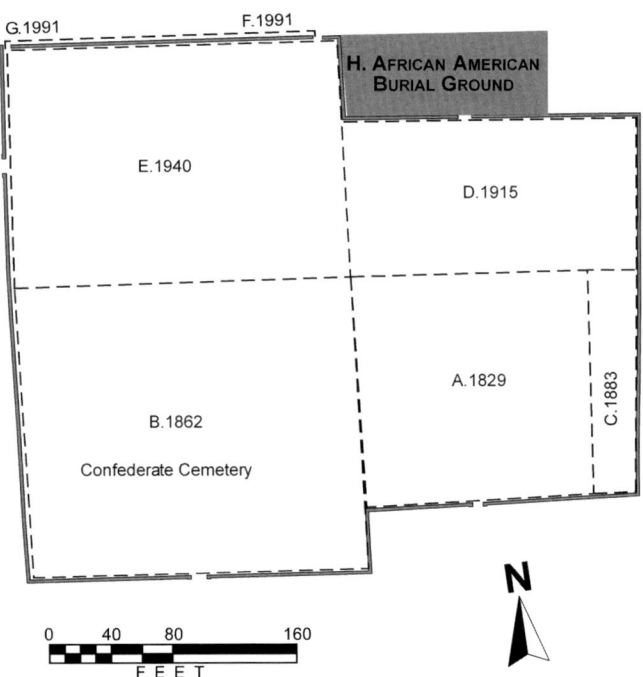

FIG. 9.5. Modern map of the university cemetery showing the various phases of expansion.

by faculty and their immediate families, the burial of several administrators, hotelkeepers, students, and other prominent and less-prominent residents implies that there were no hard-and-fast rules, and that decisions appeared to be made on an individual basis that may have been tied to a person's relationship and standing within the university community, as well as the circumstances of his or her death.

The university expanded its cemetery boundaries several times during the nineteenth and twentieth centuries (fig. 9.5). The first expansion in 1862 was added to accommodate the burial of Civil War soldiers, most of whom fought for the Confederacy, who died while being treated at the hospitals operated in Charlottesville and at the university during the war years. Additional expansions occurred in 1883, 1915, and 1940 primarily driven by an increased desire for burial at the university and a shrinking amount of space. As a university official noted in the late 1890s, "not many more graves can be placed there without crowding the already populous precincts or expanding into the tranquil pasture-grounds to the east."[14]

The nearly seventy-year history of growth and expansion of the University Cemetery throughout the nineteenth century, its informal care and management by the faculty, and the lack of any policies regarding interment prompted the faculty to petition the Board of Visitors to adopt formalized rules. Based on the recommendations of a report on the subject, in June of 1900 the Faculty Cemetery Committee recommended the following rules for adoption by the Board of Visitors.

> For a long time, a portion of the University ground, known as the University Cemetery, has, with the tacit consent of the Visitors, been used for burial purposes. In order that this ground might be kept in decent order a committee of the Faculty has for some time assumed control of it. The amount of unoccupied space is now small, and the growing community in and around the University causes a constantly increasing demand for its utilization. The committee in the absence of any fixed rules, has more or less arbitrarily to determine the nature of the burials in the cemetery. The Faculty asks the Visitors to make a rule allowing in future, with the exception of members of families already using plots of the ground, burial only to students in attendance and to members of the families of the Faculty and Officers of the University.[15]

This white-only policy was to guide all requests for burials for those associated with the university through much of the twentieth century.

AFRICAN AMERICAN BURIALS AT THE UNIVERSITY OF VIRGINIA

White faculty and students, however, were not the only individuals who lived in the Academical Village to die. From the beginning enslaved African Americans, like all others associated with the University of Virginia, died of various causes. In 1825 after an outbreak of "bilous fever," two of George Spottswood's slaves died. It is not known if Spottswood, then the operator of Hotel D, buried his slaves on land owned by the University of Virginia, or elsewhere.[16] In 1829 after the death of an unnamed slave, the proctor paid Law Professor John T. Lomax $1.50 "for plank and workmanship on a coffin for servant." It is not clear if the servant, an enslaved African American, was owned or rented by Lomax or leased by the university; nor is it clear what causes led to his or her death. Equally uncertain is where this enslaved individual was ultimately buried.[17] In numerous such examples of the death of enslaved men, women, and children who died at the university, the documents are silent about the location of their burials.

Societal norms in the antebellum South dictated the segregation of whites and blacks in both life and death. In many areas of the South, burial arrangements were typically segregated with enslaved African Americans in a separate burial ground removed from the domestic sphere, or buried outside of or adjacent to their owner's burial ground. Burial traditions varied according to region and ethnicity and many enslaved African Americans chose to retain burial customs and ceremonies from Africa. In contrast to white burial traditions, enslaved burial ceremonies often took place at night after the workday was complete and incorporated singing, drumming, and other spiritual practices. As a social event, burial was an important opportunity to bring enslaved together and to reinforce family, community, and ties to African cultural traditions.[18]

As an institution that was founded on enslaved labor, the University of Virginia was not unique in adopting the practice of segregating whites and blacks in death. At the College Graveyard, or Old Chapel Hill Cemetery at the University of North Carolina, African Americans were also buried in a segregated section. Discussion of the setting aside of a separate burial ground for the interment of enslaved individuals at the University of Virginia was never recorded in any official document. Likewise, the Board of Visitors did not provide any language clarifying what would happen when a slave owned or leased by the institution itself or a university faculty member, hotelkeeper, or staff died. While detailed university records of the general maintenance of the Academical Village grounds abound, the subject of servants' burial is never once explicitly discussed. The absence of discussion seems to have been the policy.[19]

Although official records were thus silent on the issue of burying university-associated servants, a tacitly approved burial practice for enslaved African Americans was likely already in place shortly after the establishment of the University Cemetery in 1828. At least two late nineteenth-century references note that enslaved African Americans were buried outside of and adjacent to the University Cemetery enclosure. In 1898 Col. Charles Christian Wertenbaker, son of the University Librarian William Wertenbaker, recalled that "*in old times,* the University servants were buried on the *north side of the cemetery, just outside of the wall* [emphasis added]." Born in 1834, Charles lived in Charlottesville with his father and would have been a presence at the university in the two decades prior to the Civil War.[20]

The location of servant burials to the north or rear of the University Cemetery appears to have been practiced for a number of decades, possibly extending into the post-Emancipation period as well. In the same year as Wertenbaker's recollection, the *University of Virginia Magazine* carried a colorful student-authored fiction about local election shenanigans that, as part of its plot, used the body-snatching of a recent African American burial. "We'll not have any trouble at all getting a good fresh one tonight. An old colored man was buried yesterday *just back of the University Cemetery* [emphasis added]."[21] The "back" or rear of the University Cemetery referred to in this story would have been its north side, as the original main entrance gate was located on the south side of the 1828 cemetery and would have been accessible via a segment of the old Three Notch'd Road in this location. Although a work of fiction, the story was based in the knowledge of an African American burial ground in this location, that burials of African Americans may have extended well into the post-Emancipation period, as well as a knowledge, perhaps firsthand, of the then illegal practice of grave-robbing.[22] It was rumored as well that "many of the [servant] bodies were only log of wood or stones, for the fear of having their dead taken up by medical class (then entirely dependent on their own enterprise for subjects), caused the negroes to inter their dead secretly, and hold the usual ceremonies over the dummy."[23]

REDISCOVERY OF THE UNIVERSITY AFRICAN AMERICAN BURIAL GROUND

In 2012, the university initiated plans for expanding the cemetery once again. Prior to construction work, archaeological investigations in the proposed expansion area identified sixty-seven interments under several feet of fill soil (fig. 9.6).[24] The burials were located in an area north of the 1915 cemetery expansion and outside of the existing stone-wall enclosure. Several of the burials still possessed formal markers, predominantly fieldstones, but also broken marble slabs. None of the markers bore inscriptions and the names of the individuals interred there are still unknown.

Official records of the University Cemetery do not document any burials for white individuals in this location. While it is not unusual to discover one or more interments lying outside of a cemetery enclosure, the large number of unidentified burials rediscovered north of and adjacent to the University Cemetery clearly represented a significant-sized, and most importantly an unrecorded population of individuals historically associated with the university. These two facts, combined with the documentary sources pointing to a "servant" burial ground north of the University Cemetery, argue that the

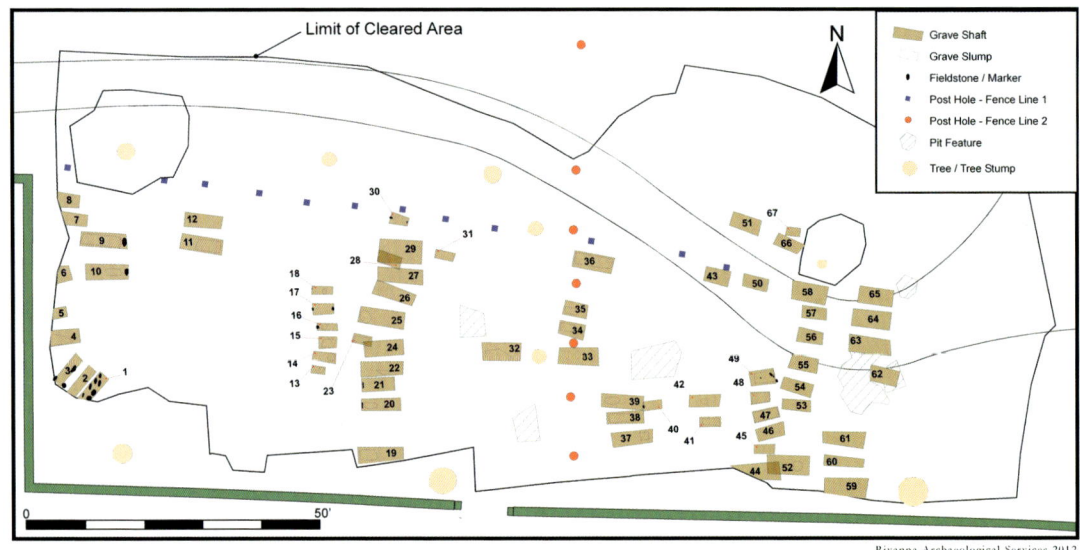

FIG. 9.6. Map locating the African American internments beyond the University Cemetery.

sixty-seven interments identified must represent at least part of enslaved African American population that lived, worked, and died at the university.

The interments varied in size, documenting that in addition to many adults, fifteen children were buried there. The large number of children, over 22 percent of the total individuals identified, certainly calls attention to the prevalence of nineteenth-century disease, but also to the fact that children, and therefore families, composed a significant portion of the people living and working in the Academical Village.

Some of the most telling evidence obtained from the rediscovery of the burials came in the analysis of their spatial patterning (fig. 9.7). While most of the graves were arranged in both short and long rows, many also appeared to be clustered in small groups suggesting family units and relationships that endured through time. This was a common African American burial practice, and one that even slaveowners sometimes acknowledged. When Milly died, her owner, Thomas Preston, an alumnus and University of Virginia visitor and rector in 1864–1865, wrote to his wife of her burial: "I am just going down to make provision for Milly's funeral & will have it performed properly. Our servants are human beings & deserve the rights of Christian sepulcher." Two days later he wrote his wife again, "we buried Milly in the *new* cemetery. She was the first, & [I] selected a section for our servants when

Fig. 9.7. Photograph of the revealed but unexcavated grave shafts from the African American Burial Ground.

should they die here, they can be buried in families. The old grave yard is full. I also selected a section for us [emphasis added]."[25] It is not known where Milly was buried, but wherever it was, she was probably buried near her family members.

The archaeological research also revealed that the northern and eastern edges of the enslaved graveyard were bounded by a post-in-ground fence-line. The simple wooden boundary fence would have been a marked contrast to the stone wall that enclosed the burial ground of the white University Cemetery to the south. The fact that the boundary fence was not found on the southern and western sides, however, suggests that the historic enclosure may have extended farther in these directions. It also implies that enslaved burials may have extended farther south and west beyond the stone wall containing the 1915 and 1940 expansions of the white burial ground. Indeed, documented enslaved graves clearly extend up to the 1915 and 1940 stone boundary walls. These facts suggest the likelihood that first half of the twentieth-century expansions in a northern direction may have encroached upon ground originally set aside for, and used as, a burying ground for enslaved African Americans. Given the total population of African Americans who are known to have lived and worked at the university between 1817 and 1865, and the relatively high death rate for children and adults in the first half of the nineteenth century, it would be expected that the total number of burials in the enslaved cemetery would far exceed the sixty-seven archaeologically identified burials.

WHY REDISCOVERY?

A question that needs to be asked is why did the African American burying ground at the university need to be rediscovered in the first place? Why and how did it recede from institutional and communal memory? Part of the answer, of course, lies in the historical context of the post-Emancipation Jim Crow era and the subsequent concerted effort by white Virginians in the late nineteenth through the first half of the twentieth century to disfranchise blacks. Racism during this period was both overt and pervasive. White-controlled government in the Commonwealth aimed at the comprehensive elimination of the socioeconomic and political gains made by blacks in the quarter century following Emancipation. The disproportionate relationships of power and wealth between blacks and whites in Charlottesville and at the University of Virginia facilitated unequal treatment in all aspects of life.

The African American Burial Ground north of the white University Cemetery suffered under repeated, intentional neglect. Where white faculty organized and received institutional monies during the late nineteenth century to maintain and beautify the white University Cemetery, the African American Burial Ground did not receive the same level of advocacy, care, and treatment. During the first decade of the twentieth century, the larger context of racial inequality and the inverse relationship of power between whites and blacks at the university likely made the institutional decision to neglect, and ultimately erase, coopt, and expand into the African American Burial Ground easier. Indeed, the silence on the subject of enslaved burials from the establishment of the university through to the institutional decision to expand into the African American burial ground in the early twentieth century can be summarized as a policy of inaction, and that resulted in rendering invisible the university's enslaved African American population.

Changing demographics too may also partly explain the abandonment of the enslaved burial ground. The population of African Americans living and working at the Academical Village in the post–Civil War period declined sig-

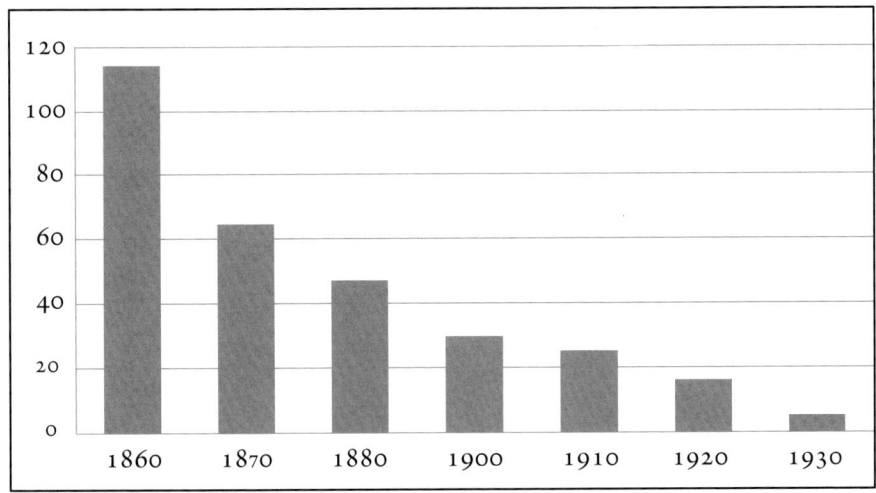

FIG. 9.8. Resident African Americans at the University of Virginia, 1860–1930.

nificantly in comparison with the prewar period (fig. 9.8). In the postbellum period, most African Americans who worked for the University of Virginia were predominantly domestic servants, washerwomen, janitors, or unskilled laborers. Census records document that the number of black residents living in white households declined significantly from an 1860 population of 114, to an 1880 population of 47, a 1900 population of 30, and a 1920 population of 16. Simply put, fewer African Americans living and working at the university meant fewer African Americans with ties to the university, an important criterion in determining access to and advocacy for this sacred space.

Part of the answer may also lie in the choices that newly emancipated African Americans made, choices that were grounded in hard-earned new opportunities and freedoms. Prior to the Civil War, few options were available to enslaved African American families for burying deceased relatives. Few early public cemeteries in Virginia and the larger South, generally operated and maintained by a white-controlled municipal government, permitted the burial of nonwhites. For enslaved African Americans working for or living at the university in the pre–Civil War period, burial north of the University Cemetery was probably one of the few options for a final resting place. Nestled into the surrounding woods, enslaved African Americans may have perceived the area north of the University Cemetery as an appropriate final resting place, albeit a decision in which they may have had little or no choice.

During the Civil War and immediately following Emancipation, however, African Americans had more burial options, a change that would have a direct impact on the university's African American Burial Ground. In 1860, the town of Charlottesville created a new cemetery, Oakwood, which was designed as a segregated burial ground. Oakwood Cemetery possessed a small portion in its southern area that was reserved for the burial of "colored" citizens.[26] In 1873 the Daughters of Zion, an African American benevolent society, purchased a two-acre parcel to be used as a cemetery. Located adjacent to and northeast of Oakwood Cemetery, it was designated for the exclusive use of African Americans.

These facts, a dramatically declining population of African Americans living at the university, and the ability of African Americans to choose where they wished to be interred in the post-Emancipation period, are likely to have led to the decline in the number of interments in the African American Burial Ground north of and adjacent to the University Cemetery. Because no institutional records were kept documenting burials outside and north of the enclosed University Cemetery, the precise date of abandonment for the African American Burial Ground may never be known. Institutionalized racism, in the form of neglect and upkeep of the cemetery, combined with a denial of its physical presence and the expansion of white burials into an area tacitly set aside for enslaved burial, completed its erasure from black and white communal memory.

FAMILY AND COMMUNITY

The presence of child burials and groupings representing families identified through archaeological research forces us to understand that the persons interred in the enslaved burial ground were not nameless individuals. It is all too easy to overlook the fact that African Americans serving faculty, hotelkeepers, or the institution itself were also members of families, relationships that they were born into or established through marriage, as well as members of larger extended kin networks. We know so little about the lives of those individuals who are buried within the enslaved burial ground. Their names are unrecorded, as are their family relations. There are many references to enslaved children in the Academical Village, hinting at the numerous family connections there must have been.

Documents held by the university have revealed the names of more than one hundred of the enslaved people who at one time lived and worked in the Academical Village, though we still know little of their lives and their relationships. There are a few exceptions that suggest the broad span of family relationships across and beyond the Academical Village. Unlike on a plantation, where choice of a spouse was frequently limited to the other people also owned by the master, at the university, enslaved people were brought together in an urban setting. In addition, as there was considerable movement between the university and town, many enslaved university residents chose to have spouses elsewhere.

One of the couples who started and raised a family within the confines of the university was William and Isabella Gibbons. William Gibbons was born enslaved in Albemarle County around 1825. Despite rules against students bringing personal attendants with them to university, later reminiscences suggest that Gibbons served that purpose. Even though the sources are silent on the identity of Gibbons's owner, it may have been a young medical student who attended the university beginning in 1842 and remained there even after his graduation, living with his brother-in-law Professor James Cabell until his death in 1851.[27]

In the 1840s, Gibbons was sold to Dr. Henry Howard, professor of anatomy and surgery, and was later hired out to Professor William McGuffey, who had married Howard's daughter, Laura, and resided with her father in Pavilion IX.[28] Gibbons served as a family butler and was taught to read by Professor McGuffey's daughter Maria.[29] The McGuffeys, who were recently from Ohio, did not embrace slavery and owned very few people: three in 1850 and one in 1860. Living in the Academical Village, however, meant that Gibbons was an integral part of a much larger enslaved community. In the early 1850s, he married Isabella, a woman owned by Francis Smith, a professor of physics. She might be the twenty-seven-year-old enslaved woman listed in the 1860 census, and the four children, then aged seven, five, three, and one, may be their children.

Like so many enslaved individuals, the Gibbonses are virtually invisible in official university documents. Most of what we know of their lives is pieced together from sources taken after the war when they both became prominent members of the free community. Isabella (fig. 9.9) became the first schoolteacher in the newly created school for emancipated slaves and William became an early minister at the African Baptist Church in Charlottes-

FIG. 9.9. Photograph of Isabella Gibbons.

ville, later moving to Zion Baptist Church in Washington, DC. William later recounted that he had become a minister in 1844, although we know little about this. Perhaps he preached to others enslaved at the university; perhaps he served a white minister by preaching to the enslaved members of a congregation in Charlottesville.[30]

The Gibbonses, living in separate white households, but both residing in the Academical Village, were able to form friendships and family across the boundaries of ownership. Their experience is a powerful reminder of the ways in which enslaved African Americans struggled to build lives and families despite the confinements of enslavement. It is also a reminder that the African Americans buried in the enslaved cemetery were also important members of families and broader communities, even though their lives and stories remain unknown to us today.

A RACIALLY CHARGED LANDSCAPE

The University Cemetery is a racially charged landscape. The presence of the African American Burial Ground adjacent to the white University Cemetery serves to humanize our often-abstract understanding of slavery and pre-Emancipation race relations, and the anonymity of black individuals owned by white residents of the Academical Village. Many of the enslaved African Americans who lived and worked at the university also died there. The groupings of adults and children seen in the patterning of graves in the university's African American Burial Ground serve as a strong reminder of the powerful family relationships of enslaved African Americans, generations of social bonds that persevered in life and survived death.

History also documents that the segregated black and white burial grounds had two distinctly different trajectories and fates. Whereas university records show an intensified focus on the care of the white cemetery by faculty committees and the Board of Visitors in the late nineteenth century, in that same period the university's enslaved cemetery was unnamed and unacknowledged in university policies and left physically unmaintained. The markers of the individuals and families interred in the enslaved burial ground disappeared from the landscape and from memory, and ultimately the sacred space itself was encroached upon.

More broadly, the rediscovery of the African American Burial Ground has served to push forward a continuing conversation about slavery at the university, one that has focused on an increased historical understanding of the lives and contributions of enslaved men and women laboring in the Academical Village, and the role of the university and its white residents in perpetuating a system upon which it was wholly dependent.

IN MEMORIAM

The symbolism of the stone boundary wall surrounding the white University Cemetery, a wall that was built by an enslaved man yet enclosing and keeping out African Americans associated with the university, is particularly poignant. Sebra was just one of the numerous enslaved individuals whose labor contributed to the creation of the buildings, structures, and landscape that compose the Academical Village. One can't help but wonder how Sebra felt about his role in creating the University Cemetery. Through his labor he constructed an enclosure, a wall that effectively separated blacks and whites as wholly and irrevocably in death as in life. The irony of the fact that he was instrumental in creating a burial ground in which he and other African Americans were prohibited from being interred was likely not lost on Sebra.

With the support of the University and Charlottesville communities, a memorial to commemorate the African American Burial Ground and those interred within was constructed on site in 2014. A pier-and-rail fence bounding the northern and eastern sides of the burial ground was reconstructed in the same location as the archaeologically identified post-in-ground fence. Trees were planted in the sod-covered burial ground, and a historical marker was erected at each of three entrances remembering and commemorating the lives of those buried there.

Sixty-seven burials, arranged in family groupings and containing adults and children, form a sacred site. The African American Burial Ground was a sacred place for the university's enslaved residents, one where ancestors provided an anchoring presence. With its rediscovery in 2012, the African American Burial Ground continues to be an important physical location where members of all races of the university and Charlottesville community can come together. Memorial services were held at the burial ground after its completion in 2014, and again most recently in 2017. This recent tradition is a moving ceremony that acknowledges in speech, prayer, and song the sacrifices made by enslaved laborers, their critical role in the creation of the university, celebrating their lives and accomplishments, and incorporating a candlelight walk to the burial ground for a libation ceremony. The African American Burial Ground, along with the Memorial to Enslaved Laborers being built in the Academical Village, will serve as important touchstones for the future of the university, reinvigorating an introspective turn, and encouraging community engagement in discussions on race and its implications in everyday life.

NOTES

Resources marked with an asterisk (*) can also be found at http://juel.iath.virginia.edu/resources.

1. Arthur S. Brockenbrough, "Receipt Book, 1824, 1825–1827," p. 53, RG-5/3/2.101, Albert and Shirley Small Special Collections Library, University of Virginia.

2. *Albemarle County Deed Book* 17:87, Albemarle County Courthouse, Charlottesville, VA.

3. Journals of Business Transactions of Central College, 1817–1819, and its successor, the University of Virginia (hereafter cited as Proctor's Journals), RG-5/3/1.111, vol. 3, August 17, 1829, p. 50, October 31, 1829, p. 55, and November 21, 1829, p. 57, Albert and Shirley Small Special Collections Library, University of Virginia; Papers of the Proctor of the University of Virginia (hereafter cited as Proctor's Papers), RG-5/3/1.111, Albert and Shirley Small Special Collections Library, University of Virginia. Note to Pay Bearer Zebra, September 29, 1829, Box 19, Bills and Accounts, July–December 1829, Albert and Shirley Small Special Collections Library, University of Virginia; Receipt of Joel Shiflett, November 2, 1829, Box 8, Receipts 1829, Albert and Shirley Small Special Collections Library, University of Virginia.

4. Other university construction projects requiring the work of a stonemason included the Anatomical Hall (1825–1827) and the Observatory (1828). On both of these important building projects, white stonemasons Samuel and Andrew Campbell were responsible for the construction of stone foundations and utilized enslaved labor to assist them.

5. Wilbur A. Nelson, "Geology and Mineral Resources of Albemarle County," *Bulletin 77*, Virginia Division of Mineral Resources (1962).

6. David Watts Jr., an Albemarle County resident, owned an enslaved man named Harry, who was leased to the university in 1821 and 1822. Harry appears in early university records under the "waggons and cart" account. It is likely that Harry was hired again from the Watts's estate to assist Sebra in the cemetery enclosure project. See Proctor's Journals, vol. 2: December 25, 1822, p. 193; Proctor's Journals, vol. 3: November 21, 1829, p. 57.

7. Save for the only/first explicit reference in the 1898 article in the *Alumni Bulletin* by James A. Harrison: "In old times, the University servants were buried on the north side of the cemetery, just outside of the wall," "The University Cemetery," *Alumni Bulletin* 4, no. 4 (February 1898): 111–15.

8. The University of North Carolina shared its cemetery with the town of Chapel Hill. See "Old Chapel Hill Cemetery," Town of Chapel Hill, North Carolina, Department of Parks and Recreation, http://www.townofchapelhill.org/town-hall/departments-services/parks-and-recreation/cemeteries/old-chapel-hill-cemetery, accessed November 23, 2017; Gretchen A. Brock, *Jackson Street Cemetery,* National Register of Historic Places Registration Form, 2009, U.S. Department of the Interior, National Park Service; Mark Auslander, "The Other Side of Paradise: Glimpsing Slavery in the University's Utopian Landscapes," *Southern Spaces*, May 13, 2010, https://southernspaces.org/2010/other-side-paradise-glimpsing-slavery-universitys-utopian-landscapes.

9. Dr. Henry William Tucker's marker is the earliest dated grave within the University Cemetery.

10. Dr. Henry William Tucker was the younger brother of George Tucker.

11. *Minutes of the Faculty of the University of Virginia, 1825–1856, vol. 2, December 1826–July 1830, February 25, 1829, pp. 256–259, Albert and Shirley Small Special Collections Library, University of Virginia.

12. *The Chairman's Journal notes: "The Chairman requested of General Cocke to have an inclosure made round the burial ground: to which he assented," Journals of the Chairman of the Faculty, 1827–1864, vol. 1, April 28, 1829, Albert and Shirley Small Special Collections Library, University of Virginia, (hereafter cited as Chairman's Journals).

13. This enclosure was near completion by year's end. Robley Dunglison noted: "The Proctor was desired to place a fastening on the gates of the Burial Ground. The Gates have been put up but they have been for weeks the sport of the winds: although a slight attention might have completed them. Almost all new undertakings are in this unfinished condition." Chairman's Journals, vol. 1, December 29, 1829, p. 203.

14. *Alumni Bulletin* 4, no. 3 (November 1897): 97; Harrison, "The University Cemetery," 111, 114.

15. *Board of Visitors Minutes, 1817–2007, June 11, 1900, pp. 364–365, 378.

16. Gessner Harrison to Dr. Peachy Harrison, November 12, 1825, Papers of the Tucker, Harrison, and Smith Families, 1790–1940, Acc. #2589, 3825, 3847, 3847 a-h, j-l, Box 2, Albert and Shirley Small Special Collections Library, University of Virginia.

17. Proctor's Journals, vol. 2, July 4, 1829, p. 45. That the University of Virginia as an institution owned enslaved persons is a fact.

18. Charlotte King, "Separated by Death and Color: The African American Cemetery of New Philadelphia, Illinois," *Historical Archaeology* 44, no. 1 (2010): 125–37.

19. *See, for instance, the University Enactments of 1825–1847. Detailed statements on grounds maintenance and by whom can also be found in the Faculty Minutes, in the same website.

20. Harrison, "University Cemetery," 112.

21. Anonymous, "The Body-Snatching of Mr. Peppers," *Virginia University Magazine* 42, no. 3 (December 1898): 133.

22. The practice of grave-robbing was largely abandoned in Virginia by the turn of the twentieth century. The Anatomical Act of 1884 passed by the General Assembly established a formal anatomical board that officially distributed unclaimed "subjects" from the Commonwealth's almshouses, prisons, morgues, hospitals, and jails to the various colleges and universities that required them.

23. Harrison, "University Cemetery," 112.

24. The archaeological investigation involved mechanically aided removal of fill soils lying on top of historic grade. Manual cleaning of the exposed surface revealed the tops of the grave shafts. The grave shafts were left preserved in place and no human remains were disturbed.

25. Thomas L. Preston to Anna M. Preston, September 15, 1863, and Thomas L. Pres-

ton to Anna M. Preston, September 17, 1863, Preston-Davis Family Papers, 1840–1930, Box 4, Folder 10, Albert and Shirley Small Special Collections Library, University of Virginia. The new cemetery referred to, while unidentified, may be a new portion of the University Cemetery. Thomas L. Preston was later buried in the University Cemetery in 1903, implying that their servants were buried there too.

26. Prior to the war, Maplewood Cemetery in Charlottesville was established as the first public cemetery. It was generally an all-white cemetery, although a few enslaved African Americans and free blacks were buried within its confines. According to the City of Charlottesville's website, two "servants," Newton Hagar and Linie Winston, were buried alongside their owners. In addition, several free black citizens from prominent Charlottesville families were interred there, including Fairfax Taylor, Robert Scott Sr., and Robert Scott Jr.

27. Orra Henderson Moore Gray Langhorne, "Southern Sketches from Virginia," *Southern Workman* 18, no. 10 (October 1889) and *Students of the University of Virginia: A Semi-Centennial Catalogue with Brief Biographical Sketches* (Baltimore: C. Harvey, 1878), quoted in Scott Nesbit, "The Education of William Gibbons," 2004, accession #13484, Special Collections, University of Virginia Library, Charlottesville, VA.

28. Papers of Philena Carkin, MSS 11123, Albert and Shirley Small Special Collections Library, University of Virginia. "Reminiscences of My Life and Work among the Freedmen of Charlottesville, Virginia, from March 1st 1866 to July 1st 1875," vol. 2, 50, cited in Nesbit, "Education," 10.

29. Alice McGuffey Ruggles, *The Story of the McGuffeys* (New York: American Book, 1950), 106, cited in Nesbit, "Education," 11–13.

30. Nesbit, "Education," 2–21.

CONTRIBUTORS

ALFRED BROPHY writes about property, trusts and estates, and race in colonial, antebellum, and early twentieth-century America. Often his work looks to the ideas of outsiders and their interaction with the legal system, sometimes as plaintiffs or defendants, and at other times as criminal defendants. His extensive writing spans empirical and quantitative methods to intellectual history (jurisprudence). His books are *Reconstructing the Dreamland: The Tulsa Riot of 1921, Race, Reparations, Reconciliation* (2002), *Reparations Pro and Con* (2006), and an expansive volume on antebellum jurisprudence, *University, Court, and Slave: Proslavery Thought in Southern Colleges and Courts and the Coming of Civil War* (2016).

BENJAMIN FORD is a principal at Rivanna Archaeological Services, LLC, a small cultural resource management firm based in Charlottesville, Virginia. With over twenty-five years of experience as an archaeologist, Ford has directed numerous archaeological investigations within the University of Virginia's Academical Village and has also conducted research on numerous prominent Virginia and national historic sites and cultural landscapes. Ford earned a BA in anthropology in 1984 from Connecticut College and an MA and PhD in 1998 in anthropology at the University of Virginia.

THOMAS HOWARD received a JD, an MEd in higher education administration, and a BA in history from the University of Virginia. While a student, he served as articles editor of the *Virginia Law Review* and president of the Jefferson Society. He was a Lawn resident, Range resident, and a member of the Raven Society. Howard has served on the staffs of Jefferson's University—Early Life (JUEL) and the Center for the Constitution at James Madison's Montpelier. He is the author of *Society Ties: A History of the Jefferson Society and Student Life at the University of Virginia* (2017). His work has also appeared in the *North Carolina Historical Review* and the *Oculus*.

ANDREW SCOTT JOHNSTON is Director of the Program in Historic Preservation and Associate Professor of Architectural History at the University of Virginia. He received his doctorate in architecture from the University of California, Berkeley. His work explores power, race, and ethnicity in the cultural landscape. He is author of *Mercury and the Making of California: Mining, Landscape, and Race, 1840–1890* (2013). His current work includes digital recordation, analysis, and interpretation of historic buildings and landscapes in Virginia and Italy and a book on contemporary historic preservation and heritage practice in China.

MAURIE D. MCINNIS is Professor of American Studies and the Jacob and Frances Sanger Mossiker Chair in the Humanities at the University of Texas at Austin. She is an award-winning author, most recently of *Slaves Waiting for Sale: Abolitionist Art and the American Slave Trade* (2011). McInnis has also worked extensively with historic sites and museums including serving as curator for "To Be Sold: Virginia and the American Slave Trade" at the Library of Virginia in Richmond in 2015. In 2012, she cofounded the digital humanities project called JUEL at the University of Virginia, from which much of the history in this book was uncovered. She currently serves as the Executive Vice President and Provost at the University of Texas at Austin.

LOUIS P. NELSON is Professor of Architectural History and the Vice Provost for Academic Outreach in the Office of the Provost at UVA. He is a specialist in the built environments of the early modern Atlantic world, with published work on the American South, the Caribbean, and West Africa. Nelson is an accomplished scholar with two award-winning monographs *The Beauty of Holiness* (2008) and *Architecture and Empire in Jamaica* (2016) and four edited collections and numerous scholarly articles. He also served two terms as Senior Coeditor of *Buildings and Landscapes*, the leading English-language venue for scholarship on vernacular architecture.

JESSICA ELLEN SEWELL is Codirector of the Center for Cultural Landscapes and Associate Professor of Urban and Environmental Planning and American Studies at the University of Virginia. She received her doctorate in architecture from the University of California, Berkeley. She is a scholar of gender, power, and the built environment across scales from objects to buildings to cities and landscapes and author of *Women and the Everyday City: Public Space in San Francisco, 1890–1915* (2011). She is currently writing a book on the relationship between bachelor pads and suburban houses in the postwar United States and working on an atlas of the cultural landscapes of Suzhou, China.

KIRT VON DAACKE is Assistant Dean and Professor in the College of Arts and Sciences at the University of Virginia. A historian, he leads both the President's Commission on Slavery and the University and the President's Commission on the University in the Age of Segregation at UVA and also serves as Managing Director of the Universities Studying Slavery consortium. In 2012, he cofounded with Maurie D. McInnis the digital humanities project called JUEL at the University of Virginia. He is the author of *Freedom Has a Face: Race, Identity, and Community in Jefferson's Virginia* (2012).

JAMES ZEHMER is a Historic Preservation Project Manager for the University of Virginia. He has led renovation projects on the pavilions, hotels, and many of the dormitory rooms in the Academical Village, which has given him a thorough knowledge of construction techniques used by the craftsmen who initially built the complex. Before coming to UVA, Zehmer worked as a restoration carpenter, including a role as carpentry foreman for the Virginia State Capitol Restoration. Zehmer serves on the Scientific Committee for the Maison des Esclaves, a UNESCO World Heritage Site on Gorée Island in Senegal focused on the Atlantic slave trade. He received a BA in architectural history from UVA in 2002.

ILLUSTRATION CREDITS

Photograph by Dan Addison: *figs. I.7, 2.11*

Colonial Williamsburg Foundation, Williamsburg, Virginia, museum purchase, 1993.100.1: *figs. I.2, 4.4*

Heritage Landscapes, LLC: *fig. I.4*

Eric Höweler/Höweler + Yoon Architecture LLP: *fig. I.9*

Kentucky Gateway Museum Center, Maysville, Kentucky: *fig.2.20*

Library of Congress Rare Books and Special Collections Division: *fig.6.2*

Photograph by Robert Llewellyn: *fig. I.3*

Collection of the Massachusetts Historical Society: *fig.2.1 (left)*

Lauren Massari: *figs. I.5, 1.1, 1.5, 2.16, 2.22, 3.2, 3.3, 3.4, 3.5, 3.9, 3.10, 3.11, 3.12, 3.13, 4.3, 5.7*

Drawing by Mesick Cohen Wilson Baker Architects, courtesy Office of the Architect, University of Virginia: *figs.5.3, 5.4*

Photograph by Louis P. Nelson: *figs. I.1, 1.3, 1.4, 1.5, 2.29, 2.32, 3.1, 3.6, 3.7, 5.2, 5.5, 5.6, 6.3, 8.2*

Plan by Nathanael Nelson: *figs. 2.2, 2.3, 3.8, 7.3*

Rivanna Archaeological Services, LLC: *figs. 2.12, 2.13, 2.14, 2.15, 2.23, 2.24, 9.2, 9.5, 9.6, 9.7*

Photograph by Zach D. Roberts: *fig. I.8*

Albert and Shirley Small Special Collections Library, University of Virginia: *figs. I.6, 1.7, 2.9, 2.10, 2.17, 2.18, 2.19, 2.21, 2.26, 2.27, 2.28, 2.30, 2.31, 4.1, 5.1, 6.4, 6.5, 7.1, 7.2, 7.4, 8.1, 8.4, 9.1, 9.3, 9.4*

© Thomas Jefferson Foundation at Monticello: *figs.2.4, 2.5, 2.6. 2.7, 2.8, 8.3*

Virginia Museum of History and Culture: *fig.4.2 (1990.114)*

Drawing by Mark Wenger: *fig.2.1 (right)*

Photograph by James Zehmer: *fig. 1.6*

INDEX

Italicized page numbers refer to illustrations.

Aaron (enslaved), 33
abolitionism, 5, 6, 141, 143, 146–47
African American Burial Ground (UVA), 22, 30, 178, 181, 231–42, *234*, *235*
Agassiz, Louis, 182
Albert (enslaved), 104, 106, 127, 140n84
Alien and Sedition Acts, 144
American Colonization Society (ACS), 143–44, 145–46, 150; certificate of membership, *144*
anatomical dissection, 171–72, 173–74, 175, 177, 178, 179, 180–88, *187*, 189, 191–93, 194n15. *See also* University of Virginia (UVA): Anatomical Theater (Hall) at
apprenticeship, 29, 36, 37, 203, 212, 222n38
Aristotle, 158
Aylett, William Roane, 157

Bacon, Edmund, 2
Bankhead, Charles, 35
Barnett, Fanny, 202, 203, 210, 211–13, 219, 222n38
Barnett, William, 203–4
Barrett (enslaved), 34
Barringer, Paul, 193
Battles, Dolly, 203
Battles, Elijah, Sr., 209–10
Battles, Elizabeth "Betsy," 206
Battles, James Franklin, 210
Battles, Robert, 216–17
Battles, Shadrach, 203

Beatley, Henry M., 177
Beecher, Catharine, 13
Bell, John, 164
Ben (enslaved), 34, 75
Birney, James, 143, 146
Bishir, Catherine, 40n2
Blaetterman, Charlotte E., *59*
Blaetterman, George, 56, 75, 79, 83, 95n1; number of enslaved individuals owned by, 74n10; property of, 68, 211–12, 219
Bledsoe, Albert Taylor, 101, 158, 159, 160
Bleeding Kansas, 161–62
Bob (enslaved), 34
Bonnycastle, Charles, 68, 102–3, 104, 199, 203
Bowles, Stephen, 203
Boyd, Thomas J., 113–14, 127
Branham, Nimrod, 204
Breckinridge, James, 5, 145
brickmaking, 34, *35*
Brock, Anselem, 84
Brockenbrough, Arthur S., 28, 29–37, 104, 208, 210; Jefferson and, 36, 63; saw fragments with name, *32*; University Cemetery and, 228; wages paid by, 29, 31, 206
Brockenbrough, J. W., 186–87
Brockman, James, 217
Brooks, Preston, 161–62; caning of Charles Sumner, *162*
Brown, Joel W., 217–18
Brown, John, 162, 163, 191
Brown, T. C., 191

Brown v. Board of Education, 20
Bruce, Philip Alexander, 178
Burnly (enslaved), 33, 35
Burwell (enslaved), 36
Burrell, Jim, 192
Burwell, William, 217
Byars, Stephen, 217–19

Cabell, Joseph Carrington, 174
Cabell, James Lawrence, 181–84, 188–89, 191, 193, 239
Calhoun, John C., 150
Campbell, Samuel and Andrew, 225
Carr, William G., 107
Carter, Richard, 129
Cary, Archibald, 171
Charles (enslaved), 80, 85
Christies, Robert, 192
Civil War, 142, 193, 230
Clay, Clement, 151
Clay, Henry, 150
Cocke, John Hartwell, 10, 35–36, 205, 217; University Cemetery and, 228–29
Colbert, Burwell, 6, 205–6
Collegian, 153, 155
Colonial Williamsburg, 48
Compromise of 1850, 155, 160, 215
Conway, Edwin, 69, 79, 82, 92, 127, 129, 130, 131–33, 137n10, 137n28; number of servants owned by, 69, 139n55
Cooper, Thomas, 174
Copeland, John A., 191
Coram, Stephen, 217
Cottrell, Dorothea, 56
Cottrell, Lucy, 56, *59,* 69, 82–83; kitchen and chamber, *83*
Crawford, John, 173
Crawford, Mr., 109–10

Daughters of Zion, 238
Davey (enslaved), 31, 33
Davis, Henry Winter, 150–51
Davis, John A. G., 11, 66, 82, 92–93, 150, 199
Davis, John Staige, 184–93
Davis, Keziah, 210–11
Day, Andra, 20
Dew, Thomas R., 166n21
Dick (enslaved), 33
Dinsmore, James, 2, 32, 40n7, 206–7
Dixon, Turner, 109–10
Dunglison, Robley, 65–66, 174, 177, 181; University Cemetery and, 228, 244n13

Eliason, Armistead, 109
Ellis, Charles, 93, 106, 127, 172
Emmet, John Patten, 65
enslaved workers at UVA: cash value of, 36–37, 225; census data on, 49–51, *52–53,* 200–201, 235–36, 239; children of, 50–51, 98, 124–25, 128; concealment of, 47–48, 54, 57, 71, 73, 89, 117; contact with students by, 13, 75, 91–92, 99, 105–7, 114, 134–35, 206; contradictory masters of, 133–36; as dissection specimens, 171–72, 173–74, 178, 180–88, 191–93; entrepreneurial activities by, 92, 93, 110, 131; euphemisms for, 2, 34; hotel duties of, 122–33; laundry duties of, 14, 42, 49, 59, 72, 84–85, 125, 132–33, 137n28, 139n72, 208; living quarters for, 65–71, *68, 69,* 72, 73, 77, 87–88, *120,* 122; medical-related duties of, 180; mobility of, 134–35; ownership of, 11, 13–14, 30, 31–33, 51, 54, 110, 133–36; racial hierarchy among, 38; runaways, 37–38, 39; scarcity of information on, 16–17, 28, 49; scholarship on, 15; surveillance of, 89–94, 105, 107; tasks of, 2, 5, 8, 10, 13–15, 28, 35, 49–50, 73, 76, 84–86, 94, 107, 115; treatment of, v, 4, 80, 87 (*see also* violence); as "Virginian Luxuries," 6–7, *7,* 107–8, *108;* wages for, 28, 29–31, 34, 84, 132, 135. *See also* Memorial to Enslaved

254 INDEX

Laborers (UVA) *and specific individuals by name*
eugenics, 193

faculty at UVA, 7, 10, 14, 16, 63, 65–67, 100–104, 111n2; free blacks and, 205, 208–9, 210–11; student violence and, 11, 102, 113–14. *See also* proslavery thought
Farrow, Thomas, 210
Fawcett, Dr., 195n33
Fermin, Robert, 3
Fielding (enslaved), 102–3, 104, 203
Fontaine, E. F., 189
Forbes, John, 123
Fossett, Joseph, *207*; and family, 206–8
Foster, Katherine "Kitty," 199–200, 202, 208, 209, 210, 215; location of residence, *200, 201*
Frank (enslaved), 35
free blacks, 29, 37, 54, 125, 143, 199–219; laws against, 214, 218
Freedmen's School, 4
French, Marinda, 213

Garden Club of Virginia, 48
Garland, Hudson S., 171
Garnett (student), 182
Garnett, Muscoe R. H., 141, 142, 153, 156, 158, 159, 161
Garrett, Alexander, 204–5, 217
Garrison, William Lloyd, 148
Gennet, Samuel, 189–90
George, Luther M., 27, 28, 32–34
Georgetown University, 5
German (enslaved), 131
Gibbons, Isabella, v, 4, 20, 22, 24n7, 77–78, 80, 239–40, *240*; kitchen, *78*
Gibbons, William, 22, 239–40
Gilmer, Francis Walker, 174
Glover, Lorri, 149
Gooch, Philip Claiborne, 182–83

Gorman, John, 36
Governor's Palace (Williamsburg), *43*, 43
grave-robbing, 171–72, 177–93, *184*, 233, 244n22
Gray, Mrs. (hotelkeeper), 71–72, 85, 87–88, 92–93, 104, 120, 125, 128, 130, 132, 133, 137n11; kitchen behind hotel, *70, 87, 88*; number of servants owned by, 139n55
Green, George E., 190
Green, Shields, 191
Green, William, 35
Gretter, John A., 114
Grigsby, William, 129
Grizzard, Frank, 40n1

Hampden-Sydney College, 183–84, 185–86, 188, 190
Hardy, George H., 109
Harpers Ferry Raid, 162, 191
Harris, W. W., 128
Harrison, Gessner, 67, 77, 80, 84, 85, 107, 146; horse-whipping of, 102
Harrison, J. H., 102, 104, 109
Harrison, James, 37
Harry (enslaved), 226, 229
Hemings, Sally, 47
Henderson, James, 27–28
Henry (enslaved), 33
Hern, Thrimston, 36–37
Hodgson, Joseph, 161
Hoffman, George, 109–10
Holcombe, James P., 101, 151, 158–60, 162, 164
Holiday, Billie, 20
Holmes, George Frederick, 158
Hooe, Thomas, 126–27
Hopkins, Alden, 48–49
Howard, Henry, 183, 239
Howell, Alfred T., 93
Hunter, Robert M. T., 13, 148–49, 151, 153

Institute of Advanced Technology in the Humanities (IATH; UVA), 15–16, 17

Jack (enslaved), 29–30, 33, 180
Jackson (free black), 209
Jefferson, Calvin, 21
Jefferson, Thomas: College of William & Mary and, 115; designs and intentions for UVA, 1–2, 5, 7–8, 14–15, 28, 42–43, 47, 54–59, 56, 57, 58, 63, 65, 69, 71, 75, 91–92, 119–20, 144–45, 174–75, 175; education views of, 1–2, 3; enslaved individuals owned by, 36, 44, 47, 56, 205–7; as first rector, 10, 12; on medical studies, 172–75, 193; on slavery and black inferiority, 5–6, 141, 142–45, 146, 148, 159, 165n8, 172–73, 193; on states' rights, 144, 150; statue (at Darden School), 3. *Writings*: A Bill for Proportioning Crimes and Punishments, 172; Declaration of Independence, 2, 142, 158, 159; *Notes on the State of Virginia*, 6, 110, 142–43, 172–73. *See also* Monticello
Jefferson Monument Magazine, 146–47, 153–56, 154
Jefferson Society (UVA), 151–53; meeting place (Hotel C), 152
"Jefferson's University—Early Life Project, 1819–1870" (JUEL), xv, xvi–xvii, 15–17; illustrations from digital model, 18, 28, 36, 55, 61, 77, 78, 79, 87, 88, 90, 91, 106, 121, 176
Jefferson Trust of the University of Virginia Alumni Association, 15
Jim Crow policies, 20, 236
John (enslaved), 33, 34
Johnson, Chapman, 188
Johnson, Colonel, 109
Johnson, Joseph, 189–90
Johnson, Thomas, 177, 181
Jones (enslaved), 38

Kean, Robert G. H., 153
Kelley, W., 37
Kemper, William, 208
Kennedy, Jack, 208–9
King, Milly (aka Milley), 203
Kinny, Sally, 210

laundry services (UVA), 14, 42, 49, 59, 72, 84–85, 125, 132–33, 137n28, 139n72, 208
Lawrence (enslaved), 127
Leake, Mr., 109
Lee (enslaved), 33
Lee, Robert E., 20
Lewis (enslaved), 34, 106
Lewis, "Anatomical," 180, 181, 182–83, 195n33
Lincoln, Abraham, 164
Lomax, John T., 66, 231
Lucy (enslaved), 87–88, 180
Lundy (enslaved), 29

Madison, James, 1, 10, 21, 34, 143, 151, 168n40
Magill, Alfred Thurston, 62, 93
Magill, Mary T., 55
Magruder, Allen B., 87
Marshall (enslaved), 75
Martin, Worthy, 15–16
Martineau, Harriet, 181–82
Massari, Lauren, 17
Maupin, Addison, 120, 214
Maupin, Socrates, 165
Maury, Matthew Fontaine, 160–61
Maverick Plan (UVA), 48–50, 49, 50, 118
McAfee, Madison, 102–3, 104
McGuffey, William, 214, 215; and family, 239
McGuffey Cottage, 72, 72
McKee, Andrew, 219
McKenney (student), 182–83
McKim, Randolph H., 164
McKinnie, Clement, 219

McLachlan, James, 167n38
McMillan, Harry, 211
Memorial to Enslaved Laborers (UVA), 22–23, *23*, 242
Miller (student), 177
Miller, Charles J., 185
Milly (enslaved), 234–35
Milton Farm, 29, 30
Minor, John B., 84, 214, 215
Minor, Lewis W., 186–88
Minor, Walter, 113–14, 127
Missouri Compromise, 45, 144
Monroe, James, 10, 21, 65, 143, 151, 168n40
Montandon, James E., 109
Montebello, 31–32
Monticello, 1, 14, 36, 43–47, *46*, *47*, *48*, 54; plans, *44*, *45*
Moon, John, 129
Moses (enslaved), 33; chalked graffiti in pavilion attic, *33*
Munroe, James, 135, 213–15; and family, 215–16; letter asking for help in purchasing his daughter Roseia, *216*

Nat Turner's Rebellion, 89, 146, *147*
Neale, John, 208
Ned (enslaved), 33
Neilson, John, 32, 35, 40n7; drawing by, *116*
Nelson (enslaved), 33, 34
Noland, Nathan B., 97–101, 103, 109
Norris, Opie, 214, 215
"not a negro" designation, 213, 223n41

Oast, Jennifer, 138n49
Oldham, James, 171–72, 181
Orr, Joseph, 151

Patterson, Robert M., 108, 109
Perrow, Daniel, 81, 128
Perry, J. M., 31, 40n7

Perry, John M., 1, 177
Peticolas, Arthur E., 186, 189–90, 192
Peticolas, Jane Braddick, view of west lawn of Monticello, *48*
Pharo, King, 204
Phil (free black), 209
Pickett, Micajah K., 81, 95n6
Poe, Edgar Allan, 151
Pratt, William A., 209; plans by, *52–53*, *64*, *98*, *179*, *200*, *205*, *226*
proslavery thought, 2, 6, 12–13, 99, 101, 141–65; UVA faculty publications on, 158
Prudence (enslaved), 177, 180

Raggi, Michele and Giacomo, 202, 203
Randolph, Septimia, 171
Randolph, Thomas Jefferson, 146, 214
Raphael (enslaved), 33
removal law, 214
Reubin (enslaved), 33, 34
Rhoda (enslaved), 30
Riley, Nancy, 212–13
Roberts, T. R., 190
Robertson, Archibald F. E., 171–72, 177, 192
Robinson, Merritt, 152–53
Roger, Professor, 93
Rose, John, 123, 125–26, 131, 211, 213; number of servants owned by, 139n55
Rose, Maria and Erasmus, 213–14
Rousseau, Jean-Jacques, 158

Sam, Old (enslaved), 30–31, 33, 34
Sam, Young (enslaved), 31, 33
Saunders, Bob, 185
Sebra (enslaved), 225–26, 229, 241–42
Seddon, James Alexander, 151
Sharper (enslaved), 34
Shaw, Charles, 158
Shiflett, Joel, 225

Shulman, Gayle, 15
Simmons, Ruth, 4
Simon (enslaved), 33
Simpson (enslaved), 180
Skepwith, Peyton, 22
Smith, Francis H., 24n7, 80, 87, 239
Smith, James, 180
Smith, Margaret Bayard, 45
Southern Rights' Association, 156–57
Spencer, Richard, 20
Spinner, Richard, 204
Spinner, William, 204–5, 206, 217, 219
Spooner, George W., 183, 204
Spottswood, George W., 65, 126–27, 131, 133–34, 231
Stowe, Harriet Beecher, 13, 158
Stuart, Alexander H. H., 151
students at UVA: class conflicts and, 11, 102, 126–17, 133–34; daily life of, 122–31; dress code for, 11, 12, 102, 177; drinking by, 11, 92, 104, 107, 134, 202, 211, 212; gambling by, 11, 92–93, 134, 211; literary magazines of, 146–47, 153–57, *154*; literary societies of, 151–53, 156, 160, 167n38; medical studies by, 171–72, 174–83, 190–92; prostitutes and, 109, 209, 212–13, 219; scholarships for, 12; social background of, 11, 13, 145, 149; tuition and fees for, 145, 180; women admitted as, 20. *See also* violence
Sturrs, Thomas, 208
Sullivan, Teresa, 21
Sumner, Charles, 161, 162; caning by Preston Brooks, *162*

Taylor, John, 131–32
Tazewell, Littleton, 130
Terrell, Lucy, 97–100, 102, 103; boardinghouse, *98*
Thelin, John, 167n27
Thomas, Howell Lewis, 185

Thornton (enslaved), 104
Thucydides, 150, 167n31
Tom (enslaved), 34
Toombs, Robert, 151, 164
Towles, Thomas, 123
Trimpson (enslaved), 104
Tucker, G., 108
Tucker, Henry St. George, 159, 214
Tucker, Henry William, 228
Tutwiler, Henry, 146, 152

Undergraduate Quarterly, 156, 168n55
"Unite the Right" rally, 20–22; march on UVA Grounds, 22
University of Virginia (UVA): "Academical Village" designation for, 6, 47; "Academical Village" aerial views/plans/maps, *8, 9, 18, 60, 66, 67,* 227; Anatomical Laboratory ("Stiff Hall") at, 179, *179*; Anatomical Theater (Hall) at, 175, *175, 176,* 177, 179–81, 225; bicentennial celebrations at, 17–21, *21*; blacks admitted to, 18; boardinghouses near, 97–98, 134; centennial poster, *19*; cisterns at, 37, 59, 62, 73, 77, *78,* 84, 86, 210; construction of, 2, 10, 27–38, 42, 63, 203–4, 225; curriculum at, 149–50; *Enactments* (rules) at, 10–11, 12, 16, 114, 122–23, 132; expansions to, 63–66, 71; food preparation/kitchens at, 14, 50, 54–59, *68,* 70, 79–81, *120*; gardens at, 49, *51,* 59, 62–63; garden walls at, *63, 65, 66, 76, 77,* 90; Gibbons Hall at, 22; hotels and hotelkeepers at, 7, *8,* 11, 13–14, 17, 28, 30–31, 69, 77, *78,* 79, 100–101, 113–36, *116, 117, 119, 120,* 152; influence and legacy of, 3–4; laundries at (*see* laundry services [UVA]); Lawn at, 7, 10, 47, 51, 58, 73, 115–17; library at, 7; livestock at, 14, 62, 76, 83–84; models for, 8; origins of, 1–2; pavilions at, 7–8, 10, 14, 17, 27, 30–32, *33,*

258

36, 40, 47–48, *51*, 54–57, *55*, *56*, *57*, *58*, *61*, *69*, *76*, *77*, *81*, *82*, *83*, *90*, *91*, *106*; population growth at, 10; privies at, 79, 86; prominent graduates of, 151; Public Hall of, *160*; quarry at, 226, *227*; Ranges at, 7; resident African Americans at, *237*; Rotunda at, 7–8, *8*, 15, 17, 22, *35*, 37, 40, 42, 47–48, 116, 164–65, 202; —, Annex (interior) *160*; —, steps (original), 37, *37*; University Cemetery at, 225–31, *226*, *227*, *228*, *229*, *230*, 241–42, 244n13; unsanitary conditions at, 14, 67, 79, 86. *See also* enslaved workers at UVA; faculty at UVA; Jefferson, Thomas; students at UVA

Varon, Elizabeth, 142
Vest, John, 185
violence: against faculty and townspeople, 11, 102, 114; against free blacks, 199–200, 202–3, 212–13, 216; against enslaved individuals, 97–104, 110, 113, 128–29, 202; against women, 107–10, 199–200, 202, 212–13; by enslaved individuals, 89, 146; whipping, 104–5, *105*, 114
Virginia Gazette, 38
Virginia Historical Society, 159
Virginia Resolution of 1798, 143–44
Virginia University Magazine, 153, 159, 162, 233

Wall, Charles Coleman, 166nn16–17
Ward, Colonel, 129, 133; number of servants owned by, 139n55
Washington Society (UVA), 152, 162
Watson, Egbert R., 215
Watson, James R., 171
Watts, David, 226
Webster, Daniel, 150
Wertenbaker, Charles Christian, 178, 191, 232–33
Wertenbaker, William, 213, 217–18, 232
White, Isaiah, 192
White, Gale Jessup, *21*
White, Thomas, 186–88, 192
Widderfield, James W., 204
Wigfall, Louis, 153
Wilder, Craig, 4
William (enslaved), 31, 33, 128
William & Mary, College of, 4, 115, 153, 227
Williams, Timothy, 151
Willis (enslaved), 34, 37–38
Wilson, Jack, 180, 195n33
Wilson, T. A., 129
Wise, Henry A., 190
Woodson, Mrs., 98, 102, 109

Yale Literary Magazine, 162, *163*

Zachariah (enslaved), 27–28, 32, 34, 210